NATURAL RESOURCES: ISSUES AND OUTLOOK

NATURAL RESOURCES: ISSUES AND OUTLOOK

A.M. BABKINA (ED.)

Nova Science Publishers, Inc.
Huntington, NY

Senior Editors: Susan Boriotti and Donna Dennis
Office Manager: Annette Hellinger
Graphics: Wanda Serrano
Information Editor: Tatiana Shohov
Book Production: Cathy DeGregory, Kay Seymopur and Jennifer Vogt
Circulation: Ave Maria Gonzalez, Ron Hedges and Andre Tillman

Library of Congress Cataloging-in-Publication Data
Available Upon Request

Copyright © 2001 by Nova Science Publishers, Inc.
        227 Main Street, Suite 100
        Huntington, New York 11743
        Tele. 631-424-6682   Fax 631-424-4666
        E Mail Novascil@aol.com

Printed in the United States of America

CONTENTS

PREFACE

Countries rich in natural resources must manage them wisely or risk a diminution of the standard of living of its citizens. A major threat, however, lurks behind every door in the form of greedy developers and other short-term thinkers. This book examines key issues related to the natural resources of the United States.

Natural Resources
Pages 1-18

WILDERNESS: OVERVIEW & STATISTICS

Ross W. Gorte

The 1964 Wilderness Act established a national system of congressionally designated areas authorized to be preserved in a wilderness condition. The National Wilderness Preservation System was created with 9 million acres of Forest Service lands. Congress has since expanded the Wilderness System to nearly 104 million acres, and more lands have been recommended for inclusion in the System. Furthermore, at the direction of Congress, several agencies are studying the wilderness potential of other federal lands. This report provides a brief history of wilderness, describes what wilderness is, identifies permitted and prohibited uses in wilderness areas, and provides statistics on wilderness designations and federal agency recommendations, as of October 31, 1996.

HISTORY OF WILDERNESS

Retaining certain lands in federal ownership, by creating national parks, national forests, and national wildlife refuges, was the first major step toward protecting the natural environment. Beginning in 1897, management of the national forests emphasized conservation -- the protection and development of the lands. However, it did not take long to recognize the need to preserve some areas in a natural state. Acting at its own discretion, the U.S. Forest Service created the first wilderness area in the Gila National Forest (New Mexico) in 1924. In the succeeding decades, the agency's system of wilderness, wild, and primitive areas grew to 14.6 million acres. However, concerns arose about the permanence of this purely administrative system. The Forest Service had relied on its administrative authority in making these designations; there was no law guaranteeing the future of wilderness.

In response to these concerns, Congress enacted the Wilderness Act[1] in 1964. The Act defines "wilderness," and prohibits or restricts certain activities in wilderness areas, while permitting other activities to occur. The Act also reserves to Congress the authority to designate areas as part of the National Wilderness Preservation System.

The Wilderness System was initially endowed with the 9.1 million acres of national forest lands that had been identified administratively as wilderness or wild areas. The Wilderness Act also directed the Agriculture Secretary to review the agency's 5.5 million acres of primitive areas, and the Interior Secretary to evaluate the wilderness potential of National Park System and National Wildlife Refuge System lands. The Secretaries were to report their recommendations to

---

[1] Act of Sept. 3, 1964, P.L. 88-577, 78 Stat. 890.

the President and to Congress within 10 years. Separate recommendations for wilderness designations were made for individual areas, and many have been designated, but some of the recommendations are still pending (and are included in table 4). The Federal Land Policy and Management Act of 1976 (FLPMA)[2] directed the Bureau of Land Management (BLM) to conduct a similar review of the lands it administers within 15 years. The BLM submitted recommendations to the President by 1991, and Presidents Bush and Clinton have submitted their recommendations to Congress.

In 1977, the Forest Service began a review (RARE II[3]) of 62 million acres of national forest roadless areas, as an acceleration of the land management planning process mandated by the Forest and Rangeland Renewable Resources Planning Act of 1974 (RPA) and the National Forest Management Act of 1976 (NFMA).[4] The RARE II Final Environmental Statement was issued in January 1979, recommending more than 15 million acres (24% of the study area) for addition to the Wilderness System. Nearly 11 million acres (17%) were to be studied further in the ongoing Forest Service planning under NFMA. The remaining 36 million acres (58% of the RARE II area) were to be available for other uses -- such as logging, energy and mineral developments, and motorized recreation -- that might be incompatible with preserving wilderness characteristics. In April 1979, President Carter presented his recommendations to the Congress, with only minor modifications in the Forest Service recommendations.

Congress began expanding the Wilderness System in 1968, as shown in table 1. Five laws were enacted by the 90th Congress, creating five new wilderness areas with 795,000 acres in four states. Wilderness areas were added by each succeeding Congress, rising to a peak of 60.8 million acres designated during the 96th Congress (1979-1980), including the largest single Act -- 56.4 million acres of wilderness designated in the Alaska National Interest Lands Conservation Act of 1980.[5] The California Desert Wilderness Act of 1994,[6] designating 7.7 million acres of wilderness in southern California, is the second largest designation since the Wilderness Act. Since the RARE II recommendations were issued, Congress has usually debated wilderness bills (especially for the National Forest System lands) for entire states. The 104th Congress enacted only one law designating wilderness areas, with less than 30,000 acres.

---

[2]Act of Oct. 21, 1976, P.L. 94-579, 90 Stat. 2743.

[3]The first Roadless Area Review and Evaluation (RARE I) was begun under the agency's administrative authority in 1970, but was abandoned in 1972 because of a lawsuit asserting the review had been restricted in ways that violated the National Environmental Policy Act of 1969 (Act of Jan. 1, 1970, P.L. 91-190, 83 Stat. 852).

[4]Respectively: Act of Aug. 17, 1974, P.L. 93-378, 88 Stat. 476; and Act of Oct. 22, 1976, P.L. 94-588, 90 Stat. 2949. 16 U.S.C. 1600-1614.

[5]Act of Dec. 2, 1980, P.L. 96-487, 94 Stat. 2371.

[6]Act of Oct. 31, 1994, P.L. 103-433, 108 Stat. 4471.

TABLE 1. Additions to the National Wilderness Preservation System

Congress Designated[a]	Number of Laws	Number of States	Number of Areas New (Additions)		Acres
88th	1	13	54	(0)	9,139,721
89th	0	0	0	(0)	0
90th	5	4	5	(1)	794,550
91st	3	12	25	(0)	305,619
92nd	9	7	8	(1)	912,439
93rd	5	22	35	(0)	1,264,594
94th	6	21	35	(0)	2,142,486
95th	7	18	28	(5)	4,555,496
96th	6	10	70	(11)	60,799,111
97th	5	5	7	(0)	83,261
98th	21	21	177	(49)	8,576,450
99th	4	4	11	(2)	97,393
100th	7	8	22	(4)	1,988,509
101st	5	5	68	(3)	1,759,479
102nd	2	2	6	(4)	424,590
103rd	2	2	79	(14)	8,272,699
104th	1	2	1	(2)	29,420
Total	88	44	631	(96)	103,784,015

[a]Column total differs from this figure, because of acreage revisions.

The wilderness designation debate was particularly intense during the 98th Congress (1983-1984). In 1980, the State of California successfully challenged Forest Service RARE II recommendations for 44 areas to nonwilderness uses, with the court decision substantially upheld on appeal in late 1982.[7] In 1983, the Reagan Administration responded by directing a re-evaluation all RARE II recommendations, except in states with wilderness laws containing certain provisions.[8] A compromise in May 1984 led to the enactment of 21 wilderness laws designating 8.6 million acres of wilderness in 21 states -- more laws and more acreage (outside of Alaska) than any Congress since the Wilderness System was created. Table 2 summarizes the major events in the development of the National Wilderness Preservation System.

[7]*California v. Bergland*, 483 F. Supp. 465 (E.D.Cal. 1980), *aff'd in part, rev'd in part*, 690 F.2d 753 (9th Cir. 1982).

[8]For a history of the debate over these "release language" provisions, see CRS Report 93-280 ENR, *Wilderness Legislation: History of Release Language, 1979-1992*.

TABLE 2. Chronology of Wilderness Events

1924 -- Forest Service establishes the first wilderness area, in the Gila National Forest of New Mexico, under its administrative authority.

1964 -- Wilderness Act is signed into law, creating the Wilderness System and directing a review of national forest primitive areas and of National Park System and National Wildlife Refuge System lands.

1968 -- Congress begins expanding the Wilderness System.

1970 -- Forest Service begins Roadless Area Review and Evaluation (RARE I) of certain undeveloped national forest lands.

1972 -- Forest Service abandons RARE I in response to legal challenge.

1976 -- FLPMA directs BLM to review wilderness potential of its lands.

1977 -- Forest Service begins second Roadless Area Review and Evaluation (RARE II).

1979 -- *Jan.*: Forest Service issues RARE II recommendations.
        Apr.: Pres. Carter transmits modified recommendations to Congress.
        June: State of California sues Forest Service over recommendations.

1980 -- *Jan.*: Judge rules for State of California; Forest Service appeals.

1982 -- *Oct.*: Appeals Court basically upholds ruling.

1983 -- *Feb.*: Dept. of Agriculture announces re-evaluation of all RARE II recommendations.

1984 -- *May*: Rep. John Seiberling and Sen. James McClure announce compromise provision for statewide wilderness bills that would halt Forest Service RARE II re-evaluation for individual States.

Since the Wilderness Act created the National Wilderness Preservation System in 1964, Congress has enacted 88 laws designating new wilderness areas or adding to existing ones, as shown in table 1. The Wilderness System now contains 631 wilderness areas totalling nearly 104 million acres in 44 states, managed by the four federal land management agencies, as shown in table 4. In addition, the agencies have recommended another 29 million acres in 26 states be added to the Wilderness System, as shown in table 5; these lands are generally managed to protect their wilderness character while Congress debates adding them to the Wilderness System. Additional lands are being studied by the agencies, to determine if they should be added to the System, but comprehensive data on lands being reviewed for wilderness potential are not available.

WHAT IS WILDERNESS?

The Wilderness Act defines wilderness as an area of generally undisturbed federal land. Specifically, §2(c) states:

> A wilderness, in contrast with those areas where man and his works dominate the landscape, is hereby recognized as an area where the earth and its community of life are untrammeled by man, where man himself is a visitor who does not remain. An area of wilderness is further defined to mean . . . an area of undeveloped

> Federal land retaining its primeval character and influence, without permanent improvements or human habitation, which is protected and managed so as to preserve its natural conditions and which (1) generally appears to have been affected primarily by the forces of nature, with the imprint of man's work substantially unnoticeable; (2) has outstanding opportunities for solitude or a primitive and unconfined type of recreation; (3) has at least five thousand acres of land or is of sufficient size as to make practicable its preservation and use in an unimpaired condition; and (4) may also contain ecological, geological, or other features of scientific, educational, scenic, or historical value.

This definition provides some general guidelines for determining which areas should, or should not, be designated wilderness, but there are no specific criteria in the law. The phrases "untrammeled by man," "retaining its primeval character," and "man's work substantially unnoticeable" are far from precise. Even the numerical standard -- 5,000 acres -- is not absolute; smaller areas can be designated, if they can be protected, and the smallest wilderness area -- Wisconsin Islands in the Green Bay National Wildlife Refuge -- is only 2 acres.

One reason for the imprecise criteria for wilderness is differing perceptions of what constitutes "wilderness." To some, a "wilderness" is an area where there is absolutely no sign of human presence: no traffic can be heard (including aircraft); no roads, structures, or litter can be seen. To others, sleeping in a camper in a 400-site campground in Yellowstone National Park is a "wilderness experience." Complicating these differing perceptions is the wide-ranging ability to "get away from it all" in various areas; in a densely wooded area, "getting away" might be measured in yards, while in mountainous or desert terrain, human developments can be seen for miles.

In an attempt to accommodate these contrasting views of wilderness, the Wilderness Act provided certain exemptions and delayed implementation of restrictions for wilderness areas, as will be discussed below. At times, Congress has also responded to the conflicting demands of various interest groups by allowing additional exemptions for certain uses (especially for existing activities) in particular wilderness designations. Ultimately, "wilderness areas" are whatever Congress designates as wilderness, regardless of developments or activities which some would argue conflict with the definition of wilderness.

PROHIBITED AND PERMITTED USES

In general, the Wilderness Act prohibits commercial activities, motorized access, and roads, structures, and facilities in wilderness areas. Specifically, §4(c) states:

> Except as specifically provided for in this Act, and subject to existing private rights, there shall be no commercial enterprise and no permanent road within any wilderness area designated by this Act and, except as necessary to meet minimum requirements for the administration of the area for the purpose of this Act (including

> measures required in emergencies involving the health and safety of persons within the area), there shall be no temporary road, no use of motor vehicles, motorized equipment or motorboats, no landing of aircraft, no other form of mechanical transport, and no structure or installation within any such area.

This section prohibits most commercial resource exploitation (such as timber harvesting) and motorized entry (*via* cars, trucks, ORVs, aircraft, or motorboats) except in emergencies. However, §4(d) provides several exceptions, including: (a) possible *continued* use of motorboats and aircraft; (b) fire, insect, and disease control measures; (c) mineral prospecting conducted "in a manner compatible with the preservation of the wilderness environment;" (d) water project developments; (e) *continued* livestock grazing; and (f) commercial recreation activities.

In addition to these exemptions, the Wilderness Act extended the mining and mineral leasing laws for wilderness areas in national forests for 20 years, through 1983.[9] New mining claims and mineral leases were permitted for many wilderness areas, and exploration and development were authorized "subject, however, to such reasonable regulations governing ingress and egress as may be prescribed by the Secretary of Agriculture." Despite this authority, no permits for on-site exploration were considered until James Watt became Secretary of the Interior in 1981.[10] Litigation halted a drilling application in Montana that year, and Congress enacted a moratorium leasing and exploration in wilderness areas in the Interior Department appropriations laws for FY1983 and FY1984. However, mineral rights existing on or before December 31, 1983 (or before the area was designated), remain valid, and can be developed if the right-holder chooses, under "reasonable regulations" determined by the Agriculture Secretary, and some mineral exploration has occurred in designated wilderness areas under such regulations.[11]

The Wilderness Act also directs that the Act not alter existing federal-state relationships with respect to state water laws or state fish and wildlife responsibilities. Specifically, §4(d) (as codified at 16 U.S.C. 1133) states:

---

[9]Most lands in the National Park System and the National Wildlife Refuge System have been withdrawn from access under the mining and mineral leasing laws, while extensive BLM wilderness designations were apparently not contemplated until FLPMA was enacted in 1976. Thus, the Wilderness Act addressed mining and mineral leasing only in the national forests.

[10]Although national forests are managed by the Forest Service in the Department of Agriculture, mining claims and mineral leases on most federal lands, including the national forests, are administered by the BLM in the Department of the Interior.

[11]Olen Paul Mathews, Amy Haak, and Kathryn Toffenetti. "Mining and Wilderness: Incompatible Uses or Justifiable Compromise?" *Environment*, v. 27 (April 1985): 12-17, 30-36.

(7) Nothing in this Act shall constitute an express or implied claim or denial on the part of the Federal Government as to exemption from State water laws.

(8) Nothing in this Act shall be construed as affecting the jurisdiction or responsibilities of the several States with respect to wildlife and fish in the national forests.

However, the extent and nature of federal water rights that might arise from wilderness designations continues to be an important issue for Congress.[12]

STATISTICS ON WILDERNESS DESIGNATIONS AND RECOMMENDATIONS, AS OF OCT. 1, 1996

The following tables present data on the federal lands managed by the four principal federal land management agencies and on the acreage designated as wilderness and recommended by the agencies for wilderness. The data were gathered from several agency sources, as described below. This section describes the agency land data shown in table 3 and the wilderness statistics shown in tables 4, 5, and 6.

Agency Land Data

Table 3 shows the area managed by each of the four major Federal land management agencies.[13] The data are not directly comparable across agencies, however, because of differences in accounting practices. The agency data also differ from the statistics maintained by the U.S. General Services Administration.[14] Differences occur in part because official ownership status often differs from managerial responsibility; for example, the Forest Service administers 462,678 acres in Oregon that are technically public lands. Another complication is partial ownership, such as "split estates," with the federal government owning only the surface (or the subsurface), and another owner for the subsurface (or surface) rights; similarly, some lands are managed by the federal government under easements and long-term leases, without federal ownership. Thus, the agency acreage statistics in table 3 probably overstate actual federal land ownership.

---

[12]For a more thorough discussion of this issue, see CRS Report 89-11 A, *Wilderness Areas and Federal Water Rights*.

[13]Other federal agencies, such as the Department of Defense, administer some federal land, but land and resource management is not their primary mission.

[14]U.S. General Services Administration, Office of Governmentwide Real Property Relations. *Summary Report of Real Property Owned by the United States Throughout the World as of September 30, 1991*. Washington, DC: Dec. 1993. p. 30.

Ross W. Gorte

TABLE 3. Total Area Managed by Federal Agencies (in acres)

	U.S.D.A. Forest Service	National Park Service	U.S. Fish & Wildlife Service	Bureau of Land Management
Alabama	662,795	14,912	16,465	110,963
Alaska	22,004,745	50,655,094	76,465,287	87,861,809
Arizona	11,250,693	2,673,233	1,676,306	14,254,175
Arkansas	2,553,342	98,198	305,826	291,166
California	20,627,691	7,560,555	243,947	14,508,453
Colorado	14,501,592	591,322	64,567	8,292,598
Connecticut	24	5,357	708	0
Delaware	0	0	25,843	0
Florida	1,146,671	2,324,805	242,343	25,277
Georgia	864,710	40,792	471,928	0
Hawaii	1	235,408	288,508	0
Idaho	20,442,651	99,154	47,061	11,855,480
Illinois	273,278	12	71,611	227
Indiana	193,939	9,972	8,159	0
Iowa	0	1,662	43,713	378
Kansas	108,175	429	29,058	0
Kentucky	688,475	93,282	2,154	0
Louisiana	603,757	10,575	449,641	309,611
Maine	53,040	63,522	46,115	0
Maryland	0	36,183	40,663	0
Massachusetts	0	32,606	12,226	0
Michigan	2,855,223	631,064	113,065	74,854
Minnesota	2,831,689	138,924	431,524	151,255
Mississippi	1,156,217	102,603	200,267	57,211
Missouri	1,492,079	54,156	49,712	2,321
Montana	16,872,610	1,220,234	608,228	8,076,062
Nebraska	352,133	5,371	163,727	7,129
Nevada	5,815,856	777,017	2,295,046	47,847,778
New Hampshire	723,906	9,489	5,872	0
New Jersey	0	35,349	58,300	0
New Mexico	9,326,599	375,012	326,597	12,864,595
New York	14,933	32,728	24,964	0
North Carolina	1,241,947	368,263	403,445	0
North Dakota	1,105,779	71,383	460,436	60,702
Ohio	221,891	17,707	7,725	0
Oklahoma	302,097	9,875	98,991	1,428
Oregon	15,664,078	194,476	535,841	16,222,461
Pennsylvania	513,229	46,840	10,006	0
Rhode Island	0	5	1,503	0
South Carolina	612,023	26,971	109,724	0
South Dakota	2,013,628	141,302	193,315	279,358
Tennessee	632,673	351,528	45,004	0
Texas	755,093	1,177,466	393,077	0
Utah	8,112,462	2,021,309	106,971	22,233,446
Vermont	355,179	8,710	6,427	0
Virginia	1,654,652	315,400	118,187	0
Washington	9,174,956	1,930,994	137,578	364,512
West Virginia	1,032,302	47,581	3,041	0
Wisconsin	1,519,832	62,432	189,237	160,167
Wyoming	9,258,281	2,392,084	57,606	18,390,633
Territories	27,978	14,790	106,601	0
U.S. Total	191,614,904	77,135,062	87,750,954	264,304,049

The data in table 3 are from agency sources; agency data, rather than GSA data, were used because they most closely match the agency wilderness data. The acreage shown in table 3 is generally limited to the lands administered by the agency or for which the agency has primary responsibility. The following list identifies the data sources for each of the agencies.

U.S. Dept. of Agriculture, Forest Service. *Land Areas of the National Forest System As of September 1995*. Report No. FS-383. Washington, DC: Jan. 1996. 123 p.

U.S. Dept. of the Interior, National Park Service. *Master Deed Listing of Acreages by State as of: 12/31/95*. Unpublished. Washington, DC: Oct. 19, 1994. 2 p.

U.S. Dept. of the Interior, Fish and Wildlife Service, Division of Realty. *Annual Report of Lands Under Control of the U.S. Fish and Wildlife Service as of September 30, 1995*. Washington, DC: U.S. Govt. Print. Off., 1995. 45 p.

U.S. Dept. of the Interior, Bureau of Land Management. *Public Land Statistics 1994/ 1995*. Vol. 179/180. Washington, DC: U.S. Govt. Print. Off., Sept. 1996. 309 p.

Wilderness Statistics: Data Description and Assumptions

The wilderness statistics presented in tables 4 and 5 are the current acreage estimates by the agencies. Table 4 is the estimated acreage for areas that have been designated by Congress. Table 5 identifies the estimated acreage of areas recommended by the agencies for addition to the Wilderness System, but which have not yet been acted upon by Congress; it includes all BLM Wilderness Study Areas in California that were not designated in the California Desert Protection Act. Table 6 is the sum of tables 4 and 5 -- the estimated acreage of designated plus recommended wilderness areas. In addition, the agencies continue to review the wilderness potential of other lands under their jurisdiction, both of congressionally designated wilderness study areas and under congressionally directed land management planning efforts. However, data on acreage being studied, particularly in the planning efforts, are unavailable.

The data sources for designated wilderness (except for the NPS) and for BLM wilderness recommendations are the same as those listed above, for general land statistics for each agency. Forest Service wilderness recommendations were presented to GAO for its review of Wilderness Study Areas.[15] The wilderness recommendations for the NPS and FWS (as well as NPS data on designated wilderness) are unpublished, but are available from the agencies.[16]

---

[15]U.S. General Accounting Office. *Federal Land Management: Status and Uses of Wilderness Study Areas*. GAO/RCED-93-151. Washington, DC: Sept. 1993.

[16]Personal communication with Peter Keller, National Park Service, U.S. Dept. of the Interior, Washington, DC, on June 17, 1994.
U.S. Dept. of the Interior, Fish and Wildlife Service. *National Wildlife Refuge System: Current Status of Wilderness*. Unpublished report. Washington, DC: Feb. 1983.

Wilderness Statistics: Summary of Data

As of October 31, 1996, Congress had designated 103.8 million acres of federal land as the National Wilderness Preservation System, as shown in table 4. More than 55% of this land -- 57.4 million acres -- is in Alaska, and includes most of the wilderness areas managed by the NPS (76%) and by the FWS (90%). A third of the Wilderness System is managed by the Forest Service, but 83% of Forest Service wilderness area is outside Alaska.

Another 29.2 million acres have been recommended by various agencies for additions to the Wilderness System on the lands they administer, as shown in table 5. Nearly half of these pending recommendations are from the NPS, and include several large, well-known areas, such as Yellowstone, Big Bend, Glacier, and Great Smoky Mountains National Parks. Congress has not acted on all the Forest Service RARE II recommendations; the recommendations shown in table 5, however, are the result of the agency's land management planning process, rather than any remaining RARE II recommendations. The BLM submitted its recommendations to President Bush by 1991, as required by FLPMA, and Presidents Bush and Clinton have forwarded recommendations for BLM wilderness to Congress.

In total, 133.0 million acres, of a total U.S. landmass of 2.271 billion acres, have been designated as or recommended for wilderness, as shown in table 6. Half of this -- 68.3 million acres -- is in Alaska, and accounts for 28% of the land in the state. The remaining 64.7 million acres are distributed among 45 other states; only Connecticut, Iowa, Kansas, and Rhode Island have no federal lands designated as or recommended for wilderness. Total land designated as or recommended for wilderness accounts for nearly 6% of all land in the United States, and more than 20% of all federal land. Outside Alaska, lands designated as or recommended for wilderness account for less than 4% of all land in the United States.

TABLE 4. Federal Designated Wilderness Acreage, by State and by Agency
(in acres and percentage of agency/Federal land)

	U.S.D.A. Forest Service		National Park Service		U.S. Fish and Wildlife Service	
Alabama	33,151	5.0%	0	0.0%	0	0.0%
Alaska	5,752,899	26.1%	32,979,370	65.1%	18,676,320	24.4%
Arizona	1,344,970	12.0%	443,700	16.6%	1,343,444	80.1%
Arkansas	116,560	4.6%	34,993	35.6%	2,144	0.7%
California	4,435,889	21.5%	5,975,052	79.0%	9,172	3.8%
Colorado	3,147,686	21.7%	55,647	9.4%	2,560	4.0%
Connecticut	0	0.0%	0	0.0%	0	0.0%
Delaware	0	n.r [b]	0	n.r	0	0.0%
Florida	74,495	6.5%	1,296,500	55.8%	51,252	21.2%
Georgia	113,423	13.1%	8,840	21.7%	362,107	77.7%
Hawaii	0	0.0%	142,370	60.5%	0	0.0%
Idaho	3,961,501	19.4%	43,243	43.6%	0	0.0%
Illinois	25,549	9.4%	0	0.0%	4,050	5.7%
Indiana	12,935	6.7%	0	0.0%	0	0.0%
Iowa	0	n.r	0	0.0%	0	0.0%
Kansas	0	0.0%	0	0.0%	0	0.0%
Kentucky	16,415	2.4%	0	0.0%	0	0.0%
Louisiana	8,679	1.4%	0	0.0%	8,346	1.9%
Maine	12,000	22.6%	0	0.0%	7,392	16.0%
Maryland	0	n.r	0	0.0%	0	0.0%
Massachusetts	0	n.r	0	0.0%	2,420	19.8%
Michigan	91,891	3.2%	132,018	20.9%	25,309	22.4%
Minnesota	807,451	28.5%	0	0.0%	6,180	1.4%
Mississippi	6,046	0.5%	4,080	4.0%	0	0.0%
Missouri	63,198	4.2%	0	0.0%	7,730	15.6%
Montana	3,371,770	20.0%	0	0.0%	64,535	10.6%

[a] 0.x% = less than 0.05%.

[b] n.r = not relevant; the agency owns no land within the state.

TABLE 4. Federal Designated Wilderness Acreage, by State and by Agency
(in acres and percentage of agency/Federal land)

State	U.S.D.A. Forest Service		National Park Service		U.S. Fish and Wildlife Service		Bureau of Land Management		Total Designated Area		Share of NWPS [a]
Nebraska	7,794	2.2%	0	0.0%	4,635	2.8%	0	0.0%	12,429	2.46%	0.x% [a]
Nevada	786,067	13.5%	0	0.0%	0	0.0%	6,458	0.x%	792,525	1.4%	0.8%
New Hampshire	102,932	14.2%	0	0.0%	0	0.0%	0	n.r	102,932	14.0%	0.1%
New Jersey	0	n.r [b]	0	0.0%	10,341	17.7%	0	n.r	10,341	11.0%	0.x%
New Mexico	1,388,063	14.9%	56,392	15.0%	39,908	12.2%	145,425	1.1%	1,629,788	7.1%	1.6%
New York	0	0.0%	1,363	4.2%	0	0.0%	0	n.r	1,363	1.9%	0.x%
North Carolina	102,634	8.3%	0	0.0%	8,785	2.2%	0	n.r	111,419	5.5%	0.1%
North Dakota	0	0.0%	29,920	41.9%	9,732	2.1%	0	0.0%	39,652	2.3%	0.x%
Ohio	0	0.0%	0	0.0%	77	1.0%	0	n.r	77	0.x%	0.0%
Oklahoma	14,431	4.8%	0	0.0%	8,570	8.7%	0	0.0%	23,001	5.6%	0.x%
Oregon	2,092,694	13.4%	0	0.0%	590	0.1%	15,694	0.1%	2,108,978	6.5%	2.0%
Pennsylvania	8,938	1.7%	0	0.0%	0	0.0%	0	n.r	8,938	1.6%	0.x%
Rhode Island	0	n.r	0	0.0%	0	0.0%	0	n.r	0	0.0%	0.0%
South Carolina	16,671	2.7%	15,010	55.6%	29,000	26.4%	0	n.r	60,681	8.1%	0.1%
South Dakota	9,826	0.5%	64,250	45.5%	0	0.0%	0	0.0%	74,076	2.8%	0.1%
Tennessee	66,208	10.5%	0	0.0%	0	0.0%	0	n.r	66,208	6.5%	0.1%
Texas	37,030	4.9%	46,850	4.0%	0	0.0%	0	n.r	83,880	3.6%	0.1%
Utah	774,328	9.5%	0	0.0%	0	0.0%	26,630	0.1%	800,958	2.5%	0.8%
Vermont	59,421	16.7%	0	0.0%	0	0.0%	0	n.r	59,421	16.3%	0.1%
Virginia	87,255	5.3%	79,579	25.2%	0	0.0%	0	n.r	166,834	8.0%	0.2%
Washington	2,572,799	28.0%	1,739,771	90.1%	839	0.6%	0	n.r	4,320,309	37.2%	4.2%
West Virginia	80,852	7.8%	0	0.0%	0	0.x%	6,900	1.9%	80,852	7.5%	0.2%
Wisconsin	42,294	2.8%	0	0.0%	29	0.x%	0	0.0%	42,323	2.2%	0.x%
Wyoming	3,080,358	33.3%	0	0.0%	0	0.0%	0	0.0%	3,080,358	10.2%	23.0%
Territories	0	0.0%	0	0.0%	0	0.0%	0	n.r	0	0.0%	
U.S. Total	34,730,828	18.1%	43,148,948	55.9%	20,685,467	23.6%	5,222,497	2.0%	103,784,015	16.7%	

[a] 0.x% = less than 0.05%.

[b] n.r = not relevant; the agency owns no land within the state.

TABLE 5. Additional Acreage Recommended for Wilderness, by State and by Agency (in acres and percentage of agency/Federal land)

	U.S.D.A. Forest Service		National Park Service		U.S. Fish and Wildlife Service		Bureau of Land Management		Total Designated Area		Share of NWPS
Alabama	0	0.0%	0	0.0%	0	0.0%	0	0.0%	0	0.0%	0.0%
Alaska	1,703,000	7.7%	9,143,005	18.0%	0	0.0%	41,000	0.1%	10,887,005	4.6%	37.3%
Arizona	62,000	0.6%	0	0.0%	0	0.0%	59,118	0.4%	121,118	0.4%	0.4%
Arkansas	0	0.0%	0	0.0%	975	0.3%	0	0.0%	975	0.x% ᵃ	0.x%
California	309,336	1.5%	0	0.0%	4,894	2.0%	1,002,901	6.9%	1,317,131	3.1%	4.5%
Colorado	0	0.0%	372,528	63.0%	0	0.0%	395,792	4.8%	768,320	3.3%	2.6%
Connecticut	0	0.0%	0	0.0%	0	0.0%	0	n.r	0	0.0%	0.0%
Delaware	0	n.r ᵇ	0	n.r	2,000	87.7%	0	n.r	2,000	7.7%	0.x%
Florida	0	0.0%	0	0.0%	0	0.0%	0	0.0%	0	0.0%	0.0%
Georgia	0	0.0%	0	0.0%	0	0.0%	0	0.0%	0	0.0%	0.0%
Hawaii	0	0.0%	0	0.0%	1,742	0.6%	0	n.r	1,742	0.3%	0.x%
Idaho	1,311,404	6.4%	9,447	9.5%	0	0.0%	972,239	8.2%	2,293,090	7.1%	7.9%
Illinois	0	0.0%	0	0.0%	0	0.0%	0	0.0%	0	0.0%	0.0%
Indiana	0	0.0%	0	0.0%	0	0.0%	0	n.r	0	0.0%	0.0%
Iowa	0	n.r	0	0.0%	0	0.0%	0	0.0%	0	0.0%	0.0%
Kansas	0	0.0%	0	0.0%	0	0.0%	0	n.r	0	0.0%	0.0%
Kentucky	0	0.0%	6,375	6.8%	0	0.0%	0	n.r	6,375	0.8%	0.x%
Louisiana	0	0.0%	0	0.0%	0	0.0%	0	0.0%	0	0.0%	0.0%
Maine	0	0.0%	0	0.0%	0	0.0%	0	n.r	0	0.0%	0.0%
Maryland	0	n.r	440	1.2%	418	1.0%	0	n.r	858	1.1%	0.x%
Massachusetts	0	n.r	0	0.0%	3,110	25.4%	0	n.r	3,110	6.9%	0.x%
Michigan	0	0.0%	0	0.0%	0	0.0%	0	0.0%	0	0.0%	0.0%
Minnesota	0	0.0%	127,436	91.7%	1,407	0.3%	0	0.0%	128,843	3.6%	0.4%
Mississippi	0	0.0%	0	0.0%	1,200	0.6%	0	0.0%	1,200	0.1%	0.x%
Missouri	0	0.0%	0	0.0%	0	0.0%	0	0.0%	0	0.0%	0.0%
Montana	798,756	4.7%	970,465	79.5%	161,580	26.6%	173,499	2.2%	2,104,300	7.9%	7.2%

ᵃ 0.x% = less than 0.05%.

ᵇ n.r = not relevant; the agency owns no land within the state.

Ross W. Gorte

TABLE 5. Additional Acreage Recommended for Wilderness, by State and by Agency (in acres and percentage of agency/Federal land)

	U.S.D.A. Forest Service		National Park Service		U.S. Fish and Wildlife Service		Bureau of Land Management		Total Designated Area		Share of NWPS
Nebraska	0	0.0%	0	0.0%	40,819	24.9%	0	0.0%	40,819	7.9%	0.1%
Nevada	0	0.0%	0	0.0%	1,751,148	76.3%	1,892,041	3.9%	3,643,189	6.4%	12.5%
New Hampshire	0	0.0%	0	0.0%	0	0.0%	0	n.r	0	0.0%	0.0%
New Jersey	0	n.r [b]	0	0.0%	0	0.0%	0	n.r	0	0.0%	0.0%
New Mexico	30,500	0.3%	0	0.0%	0	0.0%	487,186	3.8%	517,686	2.3%	1.8%
New York	0	0.0%	0	0.0%	0	0.0%	0	n.r	0	0.0%	0.0%
North Carolina	15,430	1.2%	207,647	56.4%	950	0.2%	0	n.r	224,027	11.1%	0.8%
North Dakota	0	0.0%	0	0.0%	0	0.0%	0	0.0%	0	0.0%	0.0%
Ohio	0	0.0%	0	0.0%	0	0.0%	0	n.r	0	0.0%	0.0%
Oklahoma	0	0.0%	0	0.0%	0	0.0%	0	0.0%	0	0.0%	0.0%
Oregon	0	0.0%	122,400	62.9%	46,500	8.7%	1,278,073	7.9%	1,446,973	4.4%	5.0%
Pennsylvania	0	0.0%	0	0.0%	0	0.0%	0	n.r	0	0.0%	0.0%
Rhode Island	0	n.r	0	0.0%	0	0.0%	0	n.r	0	0.0%	0.0%
South Carolina	1,969	0.3%	0	0.0%	163	0.2%	0	n.r	2,132	0.3%	0.x% [a]
South Dakota	0	0.0%	0	0.0%	0	0.0%	0	0.0%	0	0.0%	0.0%
Tennessee	0	0.0%	217,737	61.9%	0	0.0%	0	n.r	217,737	21.2%	0.8%
Texas	0	0.0%	533,900	45.3%	0	0.0%	0	n.r	533,900	23.0%	1.8%
Utah	0	0.0%	635,708	31.4%	0	0.0%	1,958,339	8.8%	2,594,047	8.0%	8.9%
Vermont	0	0.0%	0	0.0%	620	9.6%	0	n.r	620	0.2%	0.x%
Virginia	0	0.0%	0	0.0%	3,047	2.6%	0	n.r	3,047	0.2%	0.x%
Washington	0	0.0%	0	0.0%	0	0.0%	0	0.0%	0	0.0%	0.0%
West Virginia	0	0.0%	0	0.0%	0	0.0%	0	n.r	0	0.0%	0.0%
Wisconsin	0	0.0%	0	0.0%	0	0.0%	0	0.0%	0	0.0%	0.0%
Wyoming	0	0.0%	2,079,626	86.9%	0	0.0%	240,364	1.3%	2,319,990	7.7%	8.0%
Territories	6,703	24.0%	0	0.0%	0	0.0%	0	n.r	6,703	4.5%	0.x%
U.S. Total	4,239,098	2.2%	14,426,714	18.7%	2,020,573	2.3%	8,500,552	3.2%	29,186,937	4.7%	

[a] 0.x% = less than 0.05%.

[b] n.r = not relevant; the agency owns no land within the state.

TABLE 6. Federal Land Designated as or Recommended for Wilderness, by State and by Agency (in acres and percentage of agency/Federal land

	U.S.D.A. Forest Service		National Park Service		U.S. Fish and Wildlife Service		Bureau of Land Management		Total Designated Area		Share of NWPS [a]
Alabama	33,151	5.0%	0	0.0%	0	0.0%	0	0.0%	33,151	4.1%	0.x%
Alaska	7,455,899	33.9%	42,122,375	83.2%	18,676,320	24.4%	41,000	0.1%	68,295,594	28.8%	51.4%
Arizona	1,406,970	12.5%	443,700	16.6%	1,343,444	80.1%	1,464,868	10.3%	4,658,982	15.6%	3.5%
Arkansas	116,560	4.6%	34,993	35.6%	3,119	1.0%	0	0.0%	154,672	4.8%	0.1%
California	4,745,225	23.0%	5,975,052	79.0%	14,066	5.8%	4,553,212	31.4%	15,287,555	35.6%	11.5%
Colorado	3,147,686	21.7%	428,175	72.4%	2,560	4.0%	454,319	5.5%	4,032,740	17.2%	3.0%
Connecticut	0	0.0%	0	0.0%	0	0.0%	0	n.r	0	0.0%	0.0%
Delaware	0	n.r [b]	0	n.r	2,000	7.7%	0	n.r	2,000	7.7%	0.x%
Florida	74,495	6.5%	1,296,500	55.8%	51,252	21.2%	0	0.0%	1,422,247	38.1%	1.1%
Georgia	113,423	13.1%	8,840	21.7%	362,107	76.7%	0	n.r	484,370	35.2%	0.4%
Hawaii	0	0.0%	142,370	60.5%	1,742	0.6%	0	n.r	144,112	27.5%	0.1%
Idaho	5,272,905	25.8%	52,690	53.1%	0	0.0%	973,041	8.2%	6,298,636	19.4%	4.7%
Illinois	25,549	9.4%	0	0.0%	4,050	5.7%	0	0.0%	29,599	8.6%	0.x%
Indiana	12,935	6.7%	0	0.0%	0	0.0%	0	n.r	12,935	6.2%	0.x%
Iowa	0	n.r	0	0.0%	0	0.0%	0	0.0%	0	0.0%	0.0%
Kansas	0	0.0%	0	0.00%	0	0.0%	0	n.r	0	0.0%	0.0%
Kentucky	16,415	2.4%	6,375	6.8%	0	0.0%	0	n.r	22,790	2.9%	0.x%
Louisiana	8,679	1.4%	0	0.0%	8,346	1.9%	0	0.0%	17,025	1.2%	0.x%
Maine	12,000	22.6%	0	0.0%	7,392	16.0%	0	n.r	19,392	11.9%	0.x%
Maryland	0	n.r	440	1.2%	418	1.0%	0	n.r	858	1.1%	0.x%
Massachusetts	0	n.r	0	0.0%	5,530	45.2%	0	n.r	5,530	12.3%	0.x%
Michigan	91,891	3.2%	132,018	20.9%	25,309	22.4%	0	0.0%	249,218	6.8%	0.2%
Minnesota	807,451	28.5%	127,436	91.7%	7,587	1.8%	0	0.0%	942,474	26.6%	0.7%
Mississippi	6,046	0.5%	4,080	4.0%	1,200	0.6%	0	0.0%	11,326	0.8%	0.x%
Missouri	63,198	4.2%	0	0.0%	7,730	15.6%	0	0.0%	70,928	4.4%	0.1%
Montana	4,170,526	24.7%	970,465	79.5%	226,115	37.2%	179,499	2.2%	5,546,605	20.7%	4.2%

[a] 0.x% = less than 0.05%.

[b] n.r = not relevant; the agency owns no land within the state.

TABLE 6. Federal Land Designated as or Recommended for Wilderness, by State and by Agency
(in acres and percentage of agency/Federal land

	U.S.D.A. Forest Service		National Park Service		U.S. Fish and Wildlife Service		Bureau of Land Management		Total Designated Area		Share of NWPS [a]
Nebraska	7,794	2.2%	0	0.0%	45,454	27.8%	0	0.0%	53,248	10.1%	0.x% [a]
Nevada	786,067	13.5%	0	0.0%	1,751,148	76.3%	1,898,499	4.0%	4,435,714	7.8%	3.3%
New Hampshire	102,932	14.2%	0	0.0%	0	0.0%	0	n.r	102,932	14.0%	0.1%
New Jersey	0	n.r [b]	0	0.0%	10,341	17.7%	0	n.r	10,341	11.0%	0.x%
New Mexico	1,418,563	15.2%	56,392	15.0%	39,908	12.2%	632,611	4.9%	2,147,714	9.4%	1.6%
New York	0	0.0%	1,363	4.2%	0	0.0%	0	n.r	1,363	1.9%	0.0%
North Carolina	118,064	9.5%	207,647	56.4%	9,735	2.4%	0	n.r	335,446	16.7%	0.2%
North Dakota	0	0.0%	29,920	41.9%	9,732	2.1%	0	0.0%	39,652	2.3%	0.x%
Ohio	0	0.0%	0	0.0%	77	1.0%	0	n.r	77	0.x%	0.x%
Oklahoma	14,431	4.8%	0	0.0%	8,570	8.7%	0	0.0%	23,001	5.6%	0.x%
Oregon	2,092,694	13.4%	122,400	62.9%	47,090	8.8%	1,293,767	8.0%	3,555,951	10.9%	2.7%
Pennsylvania	8,938	1.7%	0	0.0%	0	0.0%	0	n.r	8,938	1.6%	0.x%
Rhode Island	0	n.r	0	0.0%	0	0.0%	0	n.r	0	0.0%	0.0%
South Carolina	18,640	3.0%	15,010	55.6%	29,163	26.6%	0	n.r	62,813	8.4%	0.1%

South Dakota	9,826	0.5%	64,250	45.5%	0	0.0%	0	0.0%	74,076	2.8%	0.1%
Tennessee	66,208	10.5%	217,737	61.9%	0	0.0%	0	n.r	283,945	27.7%	0.2%
Texas	37,030	4.9%	580,750	49.3%	0	0.0%	0	n.r	617,780	26.6%	0.5%
Utah	774,328	9.5%	635,708	31.4%	0	0.0%	1,984,969	8.9%	3,395,005	10.5%	2.6%
Vermont	59,421	16.7%	0	0.0%	620	9.6%	0	n.r	60,041	16.4%	0.x%
Virginia	87,255	5.3%	79,579	25.2%	3,047	2.6%	0	n.r	169,881	8.2%	0.1%
Washington	2,572,799	28.0%	1,739,771	90.1%	839	0.6%	6,900	1.9%	4,320,309	37.2%	3.2%
West Virginia	80,852	7.8%	0	0.0%	0	0.0%	0	n.r	80,852	7.5%	0.1%
Wisconsin	42,294	2.8%	0	0.0%	29	0.x%	0	0.0%	42,323	2.2%	0.x%
Wyoming	3,080,358	33.3%	2,079,626	86.9%	0	0.0%	240,364	1.3%	5,400,348	17.9%	4.1%
Territories	6,703	24.0%	0	0.0%	0	0.0%	0	n.r	6,703	4.5%	0.x%
U.S. Total	38,966,201	20.3%	57,575,662	74.6%	22,706,040	25.9%	13,723,049	5.2%	132,970,952	21.4%	

^a 0.x% = less than 0.05%.

^b n.r = not relevant; the agency owns no land within the state.

Natural Resources
Pages 19-76

ECOSYSTEM MANAGEMENT TOOLS & TECHNIQUES: PROCEEDINGS OF A CRS WORKSHOP

Wayne A. Morrissey

SUMMARY

The House Subcommittee on Technology, Environment, and Aviation of the House Committee on Science, Space, and Technology (103rd Congress) requested that Congressional Research Service (CRS) hold a workshop on the tools and techniques of ecosystem management. The purposes of this workshop were to demonstrate tools and techniques used in scientific research on ecosystems and to address technological aspects of developing and administering a national policy for ecosystem management.

CRS invited nationally recognized leaders to discuss practical applications such as locating boundaries of natural habitats, demonstrating temporal changes in ecosystems, and improving communication and coordination among many of the stakeholders. The workshop featured technologies used by Federal agencies to support their ecosystem management programs. Participants were also to prepare presentations which addressed five policy questions:

- What are the opportunities and limitations of these tools?
- Where is the development of these tools headed, and how rapidly are they changing?
- What are the costs associated with tools, and how do those costs compare with the cost of data acquisition?
- Is there a need for new or different data based upon the capabilities and opportunities of the tools? and,
- What is the potential of these tools for informing the public decision-making process and contributing to other national goals?

The following conclusions were drawn from the workshop:

- Many of the tools and techniques demonstrated appeared effective at analyzing functional relationships within an ecosystem, including the human component; others clearly demonstrated potential for incorporating stakeholders' concerns in assessments of ecosystems;
- New applications and technologies may be needed as project managers gain experience with an ecosystem approach;
- Stakeholders should be able to reduce redundancy in planning and to develop standardized technology-based systems for research and analysis of ecosystems, and for data management;
- Costs of procurement of technology would likely decline if collaborative approaches to ecosystem management were adopted; and
- Ecosystem data and analyses are similar to many other types of information which describe spatial changes over time; moreover, these could contribute to and benefit from other national efforts aimed at understanding the Earth and its physical systems.

INTRODUCTION

The purposes of the workshop were to demonstrate various tools and techniques of ecosystem research and to address technology-related aspects of the administration of ecosystem management programs. This workshop also explored ways technology could be helpful for developing and implementing a coordinated Federal policy on ecosystem management, one which the Clinton Administration and others have expressed hope would encompass social, economic, and cultural values in addition to environmental concerns.

The workshop focused on how technology might: 1) support better coordination of Federal agencies and their programs; 2) monitor changing conditions under an ecosystem approach; 3) be used to validate successes or failures in natural resources management which are allegedly attributable to ecosystem approaches; and 4) be used to monitor compliance with relevant environmental requirements.

Other themes of the workshop included how data derived from such ecosystem management activities could be made more readily accessible to the research community and interpreted for policymakers; and how the nature of and needs for data change over time.

Congress hopes to learn whether a Federal ecosystem management framework might help to resolve some of these conflicts; and how technology such as geographic information systems, and techniques such as spatial analysis, might be adapted to an ecosystem approach. Many Members of Congress are particularly interested in addressing conflicts in natural resources management because various Federal, State, and local laws have mandated conflicting missions. For example, some agencies have been traditionally charged with promoting natural resources development, while others protect the environment or individual species in adjacent or common sites.

The U.S. Congress also has been interested in learning how technology can enhance the science which supports the ecosystem approach and other national scientific efforts such as the U.S. Global Change Research Program, the National Biological Service, and the development of a National Spatial Data Infrastructure. Moreover, it would like to know how information can be effectively analyzed and interpreted for administrative decision makers.

Representative Tim Valentine, Chairman of the House Subcommittee on Technology, Environment and Aviation in the 103rd Congress requested that CRS hold this workshop for congressional staff. Wayne Morrissey of the Science

Policy Research Division organized and moderated this workshop, and Jeffrey Zinn of the Environment and Natural Resources Policy Division co-coordinated the workshop. The workshop took place on June 22, 1994. It was the first in a possible series of follow up workshops to the two-day CRS Symposium on Ecosystem Management which took place on March 24 and 25, 1994.[1]

BACKGROUND

The workshop was primarily focused on the tools used to describe and analyze ecosystems as part of ongoing management efforts. Demonstrations and presentations by experts explored how these might serve public decision makers. Some participants were requested to discuss practical applications of these tools, including their potential for locating natural boundaries and identifying temporal changes in ecosystems. Others participants demonstrated the potential of some of these tools to organize, analyze, and present information to support the management of ecosystems. All participants were also asked to address five questions with policy implications:

- What are the opportunities and limitations of these tools?
- Where is the development of these tools headed, and how rapidly are they changing?
- What are the costs associated with the tools, and how do those costs compare with the cost of data acquisition?
- Is there a need for new or different data based upon the capabilities and opportunities of the tools? and
- What is the potential use of these tools for informing the public decision making process and how might they contribute to other national goals?

Concurrent demonstrations for Members and staff of the practical applications of tools used in the ecosystem approach were conducted by: 1) Terrestrial Ecosystems Regional Research and Analysis Laboratory of Ft. Collins, Colorado, a U.S. Federal interagency consortium of universities and the private sector; 2) U.S. Department of Agriculture (USDA), and U.S. Fish and Wildlife Service (FWS), demonstrating the use of the Global Positioning System (GPS) for tracking non-game species on Conservation Reserve Program lands; and 3) the National Biological Survey (NBS) of the U.S. Department of the Interior -- now the National Biological Service -- in conjunction with the USGS-EROS Data Center demonstrating techniques of Gap Analysis.

After introductory remarks of Wayne Morrissey of CRS, Nancy Tosta, Chief of the Branch of Geographic Data Coordination at the National Mapping

---

[1] *Ecosystem Management: Status and Potential; Summary of a Workshop Convened by the Congressional Research Service, March 24 and 25, 1994.* Prepared by the Environment and Natural Resources Policy Division of the Congressional Research Service for the U.S. Senate Committee on Environment and Public Works [S.Prt. 103-98]. Washington, GPO, December 1994. 331 p.

Division of the U.S. Geological Survey (USGS) gave the keynote address. Ms. Tosta spoke on the role of data management and information analysis in ecosystem management. She also discussed the opportunities and limitations of ecosystem management data, and how they might serve other broad national goals. Following a discussion period, representatives of each of the demonstrations of ecosystem management technology made a brief presentation reproduced in Appendix I. TERRA Lab then demonstrated its "Active Response GIS (ARGIS)," followed by a question and answer session. Concurrent demonstrations resumed for the remaining time.

DEMONSTRATIONS

Ecosystem Management, Geographic Information Systems, and the Global Positioning System (GPS)

D. Alan Davenport, Geographic Information System (GIS) Specialist at FWS, demonstrated a GIS used interactively with a hand-held geographic position locator. The locator was in communication with the space-based satellite Global Positioning System (GPS). This suite of tools illustrated how migratory fowl, for example, could be tracked to identify their habitats and ranges.

Mr. Davenport explained how observers on the ground could spot species flying overhead and determine their location using the GPS. At the same time, aerial surveillance with an expert observer on board the aircraft is often performed in conjunction with satellite-remote sensing. Comparison of the two observations is used to validate spatial data and can help to classify broad-scale land uses and bioregions. In addition, aerial surveillance enables a trained, in-flight observer with a two-way transmitter to serve as the eyes of field experts who are unable to gather such extensive data *in situ*. In such cases, observations are radioed back to the ground and technicians scan bar-coded classifications with a wand into a notebook-PC while tracking the location of the aircraft. They may also manually input supplemental information about the ecosystem and other unique spatial attributes.

None of these technologies eliminate the work of field ecologists. At times, a field observer may have to work at a level of detail that is too great for remote-sensing technologies or aerial surveillance. Moreover, satellites and aerial surveillance cannot "see" important details of the ecosystem under forest canopies, again requiring the field observers to gather the missing information. The field expert is also important for ground-truthing and validating remotely sensed data. However, space-based technology still plays an integral role because the field experts can triangulate precise locations by GPS radio signal.

Gap Analysis

Dr. Michael Scott of the Idaho Cooperative Unit of the National Biological Service (NBS), and a current national leader in Gap Analysis, described the methodology as one which "Provides a quick overview of the distribution and conservation status of several components of biodiversity. It seeks to identify gaps (i.e., vegetation types and species that are not represented in the network of biodiversity management areas) that may be filled through establishment of new reserves or changes in land management practices."[2]

Gap Analysis relies on GIS, satellite remote-sensing, and field measurements. It entails overlaying data such as vegetation types, predicted animal distributions, and protected areas. The resulting maps can be used to identify gaps in protection of biodiversity, where biodiversity conservation might conflict with management practices. Many experts in the field are quick to point out, however, that Gap Analysis is only one technique of an ecosystem management approach and is not a substitute for a comprehensive biological survey.

Using a GIS to display and analyze spatially-referenced digital data in cartographic format, Brian Biggs of the USGS-EROS Data Center, demonstrated how NBS is currently performing Gap Analysis. Dr. Scott pointed out that the importance of this technique for ecosystem management becomes very clear when policy makers are able to visualize graphically how two different government-mandated projects, which are collecting different information or utilizing different management practices based on disparate needs, can ultimately conflict. The demonstration of the database also showed how biodiversity can often be unaccounted for in land management or environmental protection efforts, because it transcends traditional boundaries of institutions responsibilities.

In a similar vein, Gap Analysis based upon validated scientific data can demonstrate intrinsic conflicts when statutes require administrative entities to pursue differing management responsibilities. For example, currently restricted alternative land uses, including resources extraction or agriculture, might be allowed in some areas where evidence suggests that neither the environmental quality nor populations of adjacent communities are in a critical state. That is, where the ecosystem is not environmentally stressed.

Brian Biggs mentioned that only a small number of States at this time have compiled sufficient biodiversity data for inclusion in a database of Gap Analysis created by NBS for public access. Dr. Scott suggested that compilation of the database has only been made possible so far by contributions from viable, comprehensive, and detailed State and community biological surveys. NBS has made some biological survey data accessible via the Internet for a limited number of ecoregions in the United States. Dr. Scott noted that over two hundred public and private institutions are currently engaged in Gap Analysis, so the database will expand significantly in the near future.

---

[2]"Gap Analysis: A Geographic Approach to Protection of Biological Diversity," by J. Michael Scott, et al. Wildlife Monographs, no. 123, January 1993: 1-41. 1993, Blacksburg, VA., Department of Fisheries and Wildlife Sciences, Virginia Polytechnic Institute and University.

NBS is also working with the United Nations Environmental Programme's Global Resource Information Database (UNEP-GRID) Program, which has developed an extensive database of global land-use and vegetation classifications. UNEP intends to expand the biological survey concept of NBS internationally through the GRID program. Brian Biggs suggested that leveraging resources between the two institutions has helped to keep down the costs of both. Moreover, a Memorandum of Understanding (MOU) has helped NBS to enhance its Gap Analysis program with the inclusion of UNEP-GRID data on North America.

Ecosystem Management and Decision-Based Supporting Technologies

Virginia Ferreira led a group from Terrestrial Ecosystems Regional Research and Analysis Laboratory (TERRA Lab) of Ft. Collins, Colorado, in demonstrating electronic systems, some which were designed to analyze relationships of entities in the physical and geographic environment, and others which would foster a consensus-building process for stakeholders by enhancing communications. At the workshop, these technologies were adapted specifically for an ecosystem-based approach for land management.

Technologies included a hypertext-based software used interactively with a GIS, which proved to be a powerful tool for compiling spatially-referenced attributes of an ecosystem and demonstrating their functional relationships. The results of various queries could be viewed either in cartographic (map-based), encyclopedic (textual), or sophisticated graphics (computer visualization) format, and at a hierarchy of spatial resolutions. Queries could be initiated just by pointing and clicking on specific text or objects represented on a map, such as place names, water bodies, or public facilities.

TERRA Lab also demonstrated its "Modular Modeling Complex," a system which is capable of integrating independent models, and objectively giving equal weight to each model's sub-components. In this manner, the interrelationships between two (or more) physical systems, such as the local hydrological cycle and incident vegetation species, could be analyzed. Furthermore, these data were displayed in 4 dimensions, exhibiting physical changes over time (from hours to years) and space.

TERRA Lab's "Active Response GIS (ARGIS)", unlike many of the other tools demonstrated at the workshop, was primarily developed to support administrative decisions. ARGIS functions as an electronic conference tool and polling system which utilizes Structured Analysis Methodology (SAM). ARGIS has the capability of combining responses made by users who have different interests, needs, and priorities; and projecting the results as a geographically-based data display. ARGIS was touted as a non-biased means of consensus building for decision makers. At its core is a GIS, which creates possible scenarios that weigh the interests of all affected parties. TERRA Lab conducted a mock land-use planning exercise at the workshop, and final results illustrated the collective attitudes of those in attendance about sustainable economic development within a hypothetical geographic region.

PRESENTATION THEMES

The workshop revolved around six major themes: the application of technology to ecosystem management; the opportunities and limitations of technology; evolution of the technologies; characterization of the social components of ecosystem management; the potential benefits to programs from improved coordination among stakeholders; and ecosystem data management and analysis.

Applying Technology to Analyzing Ecosystems

Many presenters portrayed their demonstrations as representative of a wide array of technological approaches for addressing some of the challenges of ecosystem management. The various presentations identified the components of an ecosystem approach, including research, data management and analysis, planning for natural resources, and development of an integrated assessment of ecosystems with appropriate weights given to decisions affecting stakeholders interests. Others made a point that technology also can be used to enhance communication among the stakeholders.

TERRA Lab noted that many of their tools have already been employed successfully for such diverse purposes as environmental modeling and monitoring, meeting and conducting business electronically, and polling public opinion. Other presentations touted the benefits of integrating different technologies in an ecosystem approach. An example is FWS efforts at tracking wildlife, which draw upon the capabilities of a suite of technologies which help to identify geographic coordinates, and facilitate spatial analysis.

Technology Opportunities and Limitations

Most assessments were optimistic that technology could assist in ecosystem approaches. In the context of streamlining excessive regulations, promoting efficiency in government, and shifting toward risk-based regulatory policy, for example, one presentation discussed how GIS can show how regulations are manifested in the physical and geographic environment. Dr. Scott of NBS concentrated especially on how management practices might affect biodiversity. He suggested that GIS output can clearly demarcate where some statutes are effective, and others are conflicting, redundant, or superfluous, as measured by the apparent health of ecosystems, based on the presence of important indicator species. Many presenters described ways in which decision-makers and stakeholders could begin to build political consensus, for example, by adapting technologies such as TERRA Lab's "ARGIS" in an ecosystem-based approach which encompasses integrated assessment.

The presentations also illustrated how the purposes of the tools and techniques of ecosystem management can be as diverse as their users. D. Alan Davenport of FWS cited how some technologies help to support assessments of ecosystem function and efforts at restoring them and improving their resiliency. Others pointed out benefits from technologies which can integrate and assess the social, economic, and cultural activities of humans within the ecosystem. Such activities might help to identify human activities which foster environmental stewardship, sustainable natural resources development and planning, and long-term support of ecosystem-based management practices; or, on the other hand, identify the possible detrimental effects of humans and their institutions upon ecosystems.

One speaker suggested that although many technologies enhance scientific knowledge about ecosystems or facilitate an ecosystem approach, these tools are only one component of an ecosystem approach which requires human interface and expertise. Other limitations include the potential for data collection to outpace analytical capabilities; the high costs of developing and transferring technology to the private sector; and, the analysts' confidence in the validity of the data collected, and the quality of the metadata (auxiliary data which describe the methodologies and parameters under which data were collected).

Evolving Technologies

A recurring theme was that the technologies of ecosystem management would continue to evolve. An analogy was made in one presentation to the evolution of personal computers over the past 15 years. The tradeoff of the initially high costs of continual evolving technology is that its users are typically compensated by declining costs as the market for new technologies expands, and as the efficiency and utility of the technologies increase.

Ms. Tosta pointed out that the purpose for developing GIS systems is not only to model natural systems on a spatial basis, but also to use those models to understand how site and social interactions give value to a "place" comprised of natural systems and human, social, economic and cultural activities. She suggested that by conceptualizing ecosystems as a place containing objects with attached human values, this new approach moves spatial analysis from having to consider spatially defined areas as a series of layers which may or may not schematically relate with one another to an object-oriented GIS which defines relationships of objects in space. Using this new approach may simply require a new set of algorithms and new versions of existing GIS software programs.

Virginia Ferreira emphasized that the technological groundwork has already been laid for a consensus-building process which identifies interests and concerns of all stakeholders, and which is targeted to planning at the local community level. The essence of such a process, she suggested, is embodied in such technologies as TERRA Lab's "ARGIS", which uses structural analysis methodology.

Technology and the Social Component of Ecosystem Management

Many involved in ecosystem management, especially social scientists, have asserted that, under the evolving paradigm of an ecosystem approach, humans and their institutions should be considered an integral component of the ecosystem, rather than one operating independently and unaffected by, or dominant over the ecosystem. In her presentation, Ms. Tosta identified ecosystems as places, and as entities which encompass social, economic, and cultural functions of their human inhabitants. This concept is now generally referred to as the "human dimensions of ecosystem management." The human component of the landscape has also gained attention of those concerned with global climate change.[3] The Clinton Administration has also supported the concept of including a social and economic component in both ecosystem approaches and integrated assessments of ecosystems.

Coordination

All presentations addressed coordination among participating public and private institutions; and some of the historical impediments to inter-institutional and interdisciplinary approaches which have been encountered. An example is when social and physical scientists do not "speak the same language" or share the same terminology or research methodologies. Presenters emphasized the need for interagency and intra-governmental coordination, as well as collaboration with the academic community and the private sector to ensure that all stakeholders have an opportunity to participate in planning activities and decision making.

Nancy Tosta, in particular, explained how lack of coordination can impede the development of common tools and practices, and how it may result in institutions independently developing practices to manage and distribute data. There seemed to be a consensus that such impediments also affect private efforts. Furthermore, coordination appears to flounder when Federal laws and regulations mandate actions, or when actions are requested by the Federal government, but these are expected to be financed and managed at the sub-national level; a concern now debated under the label of "unfunded mandates".

Discussants pointed out that lack of coordination may also reflect different priorities of Federal agencies within a given ecosystem; whether it be to increase harvest of timber, to preserve the health of indigenous wildlife, or provide more scenic recreation and boating opportunities. Ms. Tosta suggested that while it might be expected that research methodologies and resultant data would differ from project to project, the intrinsic data management and other practices which administratively support research and policy decision-making should be standardized.

Other presenters commented on some of the successes of interagency and interdisciplinary coordination overcoming institutional impediments. The experiences of the NBS Gap Analysis Program and the TERRA Lab mission were offered as examples. Both activities were founded on public/private

---

[3] See, for example, *Global Environmental Change: Understanding the Human Dimensions*. Paul C. Stern, Oran Young, and Daniel Druckman, editors. Committee on Human Dimensions of Global Change, Commission on the Behavioral and Social Sciences and Education, National Research Council. Washington, 1992. National Academy of Sciences Press. 308 pp.

partnerships, and in the latter example, through a federally supported Cooperative Research and Develop Agreement (CRADA).

Ecosystem Data and Information

Discussion of the importance of data management and information analysis centered on how an ecosystem approach's spatial data needs are similar to others that require relationships within a place to be modeled; and how interpretation of these data currently depend on techniques of geospatial analysis. Issues surrounding the pricing, user-ascribed values, and criteria for data collection were also discussed.

Nancy Tosta discussed the role of the White House Federal Geographic Data Committee (FGDC) in data management, which is to promote standardization among all Federal agencies in how they archive, store, transfer, and distribute spatially related digital data. Addressing the concern that the FGDC was trying to impose a research agenda on its members, she contrasted the more philosophical and visionary aspects of how ecosystem data and information management *might* be carried out, and the more narrowly defined mandate of FGDC.

Pricing of data, and their value-added products, was also addressed by Ms. Tosta who summarized how costs often reflect values ascribed to certain data, data sets, or analyses. Moreover, the value of most raw or un-enhanced data (data as collected by the primary investigator, for example) is limited to a select group that can understand and manipulate them. Some data may be useful only in real time; other data may be more important from a historical perspective to demonstrate changes in ecosystems. Furthermore, 1) the reliability of the source, 2) the validity of the data, 3) any personal values attached to them, and 4) how they are ultimately used or interpreted by others, are other factors which may affect the pricing of data or resultant analyses. Many in the Federal data community have supported a minimal cost-of-reproduction-only policy for those who work with minimally-enhanced digital data.

Another salient issue concerns whether Federal agencies are currently collecting and preserving the "right" data, and how data collection priorities, will most likely change over time. Virginia Ferreira raised this issue in the context of detecting indicators for major global climatic change. She suggested that recent changes in water availability, which she has observed in an ecosystem she has been studying, may be one indicator of climate change. Awareness of climatic change was made possible through data collections derived from an ecosystem-based approach whose proponents are currently looking at changes in hydrologic systems over time, as one of the ecosystem's components. In this context, she suggested, both ecosystem managers and the global change community often benefit from the same data and research.

ISSUES FOR CONGRESS

Congressional Interest

Congress has shown interest in many issues relating to a Federal ecosystem management policy. In the fall of 1993, six congressional committees requested CRS organize a symposium on ecosystem management. That symposium was held on March 24-25, 1994, and was attended by many congressional staff members and over 150 experts representing science, natural resources management, public administration, environmental advocacy, and industry, as well as private land owners, such as ranchers and farmers.

Many lawmakers have raised important questions about ecosystem management. Among these were how they might support the development of a consensus-building process to serve the interests of many stakeholders, and whether technology might help to facilitate an ecosystem approach. These concerns were addressed in this workshop.

For a broader discussion of issues relating to the ecosystem approach, see *Ecosystem Management: Status and Potential; Summary of a Workshop Convened by the Congressional Research Service, March 24 and 25, 1994.* Prepared by the Environment and Natural Resources Policy Division of the Congressional Research Service for the U.S. Senate Committee on Environment and Public Works [S.Prt. 103-98]. Washington, GPO, December 1994. 331 p.

The Clinton Administration and the Ecosystem Approach

The goals of ecosystem management have been strongly supported by the Clinton Administration and are articulated in the President's FY 1995 budget submission to Congress and in *Reinventing American Government*. The Administration intends to protect biodiversity, to gain a better understanding of ecosystem dynamics, and to reduce Government costs through sharing resources. On this subject, participants discussed the need for national legislation governing domestic policy on ecosystem management in the near future.

Part of the rationale behind such legislation is the White House Office of Science and Technology Policy's (OSTP) initiative to prioritize Federal research activities in ecosystem management and environmental research and development, in general, as embodied in the President's FY 1996 budget submission. The White House Office of Environmental Policy (OEP) has been promoting a series of regional case studies to determine what is currently working in ecosystem management. The OEP has sponsored a Federal task force report on ecosystem management which will include an extensive survey of study areas.

Legislative Issues

Comments about the value of this workshop to congressional staff were offered. Generally, the value was in raising important issues that might become part of future legislative deliberations.

Some of these comments addressed how a comprehensive Federal ecosystem management approach might require a reevaluation of supporting Federal scientific research priorities and technological requirements. Participants aware of technology research, development, and transfer issues, for example, cited how impediments may arise in the development, procurement, and implementation of new technologies intended to enhance Federal efforts; and suggested that these impediments could be institutional, economic, or legal.

Many legislative staff concurred with presenters that ecosystem management programs could be better coordinated across Federal agencies and with other intergovernmental, academic, and private institutions. They said the workshop helped to make them aware of the important role for coordination in the development and utilization of these tools, processes, and data management systems.

Participants involved in ecosystem management, including Federal natural resources managers in attendance, proposed new management approaches. They concurrently requested the direction of Congress through legislation to encompass social, economic, and cultural concerns along with the promotion of healthy ecosystems in their respective programs. In addition, some attending Federal field managers urged that a national ecosystem management policy be driven from the bottom-up, and be case-sensitive. They asserted that any national policies should be flexible enough to allow for an "adaptive management" approach that can be adjusted as ecosystems change.

How the tools and techniques of ecosystem management will be used remains to be seen. However, many of these technologies demonstrated potential for contributing to an integrated assessment of ecosystems, as called for by the White House OEP and OSTP, among others. Such an assessment would require data and mathematical models, qualitative input, and conceptual models accounting for social, economic and cultural interests of stakeholders.

Most of the technologies demonstrated at the workshop and discussed in presentations appeared to be effective for relating biodiversity and physical environments within ecosystems. A demonstration of technology-assisted Gap Analysis, for example, illustrated how required management practices may be engendering conflicts within defined ecoregions; and "ARGIS", developed by TERRA Lab, demonstrated its capability for assisting with consensus building.

Remote sensing technology has accelerated the rate and increased the amount of data collected at broad spatial resolutions. This technology has facilitated spatial analysis because these data are acquired in digital format and are often compatible with GIS. With the capture of more validated spatial data, the costs of acquisition are likely to decline. Some scientists even fear that before too long there will be an inundation of data, and more will be available than they are capable of analyzing. If so, costs for value-added data and resultant analysis may begin to increase as the supply of data begins to outstrip analyses; while the costs for raw or un-enhanced data are likely to decline.

It has been argued that the costs of technology and managing data for ecosystem management activities could be leveraged among a host of stakeholders, once standardized procedures and shared practices are adopted. In this context, many speakers asserted that Federal agencies, or the Federal Government, must develop partnerships with other public and private institutions to support these efforts.

Many discussants recognized that technology alone will not resolve all the institutional barriers which currently constrain a national ecosystem effort. Obstacles are as basic as devising standard definitions for key concepts among many involved disciplines in the social and physical sciences, including a "healthy ecosystem", "adaptive management", "productive capacity", and "ecosystem restoration". Developing standards for engineering and calibrating the tools that would measure and monitor progress, and indices to validate successes or failures of the ecosystem approach, is also a formidable challenge.

Moreover, there is not total agreement among the ranks of the U.S. Federal Government and private citizens as to whether adopting an ecosystem approach--which might imply further government intervention, additional regulations and requirements for private land owners, and new responsibilities for enforcement--is the right way to proceed for future national land management policies.

However, at the conclusion of the workshop, many participants agreed that the progress of adapting technology for an ecosystem approach is at a pivotal point. They emphasized that to perpetuate such successful (albeit in some cases experimental) efforts and to implement new technology in ecosystem approaches, Congress and the public need to be aware that concepts of ecosystem management and its data and information management components will change over time and with practical experience. The technology used to acquire and analyze those data will change as well. Furthermore, the needs for data will change as knowledge about what is required for effective ecosystem management evolves. Supporters of the development of applicable technologies for Federal ecosystem approaches, therefore, must be flexible and sensitive to the evolving qualities and longevity of such programs.

APPENDIX I

PRESENTATIONS OF THE CRS WORKSHOP
ON ECOSYSTEM MANAGEMENT

I.   Wayne Morrissey
     Congressional Research Service
     Introduction to the CRS Workshop on the Tools and Techniques of Ecosystem Management

II. Nancy Tosta
     U.S. Geological Survey
     The Role of Data Management and Information Analysis for Supporting an Ecosystem Approach

III. D. Alan Davenport
     U.S. Fish and Wildlife Service
     Applications of GPS and GIS Techniques in Migratory Bird Management

IV. J. Michael Scott
     Idaho Cooperative Fish and Wildlife Research Unit
     The Gap Analysis Program (GAP) of the National Biological Survey

V.   Virginia Ferreira
     Terrestrial Ecosystem Regional Research (TERRA) Laboratory
     TERRA Tools and Techniques for Ecosystem Management

Good morning, I am Wayne Morrissey of the Science Policy Research Division of the Congressional Research Service (CRS), and moderator of the CRS workshop on the Tools and Techniques of Ecosystem Management. I would like to take this opportunity to welcome our audience and special guests who have been, and will be, demonstrating the tools and techniques of ecosystem management this morning.

Some experts have described ecosystem management as, and I quote, "An emerging and evolving paradigm which consists of a number of similar processes that seek ecological approaches for the sustainable management of the environment, including social and cultural values, and economic interests."

This workshop is the first in a series which follows the CRS Symposium on Ecosystem Management held last March. At that symposium, 150 experts including scientists, natural resources managers, Federal, State and local government representatives, and private land owners, met to discuss opportunities and concerns about developing a Federal ecosystem management policy.

A series of up to 6 CRS workshops to be held over the next year will address ecosystem management topics. Today our intention is to demonstrate that ecosystem management does not merely exist as a concept, a hope, or an aspiration, but that it has been, can be, and is actually being, done right now. However, some might concede that existing approaches are not as comprehensive or sophisticated as they will need to be to enable successful ecosystem-based management approaches.

Today, we hope to develop better understanding from those actually involved how ecosystem management, from a technological perspective, is or isn't working. We hope to learn about the potential opportunities and limitations of these tools; and, moreover, those questions relating to ecosystem management that they can and cannot answer at this time.

We have a distinguished team of experts with us today. I say team, because it will soon become clear that another purpose of today's workshop is to demonstrate how State and local governments, industry and academia are working together with the federal government both to develop the tools and techniques of ecosystem management, and to actively participate in training and research in the field.

Another theme that will also become apparent, before we finish today's workshop, is that government-wide activities in ecosystem management, and especially the data gathering and data management components of those activities, will have implications for broader national goals such as conducting the National Biological Survey, implementing Federal natural resources planning and management programs, and developing a National Spatial Data Infrastructure (NSDI), among others.

It is with great pleasure that I introduce today's guests. In the order that they will give their presentations; they are:

- Nancy Tosta, Chief of the Branch of Geographical Data Coordination, in the National Mapping Division of the U.S. Geological Survey, in Reston, Virginia;

- D. Alan Davenport of the U.S. Fish and Wildlife Service, Biologist and Geographic Information System (GIS) specialist in Laurel, Maryland;

- Dr. Mike Scott who is working for the National Biological Service, and is Leader for the Idaho Cooperative Fish and Wildlife Research Unit at the University of Idaho, in Moscow, Idaho. Dr. Scott is accompanied by Brian Biggs of the U.S. Geological Survey's Eros Data Center in Sioux Falls, South Dakota, who is also working with the United Nation Environmental Programme's Geographical Resources Information Data (GRID) program; and

- Virginia Ferreira of the Terrestrial Ecosystems Regional Research and Analysis Laboratory (TERRA LAB) of Fort Collins, Colorado. Ms. Ferreira is accompanied by a cadre of assistants whom she will introduce later.

In the audience, we also have members of the Federal Interagency Ecosystem Management Coordinating Group (IEMCG), who will be available for questions and discussion when concurrent demonstrations resume after the presentations.

CRS would also like to thank Barry Gold of the House Subcommittee on Technology, Environment, and Aviation and Gloria Dunderman of the House Committee on Science, Space, and Technology for their assistance in co-hosting this event on behalf of the Honorable Tim Valentine, Chairman of the Subcommittee, who requested CRS sponsor this workshop.

I would also like to thank Dr. Jeffrey Zinn of the CRS Environment and Natural Resources Policy Division for co-coordinating this workshop. Dr. Zinn was also a coordinator of the overall CRS Symposium on Ecosystem Management. Tom Miller, of the CRS Programs Office, was especially helpful with the logistics of pulling this workshop together. Several others at CRS who also work on various aspects of ecosystem management are here today. They include, Dr. M. Lynne Corn of the Environment and Natural Resources Policy

Division, and John Justus and Michael Simpson of the Science Policy Research Division.

And, most of all, I would like to thank you, the audience, for coming to learn about the tools and techniques of ecosystem management. We want you to ask serious questions of our guests after their individual presentations, but we also want you to have fun. You shouldn't feel guilty that you are having fun at this workshop. If you aren't having fun already, I'm sure you will, when you have a chance to view the demonstrations that our speakers will describe, and when TERRA Lab invites you to participate in their hands-on "Active Response GIS," later in the program.

Although few, if any, would concede that ecosystem management is *not* a matter of serious business, I'm sure that many of the professionals who are here demonstrating and discussing these technologies today also enjoy their work and their fields.

THE ROLE OF DATA MANAGEMENT AND INFORMATION ANALYSIS FOR SUPPORTING AN ECOSYSTEM APPROACH

Presented by Nancy Tosta[5]

There are a number of people who are likely to give you more technical perspectives on tools and techniques for ecosystem management. I am going to focus on the philosophical aspects--what we are trying to do related to coordination among institutions interested in spatial data, and how we think about the places we are trying to manage. I used to be a technologist, but now I am primarily a coordinator.

Rather than discussing the tools for ecosystem management, which I think about as being shovels, stream gauges, or controlled beams, for example, we are really addressing tools and techniques for ecosystem "information management." I would like to clarify what we in the geospatial data community are talking about when we refer to "ecosystems" and "information". E.O. Wilson's definition of biodiversity references ecosystems. He states that they (ecosystems) "comprise both the communities of organisms within particular habitats and the physical conditions under which they live." He makes it clear that it is not just the organisms, but it is very much the physical environment that impinges upon them. The physical environment relates directly to much of the work that I do in the geospatial data community, but we will come back to that.

Our concept of information is changing in the digital world. A March 1994 article in *Wired* magazine, which deals with information technology and life on the "net" (Internet), by John Perry Barlow entitled the "Economy of Ideas," examines the issues that are going to be associated with trying to copyright digital data. Barlow also provides some perspectives on information which I have found to be thought-provoking as I deal with data and technology information. He states that there are the three characteristics of information: it is an activity, a life form, and a relationship. Basically, if you think of information as an activity, you must imagine it as a verb, not a noun. He describes it as the pitch, not the ball. It is the interaction of things, of ideas with things. Data have to interact with your mind for them to be information. It is experienced, and you do not own it. You still have it, even if you give it away. It is necessarily distributed; it definitely has a half-life. It has to move. The notion of hoarding information is almost an oxymoron. In a sense information is a life form in that it definitely wants to be free; it wants to be passed around; it wants to be used; it replicates into the cracks of possibility.

Anyone who has seen a rumor spread and evolve knows that information wants to change. I have been amazed recently tracking a couple of statements that I was present at the source of and finding whole new thoughts coming back

---

[5] Nancy Tosta is Chief of Geographic Data Coordination for the National Mapping Division of the U.S. Geological Survey. This paper has been edited from a transcript of the original presentation.

any more that are not somehow tied up with human culture. All of these variables and factors must be considered to conduct ecosystem studies. The tools have to give us the ability to integrate the representations, measurements, and various values for these factors.

Another challenge with ecosystem information is that it is multi-resolutional in terms of both time and space. The kinds of measurements that must be taken must recognize that things change at different rates and must be measured at different rates. We take a human population census only once every 10 years on a national basis, although we know the population changes every minute. We know that the rates of change of certain things vary, but we often only have the resources to measure them at certain times; and I am not sure we yet have good tools to track variable rates of change. Ecosystems obviously vary spatially as well, from something that is very small--under a log or in a pond--to concepts such as the redwood belt and bioregions. How do we integrate these variable measurements and scale to yield meaningful results?

I mentioned earlier that GIS has become a very popular tool. You see variations of GIS around the room, and will hear more about them from other speakers. GIS has become a way to organize and integrate observations and measurements using location as the common denominator. Many of the origins of GIS have come from mapping and traditional map products. We are seeing an evolution away from that. Rather than maps being the primary input into GIS or spatial data models, we are seeing measurements, real time activities actually, being what we want to feed our GIS. Maps are still a primary output--the way to display the results of analyses, but we are increasingly using other data sources as the input. We also link many models, including process models, statistical models, and visualization techniques, to GIS. And we are beginning to think less of GIS as an application tool, and more as an information organizing tool. It gives us the ability to relate events, and activities, and things that occur in a common place. It may be that when you look at an ecosystem, perhaps you have multiple organisms that have been inventoried. Associated with these are a variety of taxonomic classifications that are not really linked in space, but are related by the organism. The occurrences of these classifications may be related, and defined as spatial attributes, such that future analyses can begin to show distributions of related species. GIS thus becomes a powerful organizing, as well as analysis tool.

We have come to call such data geospatial, and we are working on something called the national spatial data infrastructure. When I say "we", I refer to the entity called the Federal Geographic Data Committee. Geospatial data, as defined in an Executive Order signed by President Clinton on April 11, 1994, are any information related to a location on the surface of the earth. Obviously, geospatial data have a lot to do with ecosystem management.

The Federal government is spending considerable funds collecting geospatial data. Last year it conducted a data call asking Federal agencies how much they were spending on the collection, management, and dissemination of geospatial data. Using the definition I just mentioned, the total exceeded $4 billion to me two weeks later. Information certainly does have a half-life. There is a lot of relevance in many cases to the topics to be addressed in this workshop.

Barlow describes information as a relationship: If you think about this, you realize that the meaning of any information is unique. What you think is valuable information may not necessarily be valuable to anyone else. You have a personal relationship with information. That is one of the reasons organizations struggle over pricing data. The value of information often depends on use and context. Familiarity has value. If you are comfortable with the source of the information, it may mean more to you. There may be certain places that you are comfortable getting information from and others that you are not.

The same is true with the point of view--time, place, or space--it may be that information is more valuable because it is current rather than necessarily represents some known geography but is dated. And information is its own reward. Information often begets more information when you use it. These thoughts seem worth contemplating as we consider dealing with the information economy and information as a currency. I like to play with these ideas as we try to put policies in place that relate to the management of information.

With ecosystems, as with anything real that needs to be studied or managed, we observe and we measure. We create data when we take observations and measurements. Those data we organize and integrate, and hopefully they become information. We can interpret and understand that information to gain knowledge, and, hopefully, we can actually use that knowledge intelligently to manage the real things we were measuring -- and that in the process we might consider ourselves as gaining wisdom. One of the technology tools that we have been working with to manage ecosystem data is the Geographic Information System (GIS). GIS helps us organize data so that it becomes information. In the transformation of information to knowledge, values play a major role in how we understand it, how we interpret our point of view, and what we hold to be truth; although we don't often talk about this. I was interested to see some of the work that TERRA Lab is doing with collaborative studies, because as we try to translate our understanding of information into a basis for making decisions we must consider all of the perspectives.

Ecosystem measurements and observations fall into categories. There are the living pieces of ecosystems, such as the biological organisms, the habitats, plant associations, and vegetation. There is the physical or geographical environment, including terrain, soils, geology, the transportation infrastructure, and hydrology. There are environmental measurements that we take that often look at specific problems such as pollution or toxic sites. There are political and institutional aspects of ecosystems, such as the administrative boundaries, ownership, the basis of the economy in the ecosystem, and how the economy affects how the ecosystem is managed. And certainly there are cultural aspects of ecosystems. Aside from wilderness areas, there are relatively few ecosystems annually. We suspect this is low because it does not include all of the image activities, a lot of the sensor activities, climatological data, and so on. These data are often collected in a stovepipe approach. They are mission driven; collected by individual agencies carrying out functional responsibilities, and often over the same piece of geography. Data bases are built and analyzed, and policy recommendations are made in isolation from other agencies and levels of government that also might share an interest in that same piece of land.

Often, these data are not made readily available, or they are hard to find. The Yellow Pages do not have a listing of all the data sets that might be relevant in a specific geographic area. Even if found, these data can be difficult to access; obtaining a piece of a file with the specific measurements of interest may be costly or time-consuming. There are often questions of copyrights and data fees. This is not as true among Federal agencies, but State and local governments often set such policies. In many cases, other entities will take Federal data, build on it, add "value" to it, and then copyright it.

Over the last couple of years, data revenues have been debated as a source of funding for data collection and maintenance programs. We are going to see a lot of on-going debate in this area as data sharing becomes more prevalent. A number of major GIS meetings around the country are attracting an increasing number of lawyers. I doubt this is a good sign. The concept of recouping fees on data is obviously attractive, but there are a number of difficulties. The characteristics of the information I mentioned earlier contribute to the challenges of managing and charging for digital data. Data are hard to police and hard to track administratively. Services may be easier to charge for, and specifically attach a value to, than actual data sets.

Several other issues with geospatial data among Federal agencies are being recognized, one is that data are often out of date. This does not mean that older data are not valuable--certainly they are for trends--but often we want more current information and many parts of the country are not available in digital form at needed resolutions. Unknown quality is another issue. Often we find that when we share data, we do not know what we have: we get a data set from someone else and you do not know when it was last updated, what was actually delineated, or whether, for example, in a hydrologic data set every stream was delineated or only the perennial streams. Obviously, this creates challenges in making use of the data.

Another issue we are only just beginning to understand is that we spend a phenomenal amount of money to collect data, but very little to maintain or manage those data over time. We have not done a very good job at educating executives that beyond the need to collect data there are the requirements to manage them and keep them current. Funding must be allocated for data maintenance and management just as it is for hardware and software. Finally, data are incomplete; we do not have comprehensive digital geospatial data at the resolutions we need for many places.

Ideally, we would like to evolve to a data management model that provides in any given space or ecosystem or place a means to establish common linkages of data sets that are being collected and ways to integrate them. This is not necessarily a centralized data base. It is very much a distributed activity, but we need someway to link the data that are being collected by different agencies at a given location. Ideally, we should not just have a data base but actually be able to look at the implications of policy recommendations representing different views based on the integration of that information. I have been struggling with how to think about some of this, and I believe conceptualizing data bases based in place rather than layers may help. Ecosystems are places, and we must begin thinking about managing data, and perhaps collecting it differently than we used to.

A couple of data models are often used when talking about GIS. One is to think of space as being empty, but with things in it in different places. The other is to think in terms of layers, that there is something everywhere for soils, for vegetation, and for hydrology. In reality there may be many things in certain places; there may be fewer things in other places. As we conceptualize organizing information related to place, this should affect how we manipulate geographic data. Many GISs function based on layers of information that are overlaid, assuming that there is somewhat of linear approach to the way things are actually distributed. There are fewer that actually function based on the unique characteristics and relationships in a place, where you may not have the same information everywhere. This is more of an object-oriented approach, which establishes linkages between things in space so that rare species or unique occurrences can be taken into account.

The advantage of looking at things this way is that decisions about how we manage resources aren't made based on consistent layers; they are made on tradeoffs based on what actually exists in the geographic area. Unusual events can be easier to acknowledge when thinking about information organized this way. And the notion of organizing by place or landscape fits better with various ecosystem models. If you think of a guild or community in an ecosystem where there are relationships between feeding habitats and how individuals forage for food, and relationships between individual species, it is easier in some ways to conceptualize a series of relationships between vegetation and fauna, than to sort through layers of data that must be overlaid. I am not an expert in the software approaches for this model, but I am trying to conceptualize the approaches we need for arranging information to answer the questions we face.

What we do in the layer-based system is overlay. That's a very common GIS approach. What we might do in a place-based system would be something more akin to forming a region based on characteristics of geography. Linkages between the characteristics of things that inhabit that space would be established. Rather than necessarily resulting in a map, statistics and characteristics of those regions that were formed would be generated.

Another advantage of thinking about organizing information in terms of places is that we might better describe what is unique about that place. One of the things I have always struggled with in the use of GIS is when I look at the screen and see the various layers of rivers, and roads, and so forth--it always seems so artificial to use a cartoon representation. When I am actually walking around in that space, it is a combination of variables that makes it unique, special, and valued. It is difficult to capture that uniqueness looking at a layer of roads and a layer of rivers. And yet , we are using our GIS to conduct real analyses--to make decisions about trade-offs, the locations of businesses or toxic dumps. This picture of reality seems so artificial. Somehow I think place-based organization of data gives us an opportunity to be more definitive about what makes a place more unique, and how it fits in with other places; how it contributes to the overall value of the region; how it is representative of other places; and how it might be managed.

The tools that will contribute to being able to think about place-oriented information management are some of the ones that you're familiar with--they may be part of your operating environment now. We recognize that there are numerous institutions that are collecting data, so a means to communicate is important. Internet is an informal means of grouping individuals of like interests to exchange ideas in a "virtual community"; but certainly we are also seeing people coming together in a proliferation of watershed management councils, and bioregional activities. I think one of the first ecosystem-related workshops I encountered was on the Sierra ecoregion. We are seeing these proliferate around the country as a means for institutions and individuals to come together to think about a place, to think about the common characteristics and requirements, and to communicate about it. The concept of virtual communities on the "Net" is an interesting one, but we must consider the implications of separating community from place. Internet offers significant means to communicate about the availability of data. As a means to search for and acquire data, WAIS (Wide Area Information Servers) and Mosaic are two of the most popular tools in use now. It is also reasonable to assume that they will continue to improve with time.

New means to document and understand data quality must be found if we are going to share data, and sort and sift through all that is available. We have done quite a bit of work on something called a metadata standard. Means to consistently collect data must be improved if sharing is to be facilitated. We are increasingly moving into a world where that stovepipe approach--where data you have collected are only useful to your organization--has become a luxury. We are living in a world of limited resources, no one can collect all of the data they would like to have. We need to interact with the other likely users of the data we collect to know what their requirements may be, and put into place standards and guidelines. This is true at all levels of government. State and local governments are willing to work with commonly developed guidelines and standards for how to collect data. If we can put these into place; not necessarily to generate identical data everywhere, but based on common needs among the players in a given geographic areas; we might actually save money and have better data. Finally, for ecosystem assessment we need tools that provide means to organize data by place which GIS certainly provides; means to analyze--again GIS--and various models; and means to display--visualization tools and GIS.

Data about a place or space are inherently spatial. This is why the National Spatial Data Infrastructure (NSDI) is important, because some of its activities, though not specific to ecosystems, are the underlying fabric of place-based approaches to arranging spatial data. I work with the Federal Geographic Data Committee (FGDC). This committee was established by the President's Office of Management and Budget (OMB) and is currently chaired by Secretary of the Interior Bruce Babbitt. It has policy representation from all the major Federal agencies that have anything to do with spatial data. The major goals that we have been working on relate to facilitating access to and use of geospatial data for a variety of purposes. This means, facilitating finding of data that already exist; facilitating means to understand what data you have when you do get data from someone; and also understanding how to better integrate some of these data. We would like to see all of this done more cost effectively, rather than every ecosystem analyst digitizing the same 7-1/2 minute quadrangle.

I would like now to summarize highlights of the Executive Order (EO #12906, April 11, 1994). By January 1995, Federal agencies are to document new geospatial data with the metadata standard; the FGDC is to develop a document outlining partnership strategies; and a plan for a framework data set is to be developed. If any of the information you collect falls within the definition of geospatial data, then you are required to use the metadata standard to describe it, and you will serve that metadata to the network. This activity is referred to as the National Spatial Data Clearinghouse. Within a year of the Executive Order, by April 1995, Federal agencies are to develop plans and schedules for looking at the data already held; specifically addressing how to make it accessible to the public. Agencies will also think about adopting procedures for using this Clearinghouse to search for data before expending Federal funds for the collection of new data. The Clearinghouse is intended to involve all levels of government and a variety of institutions, public and private, and academic. It is an ambitious activity. We have just initiated a competitive agreements program to provide small financial incentives to State and local governments to establish "nodes" that will describe what data exist in their geographic area.

We have been working to adapt some of the Internet tools, such as WAIS and Mosaic, so that data can be searched for spatially. This will contribute to the ability to assess the availability of data by place. Specific coordinates or a geographic area can be defined within the network searching criteria to pose the question of what data exist. This requires that within the metadata standard, the "footprint" or geographic coverage of various data sets be defined. Given that the President has signed an Executive Order that says that federal agencies will tackle this, we are optimistic that there is progress in thinking spatially.

I mentioned that data vary by geography based on applications. We often do not design our national programs with this thought in mind. For example, the National Mapping Division of the U.S. Geological Survey has mapped the country at consistent scales. There is a 1:24,000 scale base in paper form for the entire nation that was completed about 2 years ago. It took about 100 years to complete. Actually that's not quite true. They really didn't start this series until after World War II. This would be an extremely valuable base if it was digital and current everywhere, but it is not. At current levels of funding within the USGS, it will be approximately the year 2040 before it is completely digitized. Most people think that is too long. Because it is not officially available, there is a lot of redundant digitizing going on. I often talk about students digitizing in closets, automating these maps because they are not available as a standard base.

Recently the FGDC has been exploring the concept of building a digital framework data set. There are several data sets that are critical to almost everybody using a GIS. These act as the base for additional data collection, and include roads, rivers, terrain, administrative boundaries, and elevation. Additionally these must be accurately registered to the Earth through geodetic control, and many people also want an image base. These seven "themes" are conceived of as comprising the framework data set. OMB is considering the value of creating a national framework that would have the foundation data sets required by most users, so that duplication could be minimized. This would be a shift in thinking about how we manage information and how we work with partners that might contribute spatial data in any given place.

The requirements for these data may vary quite a bit in resolution. In urban areas, we find that street centerline, for example, may be needed at a very accurate resolution, whereas in more rural areas of Montana or Alaska, one meter resolution is not necessary. The idea of variation in resolution is one characteristic of the framework that is being discussed, as well as the possibility of accelerating the digital creation of these themes of data that would form the foundation for other data collection activities.

These institutional discussions will help to put a plan into place by January 1995, as called for in the Executive Order, which could have a major effect on the activities of Federal agencies involved in geospatial data collection. The expectation is that numerous institutions would contribute to development of these data including local government. Many counties are creating street centerline files that would form part of a national database. We see the national spatial data infrastructure as content in the national information infrastructure. Additionally, NBS has conceived a national biological information infrastructure with a biodiversity clearinghouse. All of these might be thought of as tools for managing and sharing information for ecosystem management.

DISCUSSION FOLLOWING NANCY TOSTA'S PRESENTATION

Question: It is interesting how you have contrasted the concept of place to layers as the future direction of GIS function. I know current GIS technology and software is based on a layering of information. What would be different about the new GIS technology that needs to analyze data coherently on a spatial basis? Can you also use current GIS technology for that purpose?

Response: I think you can use current GIS. It is more the algorithms of the models that are fundamental in the GIS. It is establishing linkages between the data elements, and as I said, a lot of the object oriented data models are really sort of place-based or they are built on the concept of relationships between things in space. For example, you could have a river--rather than having simply a hydrology layer, that would show relationships between terrain, the water course, location of the dams, and watershed boundaries. These might be linked and represented differently within the construct of the GIS than simply "here is a hydrology layer" and "here's an elevation layer," and they can be overlaid. There would be established linkages between the features. I know there are vendors working on this. So I would not give up on GIS. GIS is the tool we have to work with.

Question: You talked about various clearinghouses for data information. I think there is a lot of duplication of effort here. There is the National Aeronautics and Space Administration's (NASA's) Global Change Master Directory, for example, the National Biological Information Infrastructure, and EPA's Environmental Mapping and Assessment Program (EMAP). Is there effort to increase interdependence between these organizations so that they might all work together?

Response: Very much so. I did not specifically say it, but the clearinghouse is distributed. There is nothing centralized here. For example, the USGS Global Land Information System (GLIS), EROS Data Center's image management system or accesses to NASA's Master Directory would be linked as nodes in the National Spatial Data Clearinghouse network. You would find this inventory of data with unique tools for the Network, such as WAIS. NASA is a member of the Federal Geographic Data Committee, and they just recently agreed to take their DIF (data interchange format) and enhance it so that it meets the requirements of the metadata standard. The metadata standard is a little more robust than what you currently find in the DIF.

So there is definitely overlap, but there are also connections and as it sorts itself out you will find agencies with Mosaic home pages pointing to every other agency. I know if you use mosaic now, you often get lost in the Net. You say, I have been here before, but I did not come this way. We will see some of that sorting out. The tools that are going to be most valuable in the future are going to be those that allow us to search and filter the information that is out there on the Net. But I will admit there is some duplication now, although there is discussion going on between the global change community, for example, and the

Federal Geographic Data Committee. We are all just learning how to do this. It is valuable to have different approaches. Also, when you look at an agency's culture you find different people sitting on different committees, and some of them talk to each other inside their organizations and some of them do not. So we are going to evolve at different rates inside the various organizations.

Question: I have a couple of questions. One is, as we move away from the layering systems, how does that affect costs? And the other more generally is how do you see the costs of data acquisition and presentation changing in the future?

Response: I'm not sure I can say. The evolution from layering systems is going to be a natural one as we demand more analysis capability. In some ways, it probably will be a cost we cannot avoid. I have no idea what that cost is likely to be. It could be that the shift to object-oriented analysis would simply an enhancement to whatever software you are using, and in the next release you would have the ability to be a little bit more sophisticated. But that's probably a naive statement because I suspect there will always be data conversion costs. We may have to rebuild our data sets to conduct these types of analyses. The costs of data acquisition are likely to go down because of the number of activities. For example, I did not say anything about small satellites, but this is a major remote sensing activity that will come on line within the next few years that will result in more data, at higher resolutions, than any of us ever knew we needed. Some of those costs now--the actual field collection costs--will probably stay the same as they always have, although if we have more specialists out there analyzing data, maybe those costs will go up. But the tools -- such as hand-held Global Positioning System (GPS) geographic locators and "Newtons" (portable fax equipment) -- will make data collection more efficient and perhaps more accurate. In the long run, we are going to have more data than we know what to do with--whether it is the right data will be one question, how we optimize how we manage it will be another.

Question: To what degree have agencies involved in the Federal Geographic Data Committee met with the management community at their agencies? It is one thing to discuss the philosophical relationship between all of these variables which, in fact, are not necessarily being communicated to those who count, namely Executive Branch managers.

Response: I assume you mean the natural research management community. What I talked about here in terms of this place-based notion is not a common discussion within the FGDC. The spatial data framework, the metadata standard, and the clearinghouse--all those are the FGDC initiatives. They are not exactly looking at how data are actually integrated in a GIS. They are facilitating access to data. They deal with data standards within the user community.

For example, the National Oceanic and Atmospheric Administration (NOAA) in the Department of Commerce has responsibility for the bathymetry subcommittee of FGDC. So NOAA is dealing with this notion of how do you represent shoreline. Is there one way to represent shoreline, and, if so, can all the off-shore resources be associated with it?

The OMB Circular (A-16) that created the FGDC, also charged various Federal agencies with coordinating thematic interests of all the other agencies that collect data related to that theme. Agencies are talking to data users to try and set standards. Every standard proposed by the FGDC goes out for very broad national review. They are announced in every GIS magazine, discussed at GIS conferences, and many of the specific subject area conferences--such as the hydrographic conference that occurred recently. So we try to involve as many viewpoints as possible in all of this. The only way you can have standards and guidelines accepted is if they come from the bottom up. My perception is that they seldom work if dictated from the top down. So we have tried to adopt the bottom up approach.

Question: Actually, I would like to make a comment while we were getting our technology demonstration together. That was a real good point to bring up. Are we collecting the right data? My thought is that it changes with topic. The right data for global change issues are very different from the right data for water quality issues, for example; and we as a society just have to be aware that our data needs change. I'm interested in rainfall which is one factor that determines water availability. Look at what's happened in the last 20 years in the Rio Puerco watershed in New Mexico. Is this possibly a harbinger of some of the things that are coming with global change? The right data is both what we collect for the problems we have to date and those we may foresee for the future.

Response: Right now, the efforts of the FGDC are focused on the minimal data sets that most people need--not all variations on themes. But you're right--data needs do change. Also, other Federal and institutional entities do consider the interdependency of efforts such as ecosystem management and global climate change research, and analyze how their respective needs for data might be similar, and where there may be overlaps and opportunities for resource sharing.

APPLICATIONS OF GPS AND GIS TECHNIQUES IN MIGRATORY BIRD MANAGEMENT

Prepared by D. Alan Davenport[6]

Biologists in the Office of Migratory Bird Management have been conducting aerial surveys since 1955 to assess breeding waterfowl populations and habitat. A large percentage of the northern breeding range (figure 1) is sampled each year. Waterfowl are counted and annual population estimates are generated. These statistics are used to establish annual hunting regulations, for example.

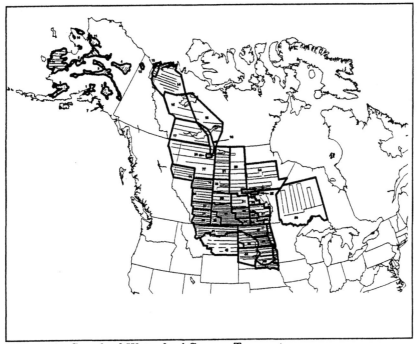

Figure 1. Standard Waterfowl Survey Transects.

One of the most important factors in conservation and wildlife management is the habitat and its condition. No organism can thrive under poor habitat conditions. Days could be spent discussing problems, progress, and other factors related to habitat studies. Global Positioning System (GPS) and Geographic Information System (GIS) techniques have the potential to bring the monitoring of wildlife populations and their associated habitat into closer focus for more detailed study and analysis.

---

[6] D. Alan Davenport is a GIS Specialist at the U.S. Fish and Wildlife Service. This paper has been edited from the transcript of the original presentation.

How can population counts be more closely related to the habitat? This should be relatively simple in a small study area, but it is much more complex when dealing with thousands of square miles of very diverse ecological compositions. Most of the survey transects are divided into segments, usually 18 miles long. Survey data are recorded by transect and segment, so the information can be analyzed by segments. However, an 18 mile segment can contain many different types of habitat.

A discussion follows on the history of some of the efforts to develop techniques to link waterfowl habitats and population counts. In 1990, researchers at Patuxent Wildlife Research Center (now Patuxent Environmental Science Center) were using hand-held LORAN units to obtain latitude and longitude data for areas of potential study. A portable computer was used to process geographic location information generated by the LORAN receiver. Researchers then posed the question: Could a similar technique be used with the LORAN navigational units in a survey aircraft?

Aerial surveys are generally conducted by two individuals, the pilot and an observer. Each counts the birds seen on his or her side of the aircraft and records the observations on audio tape. To use the LORAN there had to be some automatic way to record the location since neither the pilot nor the observer would be able to look at the instrument panel and write down the latitude and longitude. A program for a laptop computer was developed, which when connected to the LORAN unit, would continually read the location information produced. Additional micro switches were rigged with the "push to talk" switches used by the pilot and observer. Closing the switch triggered the computer to record a location and time for that individual. This procedure enabled collection of reasonably accurate locational data (figure 2 on the following page). The major problem, however, was that considerable time coordination was necessary to later be able to match the taped observations with the recorded locations.

An experimental flight was made in December, 1991, counting waterfowl encountered along a portion of the Chesapeake Bay. A basemap was created by combining a number of digital line graph maps of USGS 7.5 minute quad sheets, and the observation points and basemap were plotted using Arc/Info GIS software. The resulting plot (figure 3 on the following page) indicated that the LORAN method of recording locations was one workable solution to part of the problem. There was still the habitat issue, however, and how appropriate and usable habitat information could be obtained. The ideal solution would be to use aerial photography, satellite imagery, or perhaps some other remotely sensed information; however, for the level and scale of these experimental observations, that would be too expensive.

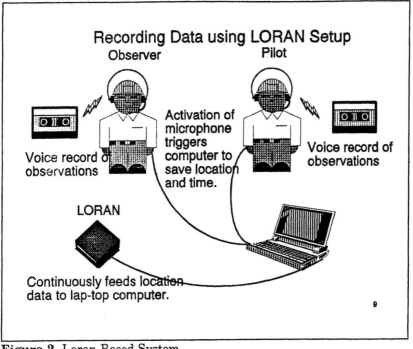

Figure 2. Loran-Based System

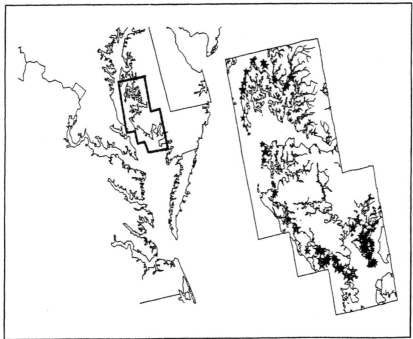

Figure 3. Plot of waterfowl sightings. The number of birds seen is related to the size of the star.

Some time after the development of the LORAN system, the office procured GPS hardware and software. The basic difference is that with GPS, location is determined by triangulation from a number of satellites positioned in stationary orbits. This system is operational worldwide. LORAN calculations, on the other hand, are based on signals from a network of communication towers on the ground, and some areas of the world are not covered. GPS, therefore, appears to be the logical navigation choice of the future.

An initial GPS application was an attempt to record habitat along Breeding Bird Survey (BBS) routes. The BBS is a permanent roadside survey that has been conducted annually by volunteers for the last 27 years. There are over 3000 randomly established routes in the US and Canada and approximately 2500 surveys are conducted annually. BBS is now being performed under the National Biological Survey.

The GPS allows us to record points, lines, and areas. The points could represent the bird observations, the lines could represent roads, and the areas could represent habitat blocks along each side of the road. Points and lines were no problem to collect, but recording an area requires that points be collected along its perimeter. This proved difficult if not impossible, especially in trees where transmission of the satellite signals could not penetrate.

The possibility of collecting habitat data from the air was considered using one of the aircraft used for waterfowl surveys. A test route was selected and a flight was made along the route in both directions. The observer recorded habitat out to 200 meters along the right side of the road.

The GPS has a wand for reading barcodes referenced to a dictionary in the Datalogger unit. This feature permits rapid data entry. A number of broad habitat classifications were set up as line features and a barcode sheet was prepared (figure 4 on the following page).

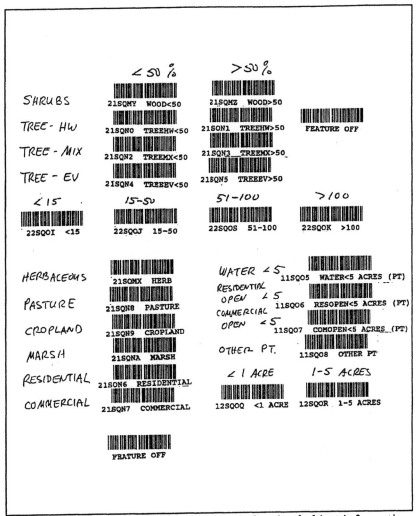

Figure 4. Sample Barcode page used for indicating habitat information.

Each "line" of habitat was mathematically converted to a polygon up to 200 meters wide. They were initially located according to the position of the plane which was usually on the opposite side of the road. It was necessary to adjust polygons relative to the center of the road (figure 5 on the following page). The habitats recorded on the test route were ultimately displayed by ARC/INFO GIS software (figure 6 on the following page).

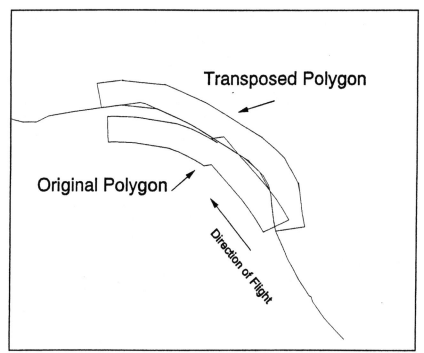

Figure 5. Relationship of original and transformed habitat polygons.

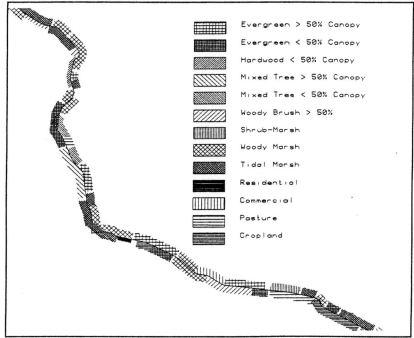

Figure 6. A portion of Maryland BBS Route 043 showing habitat classification.

Using GPS techniques for aerial population monitoring surveys has some distinct advantages over the LORAN method discussed earlier. The GPS signals are available essentially anywhere in the world, the barcode scanner permits rapid data entry, and the software provided with the system automatically prepares data for analysis by a GIS. The main disadvantage is that another person is required to enter the data (figure 7). The pilot and observer operate as before, but now the voice record is a backup. The recorder listens to the comments of the pilot and observer and enters the sightings into the datalogger with the barcode wand. The man-hours associated with the extra person on the survey are minimal when compared to the hours that were necessary with older methods used to link the audio observations to the location points, however.

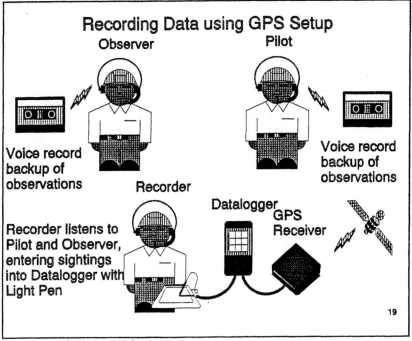

Figure 7. GPS-Based System

The GPS equipment was tested on several waterfowl population surveys in 1993 and early 1994. Survey techniques were improved with each trial of the system. Counts are recorded using a set of 36 barcodes for 1's, 10's, 100's, and 1000's. The GPS considers the entries as modifiers to the observation point which represents a species of waterfowl or whatever. Any number can be quickly entered into the system using the appropriate combination. A program was written to add them up before they get into the GIS.

The Trimble GPS unit used comes with software to process data from the datalogger. Data can be displayed on the screen, queried, edited, measured, and plotted. Each point is represented along the flight line by a cross. Any point can be queried to display the attributes that were recorded with it (figure 8). After the data are incorporated into the GIS, attributes can be displayed and queried using ArcView software. In one example, only flocks of over 500 birds were displayed along with an identification number assigned by the GIS (figure 9 on the following page).

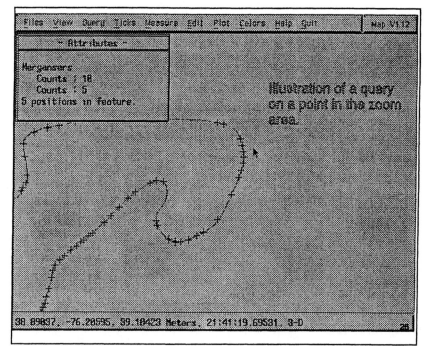

Figure 8. Flight path of a sea duck survey conducted along the east coast of the U. S. in February, 1994.

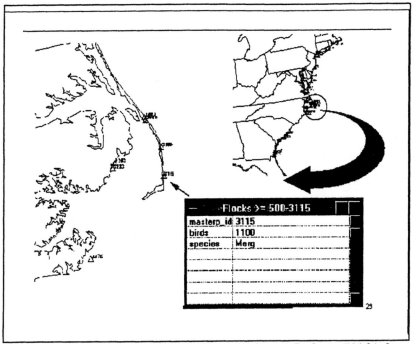

Figure 9. Sample query from ArcView display of flocks > 500 birds.

At the beginning of this year a request was made to investigate the possibilities of using GIS and Breeding Bird Survey data to explore possible relationships between the Conservation Reserve Program (CRP) lands and abundance of birds. Data were acquired for the first 11 CRP sign-ups and a quick tally disclosed that 92.7 percent of the acres were in grassland or wildlife habitat.

A framework for measurement was established by arbitrarily splitting the area into five density categories based on the number of grassland CRP acres per county: [0] No CRP acres in the county; [1] < 0.75 percent CRP (50 percent of the counties with CRP); [2] 0.75 percent - 2.35 percent CRP (20 percent of the counties with CRP); [3] 2.35 percent -7.5 percent CRP (20 percent of the counties with CRP); [4] > 7.5 percent CRP (10 percent of the counties with CRP).

Distributions of several species of grassland birds were examined, one of which is the Grasshopper Sparrow (Ammodramus savannarum) (figure 10 on the following page). Population change was estimated and patterns of change were plotted. For purposes of a simple illustration of this concept of using GIS analysis, an area was selected which was bounded on the north by 45 degrees N. Latitude, south by 40 degrees, east by 90 degrees W. Longitude and west by 95 degrees. This GIS analysis was done by overlaying the CRP data with the bird distribution data and evaluating coinciding areas.

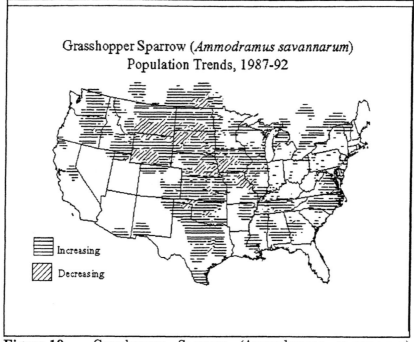

Figure 10.   Grasshopper   Sparrow   (Ammodramus   savannarum) Population Trends, 1987-92.

For example, the GIS can show and compute the size of all the areas where birds were increasing in the greatest CRP density (figure 11 on the following page). In this case, the GIS reports 6,204,258.8 hectares for the CRP of which 4,376,924.7 hectares or about 70 percent had increasing Grasshopper Sparrow populations.

Results of this nature are interesting, but must be interpreted with caution, however, because of other factors which can confound the underlying trend analyses used with the BBS data. Factors such as drought, conditions on the wintering grounds of migratory birds, sample sizes in the surveys, etc., are not reflected here. Also, the distribution of the BBS survey routes is less concentrated in the prairie areas where the greater amounts of CRP lands are found. The value of the analysis, however, is that it quantifies apparent relationships between the birds and their habitats that can then be scrutinized more closely to determine the significant relationships.

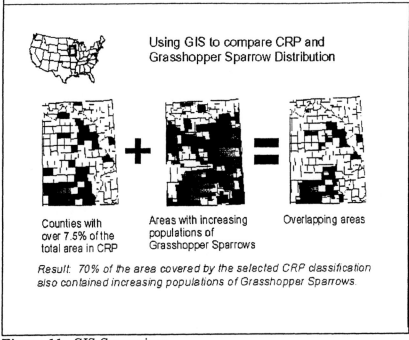

Figure 11. GIS Comparison.

In conclusion there were several policy-relevant questions that were to be addressed as they pertain to the material presented in this paper:

- What are the opportunities and limitations of these tools;
- Where is the development of these tools headed, and how rapidly are they changing;
- What are the costs associated with the tools, and how do those costs compare with the cost of data acquisition;
- Is there a need for new or different data based upon the capabilities and opportunities of the tools; and
- What is the potential use of these tools for informing the public decision making process and contributing to other national goals?

GPS equipment is limited only by its ability to receive signals from enough satellites (at least two, preferably three or more) to compute a location. GPS units are being made smaller, durable, and more reliable. GIS software is available from a number of vendors at costs commensurate with versatility and complexity. Data used in a GIS must be geo-referenced to be used, therefore older data sets may be of little value unless they can be re-worked. A number of commercial companies are involved in marketing geo-referenced satellite imagery and data from other sources at varying costs. The use of GIS techniques is rapidly expanding worldwide.

THE GAP ANALYSIS PROGRAM (GAP)
OF THE NATIONAL BIOLOGICAL SURVEY

Presented by J. Michael Scott[7]

Thank you. I will discuss the Gap Analysis program (GAP) of the National Biological Survey (NBS), which is an effort to map land cover and vertebrate distributions across the entire country. GAP is an interagency effort, involving over 200 different State and Federal agencies, and private groups. It is a bottom-up approach with national guidelines. The logic behind this approach is that we have national standards, but the people who are best suited to determine the level of detail they need and what questions they are going to ask are really at the local level--departments of fish and game or county government representatives, for example.

In dealing with ecosystem management, we are dealing with a variety of levels of biological organization at a variety of spatial scales, from the genetic to the ecosystem level. An individual Gap Analysis project operates at the community level, somewhere between the ecosystem and species level. Traditionally, wildlife biologists have operated at the smaller population level and species level when asking management questions. We have been more reactive than proactive in our managing efforts. Because of limited time and resources, managers have frequently waited until there was a problem before taking action. We can do better.

Gap Analysis is an attempt to look at the distribution of indicators of biological diversity, terrestrial vertebrates, and land cover types -- vegetation types -- and ask how those elements of diversity are distributed relative to areas that are managed for long-term maintenance of those same surrogates of biological diversity. Gap Analysis allows for participatory and proactive management of natural resources; it is not reactionary. Gap Analysis has many areas of focus, it:

- Emphasizes ecosystem based resource management, not single species;

- Identifies areas of unprotected species and community occurrence;

- Identifies areas where sensitive species do not occur so that you have the opportunity not only for proactive management, but also for identifying areas where there may not be conflicts (I believe that is equally important); and

- Places emphasis on areas of occurrence of multiple unprotected communities and species.

---

[7] J. Michael Scott is the Unit Leader of the Idaho Cooperative Fish and Wildlife Research Unit. This paper has been edited from the transcript of the original presentation.

The mix of those communities and species can be any mix that is of biological or political interest to you. You can ask what is the distribution of birds versus areas managed for them. Or, be more specific and ask what is the distribution of ponderosa pine? The results of Gap Analysis can be used to quantify habitat fragmentation and loss. Once we have a complete vegetation map for the country, we can ask the question: How has the distribution of that vegetation type changed over time? We have a baseline standard, and using some of the Landsat imagery dating back to 1972, we can go back in time as well as forward in time. It establishes a base (of data in digital format) to survey and monitor changes in land cover types. This will permit management actions to be taken on behalf of vegetation types and species while they are still common, and that's absolutely critical -- to be proactive rather than reactive.

In addition to providing information on the status of protection efforts for biodiversity, GAP provides an ecologically defensible framework for more detailed monitoring programs. Traditionally, we have established study areas for convenience. Gap Analysis allows us to look at the total distribution of ponderosa pine, for example, within an entire ecoregion. Thus, we are able to transcend traditional political boundaries such as national forests. We could look at the occurrence of ponderosa pine not only in the Boise National Forest but also in adjacent national forests in Idaho, Oregon, or elsewhere where ponderosa pine occurs, regardless of whether it is U.S. Forest Service lands, U.S. Bureau of Land Management lands, or state owned. We look at the distribution of the resource, not the distribution of the resource within a politically convenient subdivision.

The benefit of Gap Analysis is that it is standardized, systematic, hierarchical, validated nationwide, and based to a large extent on existing data. We frequently find when we start getting involved in a GAP project in a State that a lot of data sets that we didn't know about do exist, and a lot of data sets that we thought existed are not available, had been lost, or never existed. So, by working with cooperating partners to identify data sets that can be used by the entire group, we can share the data in our joint efforts to address resource issues.

Brian Biggs of the U.S. Geological Survey Eros Data Center, has been demonstrating the Mosaic Program we are using to make the GAP data sets available to a wide user community--and that is one of our biggest challenges. When you are dealing with large data sets, how do you make the information available to those people who are in a position or have a need to use that information? They may have different areas of interest. They also have different levels of sophistication in terms of how they can use the data. You can hand some people a computer tape, and everything is fine--they will slap it on their workstation and away they go. Others don't have a workstation; they just have a PC and will simply be interested in a hard copy of the data. Therefore, you really have to make your data available to the users in a format that they can understand and most importantly, can use.

GAP is about cooperative partnerships; and the structure for one state project -- the State of Washington, for example -- shows the wide range of those cooperating. Partners include the Department of Natural Resources, the Department of Energy, the Environmental Protection Agency, Washington State University, the Department of Commerce Tiger files, the Bureau of Census data files, the Nature Conservancy, the U.S. Fish and Wildlife Service, the U.S. Forest Service, and a wide variety of groups. In California, most of the program (about 80 percent) is being paid for by private individuals, private companies, development companies, and gas and electric companies. Why? Because they are interested in developing and operating in a more predictable world, and they believe some of the data sets provided by the Gap Analysis projects will help.

GAP is dynamic; it varies from State to State; and it varies because of the interest of the state cooperators. Examples of cooperators include: Biosystems Analysis, a private consulting company; National Fish and Wildlife Foundation; Department of Defense; and Maine Department of Conservation, large groups--state, federal, and private. There are over 200 of them nationally.

The national standard for map scale for GAP is 1:100,000. Many of the questions cooperators are asking require at least 1:100,000 scale, covering land units of a hundred hectare minimum. We have taken it down to 5 hectares in some states to meet the need of local cooperators. I would emphasize something else that Nancy Tosta of the U.S. Geological Survey referred to, that the scale at which you operate really is dependent on the question you are asking. We have to be very careful that we are not just asking for the delivery of the data set, but we are asking a specific set of questions and then generating the data set or sets that allow us to answer those questions. Looking at a national strategy, we would perhaps want to start at the highest levels of biological organization because those are frequently the easiest and the cheapest to gain information about. As you get more details by going from 1:1,000,000 to 1:250,000, 1:100,000, or 1:24,000, it takes more time and more money to gather that information.

How is the information from GAP being used? The Southern California Association of Governments (SCAG), in cooperation with the Gap Analysis project at the University of California-Santa Barbara, examined the occurrence of natural communities which the County Government Association had identified as being at risk. They looked at their occurrence as mapped by their Gap Analysis project, and combined the Gap Analysis maps with the information they had on local zoning and asked the question, "What is the distribution of the plant communities at risk relative to areas zoned for open space, and those areas zoned for development?" The result was a map showing where there are opportunities for change, where potential conflict might exist, and where potential conflict does not exist. I would emphasize this map was developed in response to a very specific question being asked by the organizations belonging to SCAG.

Another example of how derivative data sets can be developed can be demonstrated by a data set showing the distribution of western juniper, a particular vegetation type in Idaho relative to special management areas. What you find is very little acreage of western juniper within areas that are managed for long-term maintenance of biological diversity. Western juniper is by no stretch of the imagination on anybody's list of threatened or endangered or even sensitive communities, but I would argue that perhaps 20 or 30 years from now, there might be some species at risk associated with this community if significant acreages of western juniper are lost.

An example of a very common community type where we didn't have any problems 40 years ago and where we now do have problems is the coastal sage communities in southern California. When I grew up in southern California, coastal sage was something that you got out of the way so that you could put up a new housing development or other land improvement. Today, one endangered species and about 80 candidate species are found in coastal sage, and we have a crisis where a crisis did not exist as recently as 20 years ago. We can avoid a significant number of those types of crisis management situations if we identify the distribution of all vegetation types today and make sure that we have adequate occurrence of each in special management areas. We need to manage communities like western junipers for their long-term maintenance before a crisis situation arises. We can do it when motherhood issues are not involved, and all interests can sit down at the table as partners and deal with it in an objective, proactive manner.

TERRA TOOLS AND TECHNIQUES
FOR ECOSYSTEM MANAGEMENT

Presented by Virginia Ferreira[8]

INTRODUCTION

The Terrestrial Ecosystem Regional Research and Analysis (TERRA) Laboratory is a collaborative effort among federal, state, and private entities. The interdisciplinary staff produces tools and technologies to further global change research, which are also useful in ecosystem management. TERRA participates in integrated assessments, which complement the research program by serving as a test bed for TERRA tools.

A discussion of TERRA Laboratory includes some history and logistics of creating such a group. TERRA's two-pronged program, comprised of research and applications, is characterized. The connection between global change and ecosystem management is described. The three TERRA products demonstrated at the "Workshop on Tools and Technologies of Ecosystem Management" are described; each is a linkage between a pair of useful tools which combine to produce new dimensions in global change and ecosystem management research:

- Modular Modeling Complex linked with Computer Visualization Technology
- HyperSAM, linking hypermedia and Structured Analysis Methodology
- Active Response Geographic Information System (ARGIS), linking an electronic meeting system with a GIS.

THE TERRA LABORATORY

TERRA is an agency-and discipline-neutral space for regional-scale studies of terrestrial and human processes related to global change. TERRA's mission is to incorporate realistic consideration of land and natural resource management into terrestrial ecosystem components of earth system modeling.

The program maintains a balance between the complementary facets of development and applications. TERRA develops integrated-assessment technologies that facilitate collaboration and unite information and models. The Laboratory participates in the performance of integrated assessments by applying and testing the tools and technologies developed at TERRA.

---

[8] Virginia Ferreira is a member of the Terrestrial Ecosystem Regional Research and Analysis (TERRA) Laboratory. This paper has been edited from the transcript of the original presentation prepared by Virginia Ferreira and D. DeCoursey, U.S. Department of Agriculture, Agricultural Research Service; B. Faber, Consortium for International Earth Science Information Network; L. Knapp, IBM-U.S. Federal; and R. Woodmansee, Colorado State University. All are members of TERRA Laboratory.

Background

The Laboratory was formed by an August, 1992, Memorandum of Understanding among the USDA-Agricultural Research Service (ARS), Forest Service (FS) and Soil Conservation Service (SCS) [now the Natural Resources Conservation Service (NRCS)], and the U.S. Dept. of Interior (USDI)-Geological Survey (USGS). The Consortium for International Earth Science Information Network (CIESIN) provides systems and project engineering support. IBM Federal Systems Company, Colorado State University (CSU), USDI-Bureau of Mines (USBM), and EPA (USEPA) have contributed human and material resources at TERRA. USDA-NRCS, Utah State University, University of Montana, University of Colorado, and Optimal Decision Engineering Corporation have collaborated off-site in TERRA's technical developments. The Laboratory welcomes new participants in TERRA efforts. TERRA offices opened in November, 1992.

Guidance is provided by a Board of Directors (comprised of Agency and business leaders representing TERRA cooperators) and a Scientific Liaison Group (scientific peers representing appropriate disciplines). The TERRA staff is an interdisciplinary group representative of the wide variety of cooperative organizations listed above. Table 1, on the following page, lists on-site participants; projects also include numerous off-site cooperators.

Participation nature and levels vary among TERRA partners. One example of a cooperative arrangement with TERRA is the Cooperative Research and Development Agreement (CRADA) under which IBM-Federal Systems (a subsidiary of International Business Machines Corporation) participates: "for the purpose of broadening our technological base and by disseminating and making available new knowledge from the Federal laboratory for the development of new products and technologies" (USDA-ARS and IBM-Federal, 1993). The CRADA defines roles and responsibilities, identifies property rights, outlines copyright and patent responsibilities, and describes the symbiotic relationship established between the federal agencies and cooperator. Such agreements are authorized under the Federal Technology Transfer Act of 1986, as amended (15 USC 3710a). CRADAs have broadened the horizons of technological advancement and transfer.

Table 1. A Profile of TERRA Staff (July 1994)		
Name	**Affiliation**	**Title**
Douglas G. Fox	USDA-FS	TERRA Director/Meteorologist
Donn G.DeCoursey	USDA-ARS	Research Hydraulic Engineer
Brenda G. Faber	CIESIN	GIS/Visualization Scientist
Virginia A. Ferreira	USDA-ARS	Mathematician
Sanetta Gavette	CSU	Data Analyst
Thomas G. Goonan	USDI-USBM	Environmental Engineer
Jack Hautaluoma	CSU	Industrial Psychologist
Eugene W. Kersey	USEPA	Environmental Social Scientist
Simon Lee	CSU	GIS Analyst
Jeffrey Lundstrom	CSU	Computer Programmer
Sandy Maple	CSU	Computer Systems Coordinator
Ann N. Millard	USDA-FS	Office Manager
Jeff Miller	CSU	Computer Systems Administrator
T'Shanna Smith	USDA-ARS	Summer Intern
E.J. Soto	USDA-ARS	Summer Intern
William W. Wallace	CIESIN	Sr. Systems Analyst
Raymond D. Watts	USDI-USGS	Research Physical Scientist
Robert Woodmansee	CSU	Range Ecologist

The Global Change/Ecosystem Management Connection

Global change research and ecosystem management problems are intimately related:

- Both require integrated consideration of the entire impact of human activities on natural systems.
- Both require mathematical models to give timely answers to long-term questions of system responses to change. Traditional field research based on "do-something-and-see-what-happens" is time-and resource-intensive. Mathematical models can facilitate computerized experiments by permitting centuries of simulation in a comparatively short time, applying appropriate field-acquired knowledge as available.
- Both require a systems approach; traditional reductionist scientific research produces knowledge useful in developing process-based

models, but will not produce the broad, integrated understanding of ecosystem response that is needed for current and future challenges.
- Most global change effects are manifested as environmental (and thus ecosystem) changes.

Research Program

TERRA scientists are advancing knowledge in the following research areas:

- collaboration technology,
- socioeconomic quantification,
- conceptual modeling,
- modular modeling complex,
- networked data resources,
- scale transitions,
- expert systems for model selection and application, and for effects, determination,
- distributed modeling, and
- data and concept visualization.

The tools discussed in following sections are results of these research efforts.

Integrated Assessments and Pilot Projects

Complementing TERRA research efforts are integrated assessments and pilot projects, where the tools and technologies being developed are validated and improved under "real-world" conditions. TERRA has applied collaboration technology, in the form of a facilitated electronic meeting system (EMS), to assist various groups in problem and stakeholder identification. Two projects have been undertaken with the TERRA Active Response GIS (ARGIS): First, ARGIS is being evaluated by a TERRA/Colorado State University Psychology Department study which analyzes group response to use of the tool, and evaluates ARGIS effectiveness in facilitating group decision-making in situations where map data are part of the decision-making process. Another ARGIS pilot project involves assisting with planning for the Arapaho/Roosevelt National Forest.

An integrated assessment is being undertaken for the Rio Puerco watershed, in cooperation with a variety of groups. Located in northwestern New Mexico, the Rio Puerco is a tributary of the Rio Grande River. Its contributions include only a small fraction of the Rio Grande stream flow, and an inordinate proportion of the sediment, which is a serious Rio Grande problem.

Figure 12, on the following page, shows the watershed location in the state. The Rio Puerco joins the Rio Grande upstream of the Elephant Butte Reservoir, a major water supply for the region. Sedimentation in both the Rio Grande and Elephant Butte is a serious concern of the region, and has been studied for decades by many groups. The problem has been a classical case of "if you have a hammer, everything looks like a nail." Rangeland management has been the avenue of amelioration popular among rangeland groups; structure-building has been proposed by some groups; and some channel stabilization efforts are underway, supported by other groups. TERRA proposes a systems approach, utilizing computer simulation modeling and other tools, to coordinate the region's "hammers" in an interdisciplinary study of the integrated effect of structural and nonstructural management alternatives.

TERRA has linked with other agencies and groups with responsibilities and interests in the watershed to study potential landscape changes in response to management and/or climate changes. Touring the watershed, one finds instances of yesterday's corrective efforts creating tomorrow's problems; for example, diversions to stop flow above headcuts have started new gullies. TERRA plans to contribute to an interagency examination of the sediment production of the basin, utilizing computer simulation model experiments (including forecasting and hindcasting), and interdisciplinary, inter-institutional systems analysis using group tools. Following these steps, TERRA foresees the possibility of an integrated assessment emerging.

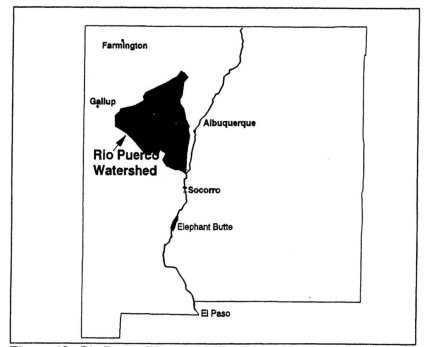

Figure 12. Rio Puerco Watershed, New Mexico

TOOLS USEFUL IN ECOSYSTEM ANALYSIS AND MANAGEMENT

Developments from TERRA include three products which are each a linkage between available products. TERRA's contributions are the concepts, logistics, and mechanics of linkage.

Modular Modeling Complex/Visualization Technology

The *TERRA Modular Modeling Complex* is an expanding collection of process models and model components (modules); their data bases, parameter values, system states, and conversion algorithms; and linkages necessary to make the assessments and comparisons needed in the decision process. The Modular Modeling System (MMS) was developed by the US Geological Survey, in cooperation with the Bureau of Reclamation and the University of Colorado (Leavesley et al., 1992). MMS is the prototype assembler for TERRA's modeling complex. It is a software system designed to support the development, linking, testing, and evaluation of algorithms, and to facilitate the incorporation of user-selected sets of algorithms into an operational model. Models and modules reside in the system "on the shelf", i.e., available for use by other than the developers. Alternative conceptualizations of processes representing different time or space scales, or different algorithms, are thus available for developing models to fit specific situations, or modules can easily be compared for a given situation. Statistical analyses are available in MMS to aid in making decisions or in comparing scenarios or model results.

The modeling complex has the potential to solve a problem common to many available models: model component imbalance. This is illustrated in figure 13. The example system conceptualization contains two components, water and plant. When implemented as a computer model, however, the system sometimes becomes more like figure 14 or figure 15, depending on if the model developer was a hydrologist or agronomist. The individual's expertise is reflected in the complexity of certain components: the hydrologist may move soil water in time steps on the order of a second, but lump plant growth into weekly accumulations, while the agronomist might be growing root hairs on each plant, but moving water weekly. The resulting system models contain mismatched component complexities. Within MMS, the components of both models in Figures 3 and 4 are available, so a model may be built using either both complex water and plant modules or both simple modules, resulting in a balanced model. As an example, the hydrologist may utilize MMS to include the expertise of the agronomist when building a "system" model (using available modules). He now has the option of using the previously developed complex plant module in MMS when first developing a complex hydrology module, avoiding the need to create a new complex plant module.

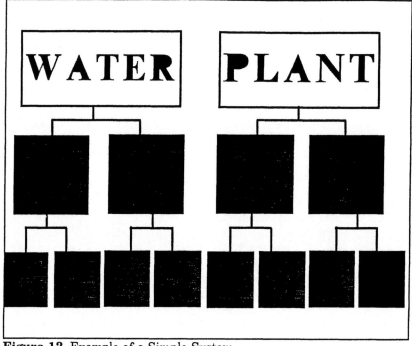

Figure 13. Example of a Simple System.

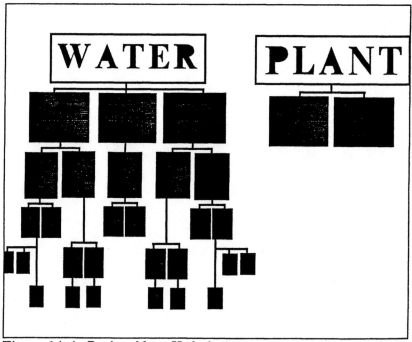

Figure 14. As Produced by a Hydrologist.

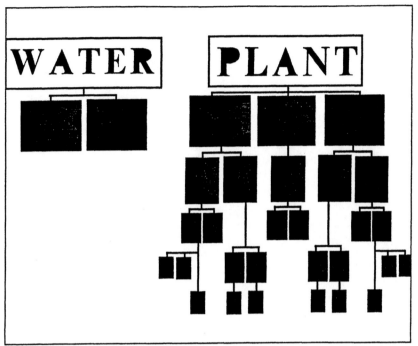

Figure 15. As produced by an agronomist.

Visualization technology provides the scientist and decision-maker with the capability to interact with large amounts of complex data through a visual format, maximizing comprehension of the information contained in the data. Three-dimensional data, such as subsurface or atmospheric phenomena, can be displayed in full dimensionality: time-dependent data can be viewed through animation, and tools for probing and manipulating the data can be provided for interactive visualization.

TERRA and IBM are cooperating on a project to link MMS with IBM's visualization software, Data Explorer. Through this link, model scenarios can be analyzed and compared through more comprehensible displays. Land managers, policy makers, and the public will be able to "see" data trends and anomalies in computer output, by using the visualization techniques available in Data Explorer[9].

TERRA is also pursuing a GIS linkage with MMS, and a PC version of the modeling complex. The final goal is to visualize MMS output together with GIS spatial data, creating more natural displays which include topography, hydrography, and other spatial variables.

---

[9]Use of product name is not an endorsement by TERRA Laboratory.

HyperSAM: a Link Between Hypermedia Software and Structural Analysis Methodology

In evaluating how best to assess environmental impacts and present the results to policy-makers and stakeholders, TERRA uses a *Structured Analysis Methodology (SAM)*. One example of steps in a SAM may be summarized as:

1. Define the issue to be analyzed;
2. Define temporal and spatial scales of the issue;
3. Determine potential effects of the decision/issue being analyzed;
4. Define a conceptual analysis of the system;
5. Develop a formal system model, sensitive to potential effects;
6. Execute model, and analyze results; and
7. Interpret and present analysis and assessment results.

Complete assessments with many steps may require different tools or computerized methodologies. HyperSAM has been developed to provide an easy means of linking appropriate software and to provide information aids to the user. HyperSAM is a linkage between Hypermedia and Structured Analysis Methodology.

Hypermedia is computerized (digital) information of various types, linked to provide users with additional information about topics. It is widely used in computerized encyclopedias, Windows "Help" applications, and other information-rich applications. An example of hypermedia is a paragraph of text that contains a "hot" word, which when selected produces a related picture, graph, map, or entire textual document. A "hot-spot" on a map might produce information about its location, in any available medium (including a more detailed map). Media may also include applications such as a spreadsheet, word processor, or GIS package.

TERRA Laboratory is developing HyperSAM to help users "navigate" through a systematic study of the Rio Puerco project. Figure 16 on the following page shows a sample of the prototype system.

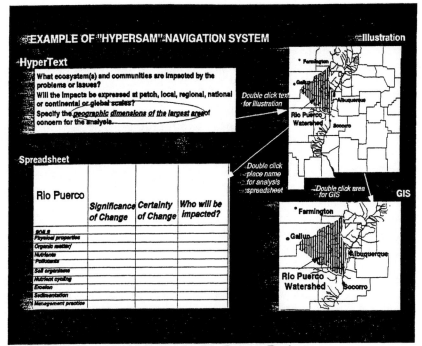

Figure 16. HyperSAM Example, Rio Puerco Project.

Active Response Geographic Information System (ARGIS)

An *Electronic Meeting System (EMS)* is software that allows participants to perform such functions as brainstorming, consensus building, and voting, through use of personal computers. The group may be together or may be scattered around the world. A "facilitator" station accumulates, stores, summarizes, and distributes information contributed by participants. Advantages of an EMS include the speed of information exchange (everyone can "talk" at once), potential anonymity, and possible lessening of psychological barriers.

A Geographic Information System (GIS) is software that stores, compares, analyzes, and manipulates map data for a single user. TERRA has developed a link connecting an electronic meeting system and a geographic information system. ARGIS (Faber et al., 1994) facilitates the exchange of information in meetings where map data are used. The system combines and analyzes participant responses, creating maps and tables summarizing group input.

ISSUES FOR CONGRESS

The U.S. Congress requested information from CRS about tools and technologies under development for ecosystem management and the issues that may be surrounding their use. The following is response to a CRS compiled list of questions, by topic.

The Limitations of These Tools

The three linkage products discussed above share the limitation of being only in developmental stages.

- HyperSAM is in an early stage, with a prototype being built around the Rio Puerco project. Utilization of HyperSAM in that project will determine if a generic navigation system should be produced.
- ARGIS has been tested, including a validation study; it is being beta-tested (used prototypically in a practical application) on a Forest Service project.
- MMS is the most mature of the three products, with years of USGS and cooperators' efforts invested. It has been initially beta-tested, and is now downloadable over Internet. Final MMS documentation is nearing publication, and TERRA documentation is complete for several enhancements. Limitations of its stage include the need to populate the system with a wide array of modules and databases, and the need to develop an expert system to assist the user in identifying appropriate concepts and modules for a given problem.

Hardware and software may be assets or limitations. HyperSAM and ARGIS are based on commercial software. Factors considered in TERRA development efforts include product availability, support, and costs.

The Direction of the Development of Tools

- HyperSAM is being developed and tailored for use in the Rio Puerco project, and is rapidly changing as more information, updated and innovative software and hardware, and project plans evolve or become available.
- ARGIS is in a more advanced stage, with an available User's Manual, and has been utilized for several projects. Refinements are being implemented.
- Modular Modeling Complex is being tested and enhanced. Recent efforts have included improving system portability, so it is now readily available for a variety of UNIX workstation models; efforts to make a PC-Unix version are under way. Graphics capabilities have been improved with a state-of-the-art visualization package linkage under development.

The Cost of Tools vs. the Cost of Acquiring Data

Federal Agencies are conducting problem-targeted research which TERRA tools may help to make relevant to global change and ecosystem management applications.

TERRA is testing and cooperating in the development of tools with a wide range of costs, from free or minimal cost (public domain and shareware) to expensive software, operating on a range of equipment from inexpensive notebook PC's to workstations. The ultimate goal is to provide easily-accessible tools, applicable on readily-available equipment. To reach this goal, TERRA is utilizing a variety of available software and equipment; as our developments on the high end of costs proceed, it is the nature of the computer industry that costs will decline, and capabilities will expand exponentially.

Data now available or now being collected will be utilized in the modeling effort; but scientists cannot simply acquire data to answer the ecosystem management/global change questions we face. Computer simulation models allow many tests and analyses of results; the real world offers only very limited scenarios in "real" time. By the time answers are available in the real world, the problems will need solutions; TERRA's goal is to provide tools and technologies to facilitate identifying strategies for prevention and/or adaptation.

The Need for New or Different Data

One need is for old (historical) data: there exists a lot of data which would be useful if it were computer-accessible. Several agencies are striving to save and process such data. The USGS is producing large quantities of geographic data, both old (from maps) and new (remotely sensed). This is a valuable resource, necessary for ecosystem-management applications.

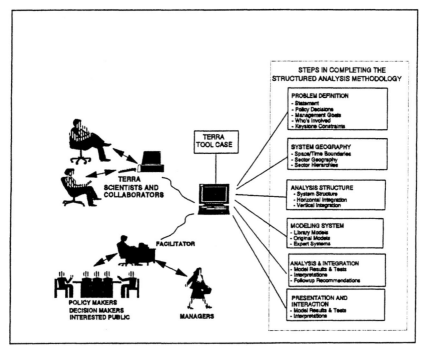

Figure 17. Structured Analysis Methodology

Another need is for overall collaboration in design of an open data archival system (one that may be freely accessed, utilized, and shared by all concerned interests).

Informing Those in the Public Decision Making Process

All of the TERRA tools have potential for transferring more scientific knowledge to the public decision-making process. In addition, HyperSAM and ARGIS are designed to facilitate the process. Figure 6. illustrates TERRA's conceptualized decision-making process, focusing on the role TERRA and TERRA tools might play in the process.

REFERENCES

Faber, B. G., R. Watts, J. E. Hauteluoma, J. Knutson, W. W. Wallace, and L. Wallace. 1994. "A Groupware-enabled GIS." *Proc. GIS '94 Symposium*, Vancouver, B.C., pp. 551-561.

Ferreira, V. A. and W. K. Lauenroth. 1993. "Computer Simulation Modeling of Pesticide Fate." In: *Pesticide Interactions in Crop Production, Beneficial and Deleterious Effects*, J. Altman, ed. CRC Press, pp. 87-111.

Leavesley, G. H., P. Restrepo, L. Stannard, and M. Dixon. 1992. "The Modular Hydrologic Modeling System - MHMS." *Proc. AWRA 28th Annual Conference and Symposium*, Reno, Nevada, pp. 263-264.

USDA-ARS and IBM-Federal Systems Company, 1993. *Cooperative Research and Development Agreement*, 27 p.

APPENDIX II

PROGRAM OF THE EVENT

**The CRS Workshop on Tools and Techniques
of Ecosystem Management**

Program

Concurrent Demonstrations of Tools and Techniques of Ecosystem Management by TERRA Lab., National Biological Service/EROS Data Center, and U.S Fish and Wildlife Service.	9:00-9:55

Intro and Welcome (Moderator)   9:55-10:00

Keynote Address: Nancy Tosta, Chief, Branch of   10:05-10:50
Geographic Data Coordination, NMD, USGS Presents
Federal Government Perspective on the Tools of
Ecosystem Management and Importance for other
National Goals including the National Biological
Survey and National Spatial Data Infrastructure.
Q&A

Discussion and Demonstrations: 10:50-11:30
-     U.S. Fish & Wildlife Service, Use of GPS in Tracking
      Non-Game Species on Conservation Reserve Program Lands.
-     The National Biological Survey and Gap Analysis.
-     An Interagency, Multidisciplinary Approach to Ecosystem
      Management, Academic and Private Sector Partnership in the
      Development of Ecosystem Management Technologies. (TERRA Lab.)

Hands-on Demonstration of
"Active Response GIS" (TERRA Lab.).   11:30-12:00

Breakaway Discussions with Guest Speakers,   12:00-12:30
Interagency Ecosystem Management Coordinating Group
Representatives, and
Concurrent Demonstrations Resume.

Nancy Tosta is the Staff Director for the Federal Geographic Data Committee (FGDC). She is also the Chief of the Branch of Geographic Data Coordination in the National Mapping Division of the U.S. Geological Survey, Reston, Virginia. Ms. Tosta is also currently editor of the "Data Data" column in *Geo Info Systems* magazine. She previously was Deputy Director of California's Teale Data Center. Prior to that she was a policy analyst on natural resources issues for the California Department of Forestry. She has experience in natural resources management and policy analysis, image processing, GIS implementation, management, and coordination, and information technology management and policy. She has B.S. and M.S. degrees from the University of California Berkeley.

D. Alan Davenport is GIS Coordinator, for the Office of Migratory Bird Management, of the U.S. Fish and Wildlife Service (FWS). He has served over 26 years as a biologist/computer specialist with FWS, this includes more than 14 years at the Northern Prairie Wildlife Research Center (Now National Biological Service's (NBS) Northern Prairies Science Center) in Jamestown, North Dakota, and more than 12 years in the Office of Migratory Bird Management in Laurel, Maryland. He was educated in Wildlife Management, receiving his B.S. in 1962 and M.S. in 1967 from Utah State University and University of Minnesota, respectively. He received his M.S. in 1982 in Computer Sciences from North Dakota State University.

Mike Scott has been Professor of Fish and Wildlife Resources, Leader of the Idaho Cooperative Fish and Wildlife Research Unit, and Research Biologist for FWS working in cooperation with the NBS, since 1986. He received his B.S. and M.S. in Biology from San Diego State University in 1966, and 1970, respectively, and he received a PhD in Zoology from Oregon State University in 1973. He has worked as Assistant Curator, for the Natural History Museum, in the Department of Zoology at Oregon State University, Corvallis, and was Instructor at Malheur Environmental Field Station of Pacific University, Malheur National Wildlife Reserve in Burns, Oregon. Formerly, he was a researcher at the Department of Fisheries and Wildlife, Oregon State University, Corvallis. He has received many distinguished professional and educational accolades. Currently, he is evaluating methods used to estimate numbers of animals, assessment of habitat selection by grizzly bears, preserve design at the continental and regional level, determining limiting factors, and designing recovery strategies for endangered species.

Brian Biggs of the U.S. Geological Survey's EROS Data Center in Sioux Falls, South Dakota graduated from the University of California at Santa Barbara with a BA in Geography. He will be attending the Utah State University working toward a Master's in Geography with an emphasis in Remote Sensing and Geographic Information Systems. He is currently working with the United Nations Environmental Programme (UNEP) in collaboration with NBS to create an electronic Encyclopedia of GAP Analysis.

Virginia Ferreira earned a Bachelor's degree in Mathematics at the University of Arizona, and a Master's in Earth Resources--Hydrology at Colorado State University. She served the U.S. Department of Agriculture's Agricultural Research Service (ARS) in Tucson, AZ and Tifton, GA before moving to Ft. Collins, CO. She is a 24-year veteran of ARS, the last year with TERRA Laboratory. Ms. Ferreira is accompanied by Sanetta Gavette, T'Shanna Smith, Bret Smith, Ernest (E.J.) Soto, and Carl Spongberg who will be assisting with TERRA Lab's demonstrations.

Natural Resources
Pages 77-92

THE ARCTIC NATIONAL WILDLIFE REFUGE

M. Lynne Corn and Lawrence C. Kuming

MOST RECENT DEVELOPMENTS

Budgetary considerations and the depressed price of Alaskan oil as a result of an export ban play a key part in the ANWR debate. On November 15, a conference committee reached an agreement on a reconciliation package (H.R. 2491) including a chapter opening the Refuge to development. The President vetoed the measure on December 6, citing the ANWR provisions as one of the reasons. On November 28, the President signed S. 395 (P.L. 104-58), which will allow the export of North Slope oil. Neither recent appropriations acts nor the Administration's proposed budget for FY1997 include ANWR development provisions. There are few signals at this time that the ANWR debate will be as active in the FY1997 budget cycle as it was in FY1996. Action, if any, still seems likely to be in the context of the new budget cycle.

BACKGROUND AND ANALYSIS

The coastal plain of the Arctic National Wildlife Refuge (ANWR) in the northeast corner of Alaska is currently the most promising U.S. onshore oil and gas prospect. This federal land (administered by the Fish and Wildlife Service in the Department of the Interior) could hold as much oil as the giant field at Prudhoe Bay, which is on state land west of ANWR. Proponents of development cite, in particular, the benefits to the Alaskan and national economies and to the balance of trade.

At the same time, the Refuge is home to a spectacular variety of plants and animals. The presence of caribou, polar bears, grizzly bears, wolves, migratory birds, and many other species in a nearly undisturbed state has led some to call the area "America's Serengeti." The Refuge and two neighboring parks in Canada have been proposed for an international park, and several species found in the area (including polar bears, caribou, migratory birds, and whales) are protected by international treaties or agreements.

The conflict between high oil potential and pristine nature creates a dilemma: should Congress open the area for oil and gas development or should the area's ecosystem be given permanent protection? What factors should determine whether to open the area? If the area is opened, how can damages be avoided, minimized, or mitigated? To what extent should Congress involve itself in the management of the area (if it is developed) and to what extent should federal agencies be allowed to manage the area under existing law?

The Clinton Administration opposes development of the Refuge. Political stability in the Middle East and comparatively low world oil prices reduce the need and make the economics less favorable for development. However, both Chairman Murkowski (AK) of the Senate Committee on Energy and Natural Resources and Chairman Don Young (AK) of the House Committee on Resources have stated that opening the Refuge to energy development is a top priority. They cite increasing oil imports and declining U.S. and North Slope output among their major reasons for wishing to open the Refuge.

History and Congressional Actions

Offsetting receipts from leasing in the Refuge are included in the assumptions in H.Con.Res. 67, the congressional budget resolution. This assumption effectively sent a recommendation to the authorizing committees either to lease in ANWR or to produce equivalent savings or revenues from other sources.

ANWR in Reconciliation: Conference Agreement. The vetoed conference agreement for the reconciliation bill (H.R. 2491) comprised Sections 5312-5344 authorizing leasing in the Refuge. Key provisions included these features.

1.   Authorized a leasing program to be established by the Secretary of the Interior through the Bureau of Land Management, in consultation with the Fish and Wildlife Service; made no explicit provision for an Alaskan effort to obtain 90%, rather than 50%, of leasing revenues.

2.   Required 50-50 split of revenues between Alaska and the U.S. Treasury (see discussion below under **Legal Issues**).

3.   Established a 12.5% minimum royalty.

4.   Forbade the requirement of any additional findings or decisions to implement the authorization, and declared that the authorized leasing program is compatible with the purposes for which the Refuge was designated.

5.   Authorized the Secretary to designate up to 45,000 acres of the 1002 area that are "of such unique character and interest...as to require special management and regulatory protection..." and allowed the seasonal closure of larger areas to exploration; these Special areas may be leased under restrictions forbidding surface occupancy.

6.   Declared the 1987 Final Legislative Environmental Impact Statement "adequate to satisfy the legal requirements of the National Environmental Policy Act of 1969 with respect to actions authorized to be taken by the Secretary to develop and promulgate the regulations for the establishment of the leasing program authorized by this chapter, to conduct the first lease sale and any subsequent lease sale authorized by this chapter, and to grant rights-of-way, and easements to carry out the purposes of this chapter."

7.   Provided for expedited judicial review of regulations promulgated under the chapter in the U.S. Court of Appeals in the District of Columbia; set deadlines for the filing of complaints.

8.   Created a Community Assistance Fund of $30 million from the federal share of leasing revenues to be placed in government securities; the interest, up to $5 million per year permanently appropriated for aid to local governments (including Native organizations) directly affected by the authorized activities; funds to provide public and social services required in connection with energy development.

9.   Created a National Park, Refuge and Fish and Wildlife Renewal and Protection Fund, consisting of 50% of ANWR revenues (the federal share) in excess of $2.6 billion (the assumptions of the budget resolution) up to $250 million over the life of the fund; amounts available "without further appropriation...." When (or if) the cumulative total (both federal revenues, and Alaska's share) reached $2.6 billion, 50% of the succeeding income flow would enter the Renewal Fund until, over months, years, or decades, a cumulative total of $250 million enters the Fund. At that point, all deposits to the Fund would cease, and any future federal share would have been simply deposited in the Treasury. The Fund's money was to be available to be spent until exhausted. The fate of the Fund is unclear if Alaska were successful in any lawsuit to obtain 90%, rather than 50%, of the

leasing revenues. It divided expenditures from fund into four equal segments: (a) infrastructure in the National Park System; (b) infrastructure in the National Wildlife Refuge System; (c) acquisition from willing private property owners of habitat for threatened and endangered species; and (d) to North American Wetlands Conservation Fund (16 U.S.C. 4401 et seq.).

Much of what is now ANWR was set aside in December 1960 by Public Land Order 2214. Section 1003 of the Alaska National Interest Lands Conservation Act of 1980 (ANILCA, P.L. 96-487) prohibits oil and gas development in the 19-million-acre Refuge unless authorized by Congress. Under Section 1002 of ANILCA, Congress required the Department of the Interior (DOI) to report on the plant and animal resources and the oil and gas potential in 1.5 million acres of the coastal plain portion of ANWR (8% of the Refuge), now generally called the "1002 area." This information was presented in the Final Legislative Environmental Impact Statement (FLEIS or 1002 report), and submitted to Congress in April 1987. DOI described leasing alternatives and recommended that the area be fully leased.

The grounding of the *Exxon Valdez* on March 24, 1989, near the southern terminal of the TransAlaska Pipeline System (TAPS) in Prince William Sound played a major role in placing the development debate on hold. Damage at the time included an estimated 300,000 to 645,000 dead seabirds; 4,000 to 6,000 dead marine mammals; and $100 million in other losses. In retrospect, some cleanup methods have been criticized as doing more harm than good. Lawsuits were abundant. One result of the lawsuits was that much of the information and research has remained secret in order to protect the interests of various parties. Today, there is still disagreement over the legacy of the spill. Some scientists note the lack of toxicity of the water, and a visitor in the area would still see rugged beauty on most beaches. But other observers stress the accumulation of oil in some species, such as mussels (which filter sea water), and the effects on species that consume contaminated organisms.

Since 1987, many hearings on development proposals and on wilderness designation of the 1002 area have been held, and many bills have been introduced. Issues covered included the FLEIS, the environmental effects of oil development in ANWR or at Prudhoe Bay, assessments of the need for additional sources of oil, the biological resources of the coastal plain, and a proposed exchange of lands with Native corporations. (For a description of the issues and bills considered since 1987, see CRS Reports 88-380 ENR, 89-266 ENR, and 91-325 ENR.)

Legislative Choices

Congress has three basic choices for ANWR legislation. One option is passing legislation permitting oil and gas leasing in the 1002 area. If the development option is chosen, Congress could also decide the pace and conditions for any oil or gas development. The current vehicle for this choice is the reconciliation process (H.R. 2491, see above).

A second option is designating the area as wilderness, thereby not allowing energy development (unless Congress later reversed the decision). This choice, like the failure to find oil, could stimulate development of alternative energy supplies and strategies.

The third option, and the one chosen since the 99th Congress, is taking no action. Because current law prohibits development unless Congress acts, this option prevents onshore energy development. Those supporting delay often argue that not enough is known about either the probability of discoveries or about the environmental impact if development is permitted. Others argue that oil deposits should be saved for an unspecified "right time." Those arguing for preservation say the Refuge is a unique national treasure. Those supporting development argue that declining oil production suggests that that time should be sooner rather than later.

Geological Variables, Economics, and Development Options

ANWR's Geology and Potential Petroleum Resources. Alaska's North Slope (ANS) coastal plain has proved abundant in oil resources, and its geology holds further promise. The oil-bearing strata extend eastward from the 2-billion-barrel Kuparuk River field, past the Prudhoe Bay field (originally 11 billion barrels (bbls), now down to about 4 billion bbls), and a few smaller fields, and may continue through ANWR's 1002 area. The smaller accumulations include some fields that have produced intermittently and others that are currently noncommercial due mainly to lack of existing infrastructure. ANWR contains the largest undrilled onshore geologic structures with petroleum potential known in the United States.

In 1991, the Bureau of Land Management (BLM) of the Department of the Interior reviewed its 1987 estimate of ANWR's recoverable petroleum resource. The review was based on updated geophysical information and four wells drilled near ANWR, as well as applicable technology recently used in the development of the Endicott and Milne Point fields on the ANS frontier.

Based on this study, BLM raised the probability distribution of field size in the 1002 area. BLM estimated a 46% chance of finding at least one economic field. If an economic field is found, the median estimate of recoverable oil is 3.57 billion barrels, with a 5% probability of finding a total of 10 billion bbl or more in the ANWR region.

In June 1995, the U.S. Geological Survey (USGS) revisited BLM's 1991 estimates, relying upon several geologic studies and data from one new well, the Tenneco Aurora, at a federal offshore location north of the 1002 Area. USGS reduced its estimates of recoverable oil reserves to between 148 and 5,150 million barrels.

The BLM estimates, both old and new, depend on limited data and numerous assumptions about geology and economics. New data, such as the Tenneco Aurora well, and how the limited information is interpreted, can dramatically change estimates of ANWR's oil potential. Another important factor is the projected price of oil, which BLM assumed would increase steadily, exclusive of inflation, over coming decades. Except briefly during the 1990 Persian Gulf crisis and some market-related events currently causing a runup during the first quarter of 1996, oil prices have been low and stable since 1986 and proved world reserves of oil have increased. Some critics argue that the price increases projected by BLM unrealistically increase the probability of finding an economic field in ANWR.

The projected price of oil, however, is only one of many factors entering into the decision on whether and how high to bid for a lease. Each prospective bidder will do its own highly sophisticated analysis of the economic and physical factors of lease offers, and industry analyses historically have led to different results than the Government's analysis. With geological evidence pointing to the presence of physically recoverable oil and gas, prospective developers are expected to be eager to bid on ANWR leases.

Economics of Alaskan Oil Production. While crude oil prices affect the economics of ANWR production, transport costs and regional market conditions -- which are unique to North Slope production -- bear on an oil prospect's commercial viability. Until recently, ANS crude could not be exported under the law. (See **Oil Export Legislation**, below.) Until 1996--when exports begin to flow under a lifting of the ban-- the export ban had contributed for years to a glut of oil on the West Coast, reducing the price received by North Slope producers. This market effect, combined with high pipeline and shipping costs, resulted in producer revenues often below $10.00/bbl, according to a Department of Energy study. (For further details on ANS and the West Coast crude pricing and export issue see CRS Report 95-214 ENR, *West Coast Oil Exports*, January 27, 1995.)

Over the years, low wellhead prices contributed to the natural decline in North Slope reservoirs' production by diminishing the incentive to drill more wells and otherwise enhance output from existing reservoirs. Low prices have reduced investment in currently producing reservoirs and caused the abandonment of exploration and development work outside the Prudhoe Bay and Kuparuk fields. Capital intensive expansion of the infrastructure would be required to access attractive geologic sites not adjacent to current production. Lacking new investment in existing fields, development of known structures and exploration, the falling output of the Prudhoe and Kuparuk fields will not be offset.

Lower production means lower TAPS throughput. Pipeline costs are largely fixed; a smaller flow of crude means higher unit pipeline rates. The effect of declining ANS oil output on transportation economics in turn aggravates the negative effect on production.

There is little chance that this self-reinforcing cycle can be altered by reducing transportation and production costs. Much of ANS transport and production infrastructure is geared to high output. Substantial fixed investment is involved, and it is not amenable to downsizing as production falls. The cycle of lower output and rising unit costs could lead to a situation in which ANS production economics are continuously eroded, clouding the outlook for existing oil fields.

Oil Export Legislation. Diminished concerns about the security of oil supply, coupled with new leadership in the 104th Congress, led to renewed interest in oil export legislation. In the Senate, an export bill (S. 395) was introduced by Senator Murkowski. On November 8, 1995, the House agreed to the conference report (H.Rept. 104-312), and the Senate approved it on November 14. The measure was signed by the President on November 28 (P.L. 104-58).

The export of the West Coast crude surplus, which was expected to raise Alaskan crude to world market levels (a $2 or $3 increment) is just beginning. At the same time, the world oil market is in the midst of an upward price fluctuation, with current prices exceeding $20/bbl, a $4 increase from late 1995. And this time the world market has taken Alaskan prices along for the ride.

Higher price of whatever origin enhance incentives for greater exploration and development on the North Slope and increase interest in, as well as the revenues which might flow from, leasing ANWR. However, it's not clear that these higher prices will be sustained. (For additional background, see CRS Report 95-214 ENR, *West Coast Oil Exports*, January 27, 1995.)

World Oil Supply and Price. In addition to uncertainty about future oil prices, and the complexities confronting ANS development and production, U.S. dependence on imported oil is another important factor in the ANWR debate. The world's total stock of proven crude oil reserves increased more than 50% in the 1980s, from 659 billion bbls in 1980 to 997 billion bbls in 1993. Global demand, measured by worldwide production, dipped to a low of 53 million barrels per day (mbd) in response to large price rises after the Iranian political upheaval, but rose to 60 mbd in 1989 and has remained essentially unchanged since.

With supply increasing nearly everywhere in the world -- except in the United States -- it is not surprising that crude prices peaked in 1981 and declined steadily until late 1985, at which point they plunged from about $26/bbl to about $14/bbl. World prices since then, except for the brief dramatics of the 1990 Persian Gulf War and a few other market driven price spikes, have hovered in the $15-$20 range.

In the context of a 22-billion-barrel-per-year market of internationally traded oil, ANWR's likely contribution would be small, even if its full potential were realized. But small contributions can have important price effects, as witnessed by the role played by declining U.S. imports in the 1980s.

ANWR, the U.S. Oil Market, and Energy Policy. Lower-48 crude production has declined consistently since its 1973 peak of 9.0 mbd. Domestic output received a boost in 1977 when TAPS was completed and ANS crude production began. In 1978, the first full year of TAPS operation, pipeline throughput averaged 1.2 mbd. ANS production peaked in 1988 at a 2.0 mbd annualized, subsequently declining to a current 1.5 mbd.

Domestic crude production now stands at 6.5 mbd, 28% below its 1973 high. The drop features a 44% decline in lower-48 production, much of which comes from very old fields, depleted by decades of production. ANS output, mostly from the Prudhoe Bay and Kuparuk fields, has declined more than 25% from its highest levels in just 6 years.

Declining domestic production has been replaced by imports, which have returned to an historic high, exceeding 8 mbd. Nearly half of the Nation's oil now comes from abroad.

Were ANWR to be leased for oil exploration and development and -- through a large discovery in the Refuge or between it and Prudhoe Bay -- a significant ANS production increase to result, how would the Nation's energy supply and security situations be affected?

Extra domestic crude production of the greatest imaginable amount would still leave the Nation dependent on imports for at least 40% of its petroleum needs. From an energy security perspective, the basic situation would be unchanged -- the Nation would still depend heavily on imports. However, at present prices, each 0.1 mbd of foreign oil replaced with domestic supply (or produced here and sold abroad) reduces the trade deficit by $700 million annually.

Exploration and Leasing Options. The main federal law governing leasing and production of petroleum on federal land is the 1920 Mineral Leasing Act. Conventional federal leases permit exploration and, after discovery, usually extend until production ceases entirely. Congress has debated whether this law, federal environmental laws, and applicable Alaskan laws are adequate for 1002 development. In past hearings, many Members were willing to consider leasing mechanisms which differed substantially from historic practices. (See also **Revenue Allocation**, below.)

To reduce uncertainty about the presence of oil, Congress could authorize exploration, without proceeding automatically to development. Such a strategy is widely opposed by both industry and environmental groups because all sides have something to lose. If oil were found, environmentalists fear that development would be virtually impossible to stop, and if it is not, that the Refuge would still be marred. Oil companies fear that if oil is found at the sites of a handful of test wells, competition could push bids to higher levels than they feel are warranted. Moreover, it is unlikely that oil companies would support or fund exploration without the right to develop any commercial quantities of oil that might be found. However, faced with the choice of participating or not, their position might change. Oil companies also fear that a few negative findings might prevent any opening of the area, even though the industry might see opportunities in other parts of the huge 1002 area, away from the test wells. The Treasury would benefit if successful exploration forced subsequent bids higher, but if oil were not found at the test wells, bids for the entire area would likely be pushed down, and the Treasury would receive less revenue.

Refuge Management

Under ANILCA, one of the purposes of ANWR is to "conserve fish and wildlife populations and habitats in their natural diversity...." The other three purposes cite fish and wildlife treaty obligations, subsistence use, and maintenance of water quality and quantity. Under current law, additional activities are allowed on refuges to the extent that they are compatible with the purposes for which the refuge was designated. Thus, energy development in the 1002 area would have to be compatible with these four purposes, or the purposes would have to be modified or over-ridden. (The latter method was chosen in H.R. 2491 in the version vetoed by the President.) In addition, environmentalists argue that the pristine quality of the refuge and the 1002 area provide an argument beyond the requirements specified in ANILCA.

On August 25, 1995, DOI released a *Preliminary Review of the Arctic National Wildlife Refuge, Alaska, Coastal Plain Resource Assessment*. Examining especially biological impacts, the report concluded "there would be major environmental impacts from oil and gas development on the coastal plain." (The report noted that it joined the earlier 1987 FLEIS in that conclusion. However, the 1987 report found relatively few major impacts and held that most of these could be mitigated and that the energy and security benefits outweighed the negative impacts.) The primary new information reported was the greater dependence of the Porcupine Caribou Herd (PCH) on the 1002 area for calving (due to greater calf survival in years when calving occurs there) and for insect relief after calving. It further noted that if development displaced the herd, calving was likely to shift to areas of higher predation. Muskoxen were reported vulnerable to winter disturbance, when their low, energy-conserving metabolism would make movement difficult. Polar bears, according to both the 1987 and 1995 reports, are vulnerable to disturbance in their maternity dens. The new report considers revegetation to be a difficult and unproven technique, and notes that a "showcase" effort to revegetate an exploratory well site near Kaktovik still bore a visible scar 8 years later. The report (like earlier reports by previous Administrations) was criticized as politically motivated.

Refuge Purposes: Plants and Animals. Development advocates note that 92% of the Refuge would remain closed to development. Environmentalists counter that the 1002 report said the area at issue "is the most biologically productive part of the Arctic Refuge for wildlife and is the center of wildlife activity." If development were authorized, Congress would have to weigh how the various activities that would necessarily accompany development would affect the Refuge's resources. The importance of these resources (such as caribou, polar bears, grizzly bears, wolves, snow geese, wildflowers, water quality and quantity, etc.) in the debate derives from their value for subsistence take, sport hunting and fishing, their ecological roles, and/or aesthetic enjoyment, depending on the observer's point of view. Management of particular species, siting of facilities, and timing of development could all be issues.

Fewer Listed Species than in 1987. At the time of the 1002 report, 3 species were listed under the Endangered Species Act (ESA): the endangered bowhead and gray whales, and the threatened arctic peregrine falcon. The bowhead is still listed as endangered; according to the report, the activities most likely to affect this species would be summer-time noise and disturbance, though these effects were not deemed to be serious. This species, one of the largest marine mammals, is an important cultural and subsistence resource for Native people, and they have expressed concern that development activities take careful account of the needs of this species. The gray whale population for this area was de-listed on June 15, 1994, although ESA still requires that the species be monitored until 1999. The Arctic peregrine was de-listed on October 5, 1994, and must likewise be monitored for 5 years.

Caribou and Other Species. Opponents of development argue that the entire, balanced complex of caribou, polar and grizzly bears, wolves, falcons, wildflowers, and so on, is worth preserving intact, especially since it represents the least disturbed Arctic coastal area under U.S. ownership, and one of the "wildest" habitats of any type left in the United States. Scientists and sport hunters both stress the importance of the summer habitats on the plain for migratory game birds taken in both Canada and the United States. Game birds, especially snow geese, use the area for feeding before starting their journey south, and some hunters fear that summer development, especially overflights, could interfere with feeding enough to prevent the geese from gaining adequate weight for migration. The 1002 report notes some studies supporting that view and says that this and other possible consequences to birds could be minimized by controlling transportation and siting of facilities.

The species which has drawn the most attention in this debate is the caribou. The PCH calves in or near the 1002 area, and winters south of the Brooks Range in Alaska or Canada; in 1994, the herd numbered 152,000. In both areas it is an important food source to Native people and others -- especially since other meat is either expensive or unavailable. Some observers fear that development and production could cause cows to calve in less desirable locations or prevent the herd's access to sites where they can escape from the voracious insects common in early summer. Oil companies counter with a comparison to the Central Arctic Herd (CAH) that summers near Prudhoe, whose population has grown significantly since oil was discovered, and in 1994 numbered about 25,000. Environmentalists and some Natives counter that the CAH has a much larger area in which to calve, that caribou cows with young calves tend to avoid developed areas, and that predators have been controlled in that herd's area. The effect of oil development on the PCH is likely to remain one of the hotly contested issues in a new round of debate over the Refuge.

Pristine and Untrammelled? To follow the Refuge debate, it is important to understand that those who wish to prevent development are not basing their arguments primarily on economic tests nor pollution risks, though they may view those issues as favoring their side of the debate. Rather, they argue that "pristine" is a relative term and that the word has lost all meaning if it does not include a place like the Arctic Refuge. In terms that emphasize deeply held values, supporters of wilderness designation argue that few places as untrammelled as the 1002 area remain on the planet, and fewer still on the same magnificent scale. Any but the most transitory intrusions (e.g., visits for recreation, hunting, fishing, subsistence use, research, etc.) would, in their view, damage the "child-like sense of wonder" they see the area as instilling. The mere knowledge that a pristine place exists, whether one ever visits it, can be important to those who view the debate in this light.

Thus, even if a number of measures of biodiversity were to remain stable in the face of development, from their perspective, the peace of the area as a place where a larger truth may be sought would be seriously corrupted. Similarly, when told that the total "footprint" of development (the area actually occupied by drill pads, roads, etc.) would be smaller than Dulles International Airport, they note that the infrastructure would actually be scattered like a fine net thrown over the entire area, disrupting the terrain, the ecosystem, and the sense of lonely grandeur.

Development advocates counter this argument by noting the presence of the Native village of Kaktovik, the nearby DEWline station, and the remnants of other DEWline installations, and argue that the area is not pristine. Moreover, many Natives of Kaktovik respond that an argument about the value of pristine nature relegates their village to the margins of the debate.

The 1002 debate sometimes takes on a feud-like aspect due to the clash of two deeply held values: a belief in wilderness as teacher and guide in the quest for important values and sustenance of the planet over the long term, versus the value of work and of supporting a family. The re-injection of drilling wastes and similar issues would not raise the temperature of the debate higher than these issues.

Areas of Special Environmental Significance. The wildlife debate has focused mainly on the migratory Porcupine Caribou Herd. However, some believe other species, such as polar bears, grizzly bears, wolves, or migratory birds, may be at greater risk. Congress could consider special protection (e.g., wilderness designation, delayed exploration, or a special regulatory regime) of the most important habitats. The areas most often mentioned for some special status include the major calving area of the PCH, the area around Sadlerochit Spring (a warm spring that flows all year), and the overlapping areas near the coast where substantial bird populations occur in the summer and where pregnant female polar bears make their winter dens. From 1981-

1991, 90 dens of female polar bears were found in the latter area, making up about 43% of the dens of this population.

Control of Access. One access issue could be the logistical conflict between the area's management as an industrial site versus its current management as a refuge devoted not only to wildlife conservation but also to recreation (including sport fishing and hunting) and subsistence uses, among other functions. This conflict would become more intense as human populations and road networks increased with development. In contrast to the current open but difficult access at ANWR, access to the state-owned Prudhoe Bay complex is strictly (if not always effectively) controlled. Visitors' and workers' belongings are searched for firearms, alcohol, and drugs, which are prohibited. (None of these requirements now applies to the 1002 area.) Moreover, hunting, even for subsistence, is forbidden at Prudhoe and limited in other developed areas. Similar restrictions are not found in the 1002 area and may conflict with the Refuge's purposes as currently interpreted.

Environmental Quality Management

The grounding of the *Exxon Valdez* increased concern among environmentalists and others over oil spills and other potential sources of pollution, whether in Prince William Sound, along the length of TAPS, or at the North Slope. These environmental quality management issues can be divided into three categories: resource management, pollution, and waste disposal. Congress could choose to leave these matters to administrative agencies under authorities of existing laws. Alternatively, Congress could opt to impose a higher standard of environmental protection because the area is in a national wildlife refuge or because of the fragility of the Arctic environment. At issue would be the use of gravel and water resources essential for oil exploration and development; and setting fees for and allocating any revenues from exploiting these resources.

In addition, air and water pollution (whether chronic or acute) primarily raise questions of subtle, long-term ecological effects. Potential legislative issues include the adequacy of existing standards, research needs, monitoring, prevention and treatment of spills, the adequacy of current waste disposal requirements, the development of alternatives to landfills, and liability concerns that can make consolidation of disposal facilities unattractive to oil companies. (For a range of specific environmental quality issues, see CRS Videotape *Arctic Oil, Arctic Refuge.*)

Management of Support Services. Activities of the independent support service industry in the Prudhoe Bay area, particularly at Deadhorse, have been widely criticized. (Firms in this industry are generally employed by, rather than part of, major oil companies.) At Deadhorse, the state leases land for these independent services (repair, cleaning, laundry, aircraft supply, etc.). Management and control of support facilities, while a complex subject, could be one of the areas where oil companies and environmentalists might reach common ground, if development were authorized by Congress.

Section 1003 of ANILCA does not cover the role the 1002 area might play as a land base for state or federal offshore activity. Both the United States and Alaska are proceeding with offshore leasing near the 1002 area. But despite occasional small flurries of interest, no well has been commercially developed offshore from the Refuge.

Long-Term Cleanup. If Congress authorized development, but no commercial quantity of oil were found, the ecosystem is likely to recover substantially from exploratory activities in only a few years. If major quantities of oil and gas were found, development would probably last for decades or perhaps even a century, if natural gas production becomes commercially feasible. Substantial recovery from the much higher level of disturbance might then take further centuries in the harsh Arctic environment and could be a herculean task. Thus, Congress might be debating rehabilitation that would not begin until 2060 or 2090. Furthermore, some types of cleanup might not even be desirable or practical: deep gravel roads and drilling pads, for example, might be impossible to remove without creating further damage, and thus might necessarily become a permanent feature of the landscape. No existing federal laws are known to cover such long terms in planning for a cleanup whose cause may never occur, and the exact nature of which is unknown.

Congress may consider various proposals on assuring the long-term environmental quality of the area. Central to any decision on these proposals is determining what the ultimate rehabilitation goal(s) should be. Environmentalists would want strong standards, but would simultaneously argue that complete recovery is nearly impossible. Development advocates would argue that existing and future practices are adequate.

Subsistence Use and Access

The village of Kaktovik (over 200 people) and the lands of the Kaktovik Inupiat Corporation (KIC) lie along the coast within the Refuge and mostly adjacent to the 1002 area. Natives of Kaktovik are the major users of the resources in the coastal plain, although they focus significantly on marine resources. Kaktovik Natives support leasing generally but oppose both leasing in the primary caribou calving area in the east-central 1002 area and restrictions on discharging firearms. There is also a U.S. military Distant Early Warning (DEW) station near Kaktovik, with about a dozen employees. The DEW network has several unoccupied sites of former or uncompleted developments scattered in or near the 1002 area. Together with Kaktovik, the DEW site operates a garbage dump and a runway.

Subsistence hunters in the interior of Alaska and Canada (including especially the Gwich'in people who hunt the herd in its winter range) and the Canadian government oppose leasing in the calving area of the herd and support wilderness designation. If the area is opened to leasing, Congress may be asked to consider whether the current access or hunting rights of Native users should be restricted to protect pipeline safety; whether subsistence users should have a special voice in new regulations as 1002 exploration or development evolve and what provision might be made to minimize any harmful impacts of development on Native culture among both north slope and interior Alaska groups.

Revenue Allocation

If oil is present, ANWR development revenues from bonuses, rents, and royalties, as well as from sales of gravel and water, could generate billions of dollars for the landowners. Peak annual royalties alone might range from $200 million to $2.5 billion, followed by declining revenues for 30-50 years. If Alaska owns submerged lands in the Refuge, it could receive substantial revenues directly. (See **Legal Issues**, below.) Whatever the federal income, Congress would need to decide:

1.   If development is permitted, should Alaska receive its current statutory 90% share
      of certain revenues from mineral leases on federal lands; and considering the terms
      of the Alaska Statehood Act, could Congress change Alaska's share? (See CRS
      Report 87-63 A.)

2.   Should any federal revenues from ANWR be used for land acquisition in Alaska
      or elsewhere as part of the mitigation for reduced habitat values in a developed
      1002 area as some have suggested? If so, how should the revenues be allocated?

Legal Issues

The United States and Alaska dispute the ownership of submerged lands beneath
waters within and offshore of ANWR. Depending on how the legal issues are decided,
Alaska may own significant subsurface inholdings within ANWR. If these inholdings
were opened to leasing, not only would management of the remaining Refuge lands be
complicated, but substantial revenues from any oil on those inholdings would accrue
to Alaska, rather than the United States. P.L. 100-395 addressed these issues in part,
but significant issues remain. (For further information, see CRS Report 87-673 A.)

A court held that DOI should have prepared a Supplemental Environmental
Impact Statement (SEIS) encompassing new information about the 1002 area in
connection with the Department's recommendation that Congress legislate to permit
development. The last EIS was prepared in 1987 and it seems clear that, under current
law, either an SEIS or a new EIS would have to precede development, unless Congress
eliminates this requirement, as would have occurred under Section 5335 of the
conference agreement on H.R. 2491. The Section stated that the 1987 EIS was
adequate for development of the regulations, for conducting the first and subsequent
lease sales, and for granting rights-of-way.

The bill also called for a 50/50 split of revenues from the development of ANWR.
Alaska has indicated that the state will dispute any distribution of revenues from
ANWR leases that deviates from the 90/10 share to which Alaska is entitled under a
1976 Act and, allegedly, under the Alaska Statehood Act. It can be argued, however,
that that split was intended to reflect the usual share of western states under the 1920
Mineral Leasing Act, which allows a 50/50 direct split and an additional 40% returned
to the states indirectly through the Reclamation Fund; and that Congress has at times
prescribed other disposition of revenues, e.g., with respect to the Naval Petroleum
Reserves.

LEGISLATION

P.L. 104-58, S. 395
Allows oil from TAPS to be exported; restricts transport to U.S.-flagged tankers
with U.S. crews; and for other purposes. Introduced February 13, 1995; referred to
Committee on Energy and Natural Resources; reported April 27, 1995 (S.Rept. 104-78).
Passed Senate (amended) May 16, 1995 by 74-25 (Rec. vote 170). Passed House (text
of H.R. 70 inserted in lieu) July 25, 1995. Conference report (H.Rept 104-312) filed in
House November 6, 1995. House agreed to conference report November 8, 1995 (289-

134, Rec. vote 772). Senate agreed November 14, 1995 (69-29, Rec. vote 574). Signed by President, November 28, 1995.

H.R. 70 (Thomas)

Amends Mineral Leasing Act to permit export of North Slope Oil; requires oil to be carried on U.S. vessels except in certain cases. Introduced January 4, 1995; referred to Committees on Resources and on International Relations. Reported (amended) from Committee on Resources June 15, 1995 (H.Rept. 104-139, Part I). Passed House (amended) July 24, 1995 (324-77, Roll Call No. 557). See P.L. 104-58 for further action.

H.R. 1000 (Vento)

Designates the 1002 area as wilderness. Introduced February 21, 1995; referred to Committee on Resources.

H.R. 2491 (Kasich)

Provides for reconciliation of the concurrent budget resolution on the budget for FY1996. Introduced October 17, 1995; Committee on the Budget reported an original measure (H.Rept. 104-280). Passed by House October 26, 1995. Passed Senate (text of S. 1357 inserted in lieu) October 28, 1995. Conferees agreed to report (H.Rept. 104-347) November 15, 1995. Vetoed December 6, 1995.

S. 428 (Roth)

Amends Refuge Administration Act of 1966 to designate 1002 area as wilderness. Introduced February 16, 1995; referred to Committee on Environment and Public Works.

FOR ADDITIONAL READING

ARCO Alaska, Inc. *Oil in the Arctic: The Environmental Record of Oil Development on Alaska's North Slope -- Comments and Critique.* Natural Resources Defense Council, National Wildlife Federation, and Trustees for Alaska. 1988. 24 p.

Speer, Lisa, and Sue Libenson. *Oil in the Arctic: The Environmental Record of Oil Development on Alaska's North Slope.* Natural Resources Defense Council, Inc., 1988. 78 p.

Speer, Lisa. *Tracking Arctic Oil: The Environmental Price of Drilling in the Arctic National Wildlife Refuge.* Natural Resources Defense Council, National Wildlife Federation, and Trustees for Alaska. New York. 1991. 36 p.

U.S. Department of the Interior. Bureau of Land Management. *Overview of the 1991 Arctic National Wildlife Refuge Recoverable Petroleum Resource Update.* Washington, April 8, 1991. 8 p., 2 maps.

U.S. Department of the Interior. Fish and Wildlife Service. Arctic Refuge website. *http://bluegoose.arw.R9.fws.gov/NWRSFiles/RefugeSystemLeaflets/R7/Arctic/ArcticIndex.html.* Hypertext links to numerous other relevant information, and maps and photographs from a variety of sources and viewpoints. Revised frequently.

U.S. Department of the Interior. Fish and Wildlife Service, Geological Survey, and Bureau of Land Management. *Arctic National Wildlife Refuge, Alaska, Coastal Plain Resource Assessment.* Report and Recommendation to the Congress of the United States and Final Legislative Environmental Impact Statement. Washington, 1987. 208 p.

U.S. General Accounting Office. *Arctic National Wildlife Refuge: An Assessment of Interior's Estimate of an Economically Viable Oil Field.* Washington, D.C. July, 1993. 31 p.
    GAO/RCED-93-130

U.S. Library of Congress. Congressional Research Service. *West Coast Oil Exports.* Lawrence C. Kumins. [Washington] 1995. 7 p.
    CRS Report 95-214 ENR

----- *ANWR Development: Analyzing its Economic Impact.* Bernard A. Gelb. [Washington] 1992. 6 p.
    CRS Report 92-169 E

----- *Arctic Oil, Arctic Refuge.* Videotape by Lynne Corn, Bob Nickel, et al. 53 minutes. [Washington] 1991. (Available to congressional requestors only.)

----- *Arctic National Wildlife Refuge: Congressional Consideration Since the 99th Congress*, by M. Lynne Corn and Ted L. Burch. [Washington] 1991. 21 p.
    CRS Report 91-325 ENR

----- *The Arctic National Wildlife Refuge: Major Oil Development or Wilderness?* ed. by John E. Blodgett and John L. Moore. [Washington] 1988. 162 p.
    CRS Report 88-161 ENR

----- *Legal Issues Related to the Ownership of the Submerged Lands within and off the Coast of the Arctic National Wildlife Refuge*, by Pamela Baldwin. [Washington] 1987. 36 p.
    CRS Report 87-673 A

----- *Whether Congress Unilaterally May Amend a Mineral Lease Revenue Distribution Formula that Appeared in the Alaska Statehood Act*, by Thomas J. Nicola. [Washington] 1987. 12 p.
    CRS Report 87-63 A

Natural Resources
Pages 93-108

THE ARCTIC NATIONAL WILDLIFE REFUGE: THE NEXT CHAPTER

M. Lynne Corn

MOST RECENT DEVELOPMENTS

Budgetary considerations and the increasing price of imported oil as a result of cutbacks in foreign production play a key part in the reawakening of the ANWR debate. Bills to designate the key northern portion of the refuge as wilderness, and others to open the refuge to energy development have been introduced. Assumptions about revenues from ANWR leasing were included in the FY2001 budget resolution (S.Con.Res. 101) as reported by the Senate Budget Committee on March 31, 2000. An amendment to remove the language was tabled (51-49) on April 6, 2000. However, conferees rejected the language; the conference report on H.Con.Res. 290 did not contain this assumption, and the report was passed by both House and Senate on April 13. S. 2557, introduced May 16, 2000, includes a title to open the refuge to development.

BACKGROUND AND ANALYSIS

The Arctic National Wildlife Refuge (ANWR) consists of 19 million acres in northeast Alaska. The 1.5 million acre coastal plain of the refuge is currently one of the most promising U.S. onshore oil and gas prospects. This federal land (administered by the Fish and Wildlife Service (FWS) in the Department of the Interior (DOI)) could hold as much oil as the giant 11 billion barrel field at Prudhoe Bay, found in 1967 on state land west of ANWR.

At the same time, the Refuge, and especially the coastal plain, is home to a wide variety of plants and animals. The presence of caribou, polar bears, grizzly bears, wolves, migratory birds, and many other species in a nearly undisturbed state has led some to call the area "America's Serengeti." The Refuge and two neighboring parks in Canada have been proposed for an international park, and several species found in the area (including polar bears, caribou, migratory birds, and whales) are protected by international treaties or agreements. The analysis below covers, first, the economic and geological factors that have triggered new interest in development, followed by the biological and environmental quality factors that have triggered opposition to it.

The conflict between high oil potential and pristine nature creates a dilemma: should Congress open the area for oil and gas development or should the area's ecosystem be given permanent protection from development? What factors should determine whether to open the area? If the area is opened, how can damages be avoided, minimized, or mitigated? To what extent should Congress legislate special management of the area (if it is developed) and to what extent should federal agencies be allowed to manage the area under existing law? (Information, including maps of the refuge, can be found at the FWS web site, [http://www.r7.fws.gov/nwr/arctic]. Links to a number of other organizations interested in the area can be found at [http://www.r7.fws.gov/nwr/arctic/devlinks.html].)

Rapidly rising oil prices have fueled the debate. The Clinton Administration opposes development of the Refuge. In the key Committees, Chairman Murkowski (AK) of the Senate Committee on Energy and Natural Resources and Chairman Don Young (AK) of the House Committee on Resources have stated that opening the Refuge to energy development is a top priority. They cite high energy costs, increasing oil imports, and declining U.S. and North Slope output among their major reasons for wishing to open the Refuge. (For additional information on high energy prices, see CRS Rept. RL30459, *Coping With High Oil Prices: A Summary of Options*.)

History and Congressional Actions

Early History of Arctic Refuge. Much of what is now ANWR was set aside in December 1960 by Public Land Order 2214; protection of the area's wildlife was named as one of the new refuge's purposes. Section 1003 of the Alaska National Interest Lands Conservation Act of 1980 (ANILCA, P.L. 96-487) prohibits oil and gas development in the 19-million-acre Refuge unless authorized by Congress. Under Section 1002 of ANILCA, Congress required DOI to report on the plant and animal resources and the oil and gas potential in 1.5 million acres of the coastal plain portion of ANWR (8% of the Refuge, where any oil is most likely to be found), now generally called the "1002 area." This information was presented in the Final Legislative Environmental Impact Statement (FLEIS or 1002 report), which was submitted to Congress in April 1987. At that time, DOI described leasing alternatives and recommended that the area be fully leased.

Since 1987, many hearings on development proposals and on wilderness designation of the 1002 area have been held, and many bills have been introduced. Issues covered included the FLEIS, the environmental effects of oil development in ANWR or at Prudhoe Bay, assessments of the need for additional sources of oil, the biological resources of the coastal plain, and a proposed exchange of lands with Native corporations. (For a description of the issues and bills considered since 1987, see CRS Report 88-380 ENR, CRS Report 89-266 ENR, and CRS Report 91-325 ENR.) In the intervening years, low oil prices played a major role in dampening enthusiasm for energy development in the refuge. In addition, new opportunities in the former Soviet republics and in the developing world have focused industry attention elsewhere. Another industry focus has been the lease sales held in the National Petroleum Reserve-Alaska (NPRA), to the west of the Prudhoe Bay area. These sales were supported by industry and the Administration, but not by the environmental community.

The grounding of the *Exxon Valdez* on March 24, 1989, near the southern terminal of the TransAlaska Pipeline System (TAPS) in Prince William Sound played a major role in placing the development debate on hold. Damage at the time included an estimated 300,000 to 645,000 dead seabirds; 4,000 to 6,000 dead marine mammals; and $100 million in other losses. Some cleanup methods were criticized as doing more harm than good. Lawsuits were abundant. One result of the lawsuits was that much of the research on the effects has remained secret in order to protect the interests of various parties. Today, there is still disagreement over the legacy of the spill. Some scientists note the lack of toxicity of the water, and a visitor in the area would still see rugged beauty on most beaches. But other observers stress the accumulation of oil in some species, such as mussels (which filter sea water), and the effects on species that consume contaminated organisms.

Due to reduced attention to the 1002 Area, research and investigation across a number of fronts have not maintained the intensity of the 1980s. As a result, the best available data on a number of topics may be several years old.

ANWR Consideration in the 104th Congress. Congress attempted to authorize the opening of ANWR in the FY1996 reconciliation bill (H.R. 2491, §§5312-5344), but the measure was vetoed. President Clinton cited those sections as one of his reasons for vetoing the measure. (For key provisions of that legislation, see Archived Issue Brief 95071.) Key votes occurred on May 24 and October 27, 1995, on motions to table amendments that would have stripped ANWR development titles from the Senate version of the bill. Both motions succeeded. The ANWR issue was not raised in the 105th Congress.

Legislative Choices

Congress has three basic choices for ANWR legislation. One option is passing legislation permitting oil and gas leasing in the 1002 area. If the development option is chosen, Congress could also specify the pace and conditions for any oil or gas development, or it could allow these decisions to be made under other laws governing development on federal land generally.

A second option is designating the area as wilderness, thereby not allowing energy development (unless Congress later reversed the decision).

The third option, and the one chosen since the 99th Congress, is taking no action. Because current law prohibits development unless Congress acts, this option prevents energy development. Those supporting delay often argue that not enough is known about either the probability of discoveries or about the environmental impact if development is permitted. Others argue that oil deposits should be saved for an unspecified "right time." Those arguing for preservation say the Refuge is a unique national treasure. Those supporting development argue that declining oil production suggests that that time should be sooner rather than later.

Current Bills and Budget Resolution, FY2001. Four bills have been introduced concerning ANWR. S. 867 would designate the 1002 Area as wilderness; H.R. 2250, S. 2214, and S. 2557 would repeal the prohibition on energy exploration and development in current law and would create programs for competitive oil and gas leasing in the area. Offsetting receipts from leasing in the Refuge were included in the assumptions in the FY2001 Senate budget resolution (S.Con.Res. 101, S.Rept. 106-251). This assumption effectively sent a recommendation to the authorizing committees either to lease in ANWR or to produce equivalent savings or revenues from other sources. An amendment to delete this recommendation from the report was tabled (51-49, roll call #58) on April 6, 2000. However, the assumption was rejected in H.Con.Res. 290, the final budget resolution that was passed by both House and Senate on April 13, 2000.

Geological Variables, Economics, and Development Options

ANWR's Geology and Potential Petroleum Resources. Parts of Alaska's North Slope (ANS) coastal plain have proved abundant in oil resources, and its geology holds further promise. The oil-bearing strata extend eastward from structures in the NPRA, to the 2 billion barrel Kuparuk River field, past the Prudhoe Bay field (originally 11 billion barrels, now down to about 4 billion barrels), and a few smaller fields, and may continue through ANWR's 1002 area. Further east in Canada's Mackenzie River delta, once promising structures have not produced significant amounts of oil. The smaller accumulations include some fields that have produced intermittently and others that are currently noncommercial due mainly to lack of existing infrastructure. ANWR contains one of the most promising undrilled onshore geologic structures with petroleum potential known in the United States.

Estimates of ANWR oil potential, both old and new, depend on limited data and numerous assumptions about geology and economics. (Actual exploration in the refuge remains illegal under §1003 of ANILCA.) New data from outside the boundaries and the interpretation of the old, limited LEIS information can dramatically change estimates of ANWR's oil potential. Another important factor is the projected price of oil, which the Bureau of Land Management (BLM) in 1987 assumed would increase steadily (excluding inflation), over coming decades. In actuality, the price of oil has stayed fairly low and stable since 1986 (corrected for inflation), with intervals of spiking – briefly during the 1990 Persian Gulf crisis, a period during 1996, and the recent rise. Proven world reserves of oil have increased during the same period. A third factor is falling production costs, as technology improves – structures which were once unprofitable may become so, and this has occurred at Prudhoe Bay through several new technologies.

What the Numbers Mean. There are many wildly varying estimates of oil quantity in ANWR. Here is a guide to these estimates and their meaning.

Minimum field size is the amount of oil that must be present in at least one field to make a defined area profitable. Embedded in this concept are assumptions about future oil prices, technology development, and costs of production; if these change, this estimate will change. At ANWR, the minimum field size is usually estimated at several hundred million barrels. Many little fields, very close together, might substitute for a larger one.

How much oil might be present? This number is not particularly useful, since it is not possible to extract every drop of oil in a field. The response is almost never given as a single number, but instead, usually as two and sometimes three numbers. First, analysts ask "what quantity of oil are we confident of finding?" Logically, there is a good chance of finding a small amount (or more), and only a small chance of finding a large amount (or more). These probabilities are fixed (by tradition) at 95% (chance of at least a certain small amount), and 5% (chance of at least a certain large amount). The third number is the median (50%) estimate: it is equally likely that any oil found will be above or below this amount.

How much oil is technically recoverable? This number assumes that cost of recovery and price of oil are irrelevant, and that only current technology is used. Like the previous estimates, it gives the large (95%) chance that a certain small amount (or more) of oil is present, the small chance (5%) that a large amount (or more) is present, and the median (50%) estimate. These three numbers are always smaller than the estimates of oil that might be present.

How much oil is economically recoverable? These numbers are the most useful, and could exceed technically recoverable amounts if technology advances. They include assumptions about oil prices, advances in technology, costs of production, etc. They are also given as 95%, 50%, and 5% estimates (of small or more, median or more, and large or more amounts).

Geological Studies, 1991-Present: Understanding the Numbers. In 1991, the Bureau of Land Management (BLM) of the Department of the Interior reviewed its 1987 estimate of ANWR's recoverable petroleum resource. The review was based on updated geophysical information and four wells drilled near ANWR, as well as applicable technology used in the development of the Endicott and Milne Point fields on the ANS frontier. Based on this study, BLM increased its estimates of possible oil resources in the 1002 area. BLM estimated a 46% chance of finding at least one minimum field. It estimated that if a minimum field is found, the median estimate of economically recoverable oil would be 3.57 billion barrels, with a small chance (5%) of finding 10 billion barrels or more in the area.

In June 1995, the U.S. Geological Survey (USGS) revisited BLM's 1991 estimates, relying upon several geologic studies and data from one new well, the Tenneco Aurora, at a federal offshore location north of the 1002 Area. USGS reduced its estimates of recoverable oil reserves to between 148 and 5,150 million barrels.

The most recent government study of oil prospects in ANWR is the 1998 study by USGS *Arctic National Wildlife Refuge, 1002 Area, Petroleum Assessment, 1998* (USGS Fact Sheet FS-040-98, May 1998). USGS scientists gathered new data from nearby fields both onshore and offshore and examined the reprocessed seismic data collected in the refuge in 1984-1985. Table 1 shows the results of this study. The results assume that at least one commercial-size field is discovered. (The USGS study does not give a probability that such a minimum field would be found.)

According to USGS, there is an excellent chance (95%) that at least 11.6 billion barrels is present. There is also a small chance (5%) that 31.5 billion barrels or more could be found. With current technology, and if cost were no object, USGS estimates that there is an excellent chance (95%) that 5.7 billion barrels or more is technically recoverable. And there is a small chance (5%) that 16.0 billion barrels or more could be technically recoverable.

However, especially in the extreme conditions of the North Slope, cost is inevitably an object. Thus, the third question is *how much oil can be extracted profitably?* The higher the price of crude oil, the greater the proportion that would be economically recoverable. The USGS study did not estimate future oil prices and therefore did not determine that proportion. (Thus, this figure is not addressed in Table 1.)

Table 1. Probability of the presence of given quantities of oil and the recoverability of the oil. (billions of barrels)

	95% chance this much or more	50% chance this much or more	5% chance this much or more
Oil actually present	11.6	20.7	31.5
Oil technically recoverable	5.7	10.3	16.0

Source: U.S. Geological Survey. *Arctic National Wildlife Refuge, 1002 Area, Petroleum Assessment, 1998.* USGS Fact Sheet. FS-040-98. May 1998. 6 p.

The projected price of oil, however, is only one of many factors entering into the decision on whether and how high to bid for a lease. Efforts to reduce production costs through new technologies play a key role, for example. Each prospective bidder will do its own highly sophisticated analysis of the economic and physical factors of lease offers, and industry analyses historically have led to different results than the government's analyses. With geological evidence pointing to the presence of physically recoverable oil and gas, prospective developers are expected to be eager to bid on ANWR leases.

Economics of Alaskan Oil Production. While crude oil prices affect the economics of ANWR production, transport costs, production costs, and regional market conditions – which are unique to North Slope production – bear on an oil prospect's commercial viability. Until 1995, ANS crude could not be legally exported and the export ban contributed to a glut of oil on the West Coast, reducing the price received by North Slope producers. (See **Oil Export Legislation,** below.) The market effect of the ban, combined with high pipeline and shipping costs, resulted in producer revenues often below $10.00/barrel, according to a Department of Energy study. In 1996, exports began to flow after a lifting of the ban. West Coast prices rose, as did the prices paid for Alaskan crude. (For further details on ANS and the history of the West Coast crude oil pricing and export issue, see CRS Report 95-214 ENR, *West Coast Oil Exports.*)

Over the years, low wellhead prices contributed to the natural decline in North Slope production by diminishing the incentive to drill more wells and otherwise enhance output from existing reservoirs. Low prices reduced investment in producing reservoirs and caused the abandonment of some exploration and development work outside the Prudhoe Bay and Kuparuk fields. Even so, some development has continued with discoveries as recent as 1998, and development has begun in the eastern portion of the NPRA, near the existing Kuparuk field. Capital intensive expansion of the infrastructure is required to access attractive geologic sites not adjacent to current production. With reduced investment in existing fields, development of known structures, and exploration, the falling output of the Prudhoe and Kuparuk fields would not be offset. A major contributor to efforts to prevent that fall is the development of technologies to improve extraction efficiency. (Arco Corporation has a description of these technologies at [http://www.arco.com/world/no_amer/expl_prod_ala.html].)

Lower production means lower shipments through TAPS. Pipeline costs are largely fixed; a smaller flow of crude means higher unit pipeline rates. The effect of declining ANS oil output on transportation economics in turn aggravates the negative effect on production. There is little chance that this self-reinforcing cycle can be greatly altered by reducing transportation and production costs for the pipeline itself. Much of ANS transport and production infrastructure is geared to high output. Substantial fixed investment is involved in TAPS, and it is not amenable to downsizing as production falls. The cycle of lower output and rising unit costs could lead to a situation in which ANS transportation economics are continuously eroded, clouding the outlook for existing oil fields. Rising oil prices might provide some temporary respite, however.

Oil Export Legislation. Diminished concerns about the security of oil supply, coupled with new leadership in the 104th Congress, led to renewed interest in oil export legislation. A measure lifting the export ban was signed by the President on November 28, 1995 (P.L. 104-58). The export of the West Coast crude surplus helped to raise Alaskan crude oil prices to world market levels. Some have proposed a repeal of this legislation in order to ease oil prices on the West Coast – the primary market for Alaskan crude if foreign sales are forbidden. Alaskan oil companies, not unexpectedly, oppose such a move.

World Oil Supply and Price. In addition to uncertainty about future oil prices, and the complexities confronting ANS development and production, U.S. dependence on imported oil is another important factor in the ANWR debate. The world's total stock of proven crude oil reserves increased more than 50% in the 1980s, from 659 billion barrels in 1980 to roughly one trillion barrels currently.

While prices were low or falling, little interest was focused on oil potential in the 1002 area. However, in 1999, the Organization of Petroleum Exporting Countries (OPEC), and certain other oil-exporting nations, agreed to cut crude oil production. World oil prices went from $9.84 to about $33 per barrel in 5 years and back down to about $26 per barrel in recent weeks. While ANWR development would be one of the longer term responses to the increased price of heating oil and gasoline, interest in Alaskan oil has increased markedly. The OPEC production agreement has renewed demand for U.S. policies that might reduce dependence on foreign oil producers. (For additional information on world oil prices and the OPEC agreement, see CRS Report, RS20487, *OPEC Oil Production - Facts and Figures*.)

ANWR, the U.S. Oil Market, and Energy Policy. Crude oil production in the 48 states has declined consistently since its 1973 peak of 9.0 million barrels per day. If ANWR were leased and developed and a significant ANS production increase resulted, how would the nation's energy supply and security situations be affected? First, ANWR development would constitute a long term response to current oil supply problems, since the production cycle for that area is about 15 years from leasing to production. Second, extra domestic crude production of the most optimistic amount would still leave the nation dependent on imports for well over 50% of its petroleum needs. From an energy security perspective, the basic situation would be largely unchanged – the nation would still depend heavily on imports. However, at $28/barrel, each 0.1 million barrels per day of foreign oil replaced with domestic supply (or produced here and sold abroad) reduces the trade deficit by $1.0 billion annually. (For additional information on the U.S. market, see CRS Rept. RL30421, *Home Heating Oil: Price and Supply in the Winter of 1999-2000*; and RL30290, *Domestic Oil and Gas Producers: Public Policy When Oil Prices Are Volatile*.)

Exploration and Leasing Options. The main federal law governing leasing and production of petroleum on federal land is the 1920 Mineral Leasing Act. Conventional federal leases permit exploration and, after discovery, usually extend until production ceases entirely. Congress has debated whether this law, federal environmental laws, and applicable Alaskan laws are adequate for 1002 development. In past hearings, many Members were willing to consider leasing mechanisms which differed substantially from historic practices. (See also **Revenue Allocation**, below.)

To reduce uncertainty about the presence of oil, Congress could authorize exploration, without proceeding automatically to development. However, such a strategy is widely opposed by both industry and environmental groups because all sides have something to lose. If oil were found, environmentalists fear that development would be virtually impossible to stop, and if it is not, that the Refuge would still be marred. Oil companies fear that if oil is found at the sites of a handful of test wells, competition could push bids to higher levels than they feel are warranted. Moreover, it is unlikely that oil companies would support or fund exploration without the right to develop any commercial quantities of oil that might be found. However, faced with the choice of participating or not, their position might change. Oil companies also fear that a few negative findings might prevent any opening of the area, even though the industry might see opportunities in other parts of the 1002 area, away from the test wells. The U.S. Treasury and the State of Alaska (which would receive 90% of the revenues under current law) would benefit if successful exploration forced subsequent bids higher, but if oil were not found at the test wells, bids for the entire area would likely be pushed down, and the Treasury would receive less revenue.

Refuge Management

Under ANILCA, one of the purposes of ANWR is to "conserve fish and wildlife populations and habitats in their natural diversity...." The other three purposes cite fish and wildlife treaty obligations, subsistence use, and maintenance of water quality and quantity. Under current law, additional activities are allowed on refuges to the extent that they are compatible with the purposes for which the refuge was designated; in the case of ANWR, energy development was forbidden unless authorized by Congress (§1003). Thus, if Congress authorizes energy development in the 1002 area it would have to include provisions to address the compatibility tests by modifying or over-riding them. (This was the method chosen in the 104th Congress in H.R. 2491, which was vetoed by the President.)

Refuge Purposes: Plants and Animals. Development advocates note that 92% of the Refuge would remain closed to development. Environmentalists counter that the 1002 report said the area at issue "is the most biologically productive part of the Arctic Refuge for wildlife and is the center of wildlife activity." If development were authorized, Congress would have to weigh how the various activities that would necessarily accompany development would affect the Refuge's resources. The importance of these resources (such as caribou, polar bears, grizzly bears, wolves, snow geese, wildflowers, water quality and quantity, etc.) in the debate derives from their value to Native peoples for subsistence take, sport hunting and fishing, their ecological roles, and/or aesthetic enjoyment, depending on the observer's point of view. Management of particular species, siting of facilities, and timing of development could all be issues.

Different Listed Species Than in 1987. In 1987, when the 1002 report was issued, three species were listed under the Endangered Species Act (ESA): the endangered bowhead and gray whales, and the threatened arctic peregrine falcon. The bowhead is still listed as endangered; according to the report, the development activities most likely to affect this species would be summer-time noise and disturbance, though these effects were not deemed to be serious. This species, one of the largest marine mammals, is an important cultural and subsistence resource for Native people, and they have expressed concern that development activities avoid harm to this species. The gray whale population for this area was de-listed on June 15, 1994. The Arctic peregrine was de-listed on October 5, 1994. Two other species have been added. The spectacled eider (a large diving duck) was listed as threatened throughout its range on June 9, 1993; Stellar's eider was listed as threatened on July 11, 1997. The latter once nested in significant numbers in the 1002 area, but it may not be present any more. In neither case is the cause of the decline well-understood.

Caribou and Other Species. Opponents of development argue that the entire, balanced complex of caribou, polar and grizzly bears, wolves, falcons, wildflowers, etc., is worth preserving intact, especially since it represents the least disturbed Arctic coastal area under U.S. ownership, and one of the "wildest" habitats of any type left in the United States. Scientists and sport hunters both stress the importance of the summer habitats on the coastal plain for migratory game birds taken in Canada and the United States. Game birds, especially snow geese, use the area for summer feeding, and some hunters fear that summer development, especially aircraft overflights, could interfere with feeding enough to prevent the geese from gaining adequate weight for migration. The 1002 report notes some studies supporting that view and says that this and other possible consequences to birds could be minimized by controlling transportation and siting of facilities.

The species which has drawn the most attention in this debate is the caribou. The Porcupine Caribou Herd (PCH) calves in or near the 1002 area, and winters south of the Brooks Range in Alaska or Canada; in 1994, the herd numbered 152,000 and is currently estimated at 130,000 according to the international Porcupine Caribou Management Board. In both areas it is an important food source to Native people and others – especially since other meat is either expensive or unavailable. Some observers fear that development and production could cause cows to calve in less desirable locations or prevent the herd's access to sites where they can escape from the voracious insects common in early summer. Oil companies counter with a comparison to the Central Arctic Herd (CAH) that summers near Prudhoe, whose population grew from about 13,000 when oil was discovered to a peak of about 25,000, and in 1995 declined to about 18,000. Environmentalists and some Natives note that the CAH has a much larger area than the PCH in which to calve, that caribou cows with young calves tend to avoid developed areas, and that predators have been controlled in that CAH's area. The effect of oil development on the PCH is likely to remain one of the hotly contested issues in a new round of debate over the Refuge.

Review of 1987 Assessment. On August 25, 1995, DOI released a *Preliminary Review of the Arctic National Wildlife Refuge, Alaska, Coastal Plain Resource Assessment.* Examining especially biological impacts, the report concluded "there would be major environmental impacts from oil and gas development on the coastal plain." (The report noted that it joined the earlier 1987 FLEIS in that conclusion. However, the 1987 report held that most of these could be mitigated and that the energy and security benefits outweighed the negative impacts.) The primary new information reported was the greater dependence of the PCH on the 1002 area for calving (due to greater calf survival in years when calving occurs there) and for insect relief after calving. It further noted that if development displaced the herd, calving was likely to shift to areas of higher predation. Muskoxen were reported vulnerable to winter disturbance, when their low, energy-conserving metabolism would make movement difficult. Polar bears, according to both the 1987 and 1995 reports, are vulnerable to disturbance in their maternity dens. The newer report considers revegetation to be a difficult and unproven technique, and notes that a "showcase" effort to revegetate an exploratory well site near Kaktovik still bore a visible scar 8 years later. (See Archived IB91011 for a history of this well on an area of Native inholdings within the 1002 area.) The report (like earlier reports by previous Administrations) was criticized as politically motivated.

Pristine and Untrammeled? To follow the Refuge debate, it is important to understand that those who wish to prevent development are not basing their arguments primarily on economic tests nor pollution risks, though they may view those issues as favoring their side of the debate. In terms that emphasize deeply held values, supporters of wilderness designation argue that few places as untrammeled as the 1002 area remain on the planet, and fewer still on the same magnificent scale. Any but the most transitory intrusions (e.g., visits for recreation, hunting, fishing, subsistence use, research, etc.) would, in their view, damage the "child-like sense of wonder" they see the area as instilling. The mere knowledge that a pristine place exists, whether one ever visits it, can be important to those who view the debate in this light.

Thus, even if a number of measures of biodiversity were to remain stable in the face of development, from their perspective, the peace of the area as a place where a larger truth may be sought would be seriously corrupted. Similarly, when told that the total "footprint" of development (the area actually occupied by drill pads, roads, etc.) would be smaller than Dulles International Airport, they note that the infrastructure would actually be scattered like a fine net thrown over the entire area, disrupting the terrain, the ecosystem, and the sense of lonely grandeur.

Development advocates counter this argument by noting the presence of the Native village of Kaktovik, the nearby DEWline station, and the remnants of other DEWline installations, and argue that the area is not pristine. Moreover, many Natives of Kaktovik (population about 250) respond that an argument about the value of pristine nature relegates their village to the margins of the debate.

Taken together, these issues mean that the 1002 debate sometimes takes on a feud-like aspect due to a culture clash: those who believe in wilderness as teacher and guide in the quest for important values and sustenance of the planet over the long term, versus those who place a higher value on job creation or economic development. The re-injection of drilling wastes and similar issues would not raise the temperature of the debate higher than these issues.

Areas of Special Environmental Significance. The wildlife debate has focused mainly on the areas important to the migratory Porcupine Caribou Herd. However, some believe other species, such as polar bears, grizzly bears, wolves, or migratory birds, may be at greater risk. Congress could consider special protection (e.g., wilderness designation, delayed exploration, or a special regulatory regime) of the most important habitats. The areas most often mentioned for some special status include the major calving area of the PCH, the area around Sadlerochit Spring (a warm spring that flows all year), and the overlapping areas near the coast where substantial bird populations occur in the summer and where pregnant female polar bears make their winter dens. From 1981-1991, 90 dens of female polar bears were found in the latter area, making up about 43% of the dens of this Beaufort Sea population of eastern Alaska and western Canada. The effect on development would depend on the size and placement of these areas.

Control of Access. One access issue could be the logistical conflict between the area's management as an industrial site versus its current management as a refuge devoted not only to wildlife conservation but also to recreation (including sport fishing and hunting) and subsistence uses, among other functions. This conflict would become more intense as human populations and road networks increased with development. In contrast to the current open but difficult access at ANWR, access to the state-owned Prudhoe Bay complex is strictly (if not always effectively) controlled. Visitors' and workers' belongings are searched for firearms, alcohol, and drugs, which are prohibited. (None of these requirements now applies to the 1002 area.) Moreover, hunting, even for subsistence, is forbidden at Prudhoe and limited in other developed areas. Similar restrictions are not found in the 1002 area and may conflict with the Refuge's purposes as currently interpreted.

Environmental Quality Management

The grounding of the *Exxon Valdez* increased concern among environmentalists and others over oil spills and other potential sources of pollution, whether in Prince William Sound, along the length of TAPS, or at the North Slope. These environmental quality management issues can be divided into three categories: resource management, pollution, and waste disposal. Congress could choose to leave these matters to administrative agencies under existing laws. Alternatively, Congress could impose a higher standard of environmental protection because the area is in a national wildlife refuge or because of the fragility of the Arctic environment. One issue would be the use of gravel and water resources essential for oil exploration and development; another would be setting fees for and allocating any revenues from exploiting these resources.

In addition, air and water pollution (whether chronic or acute) may involve questions of subtle, long-term ecological effects. Potential legislative issues include the adequacy of existing standards, research needs, monitoring, prevention and treatment of spills, the adequacy of current waste disposal requirements, the development of alternatives to landfills, and liability concerns that can make consolidation of disposal facilities unattractive to oil companies. (For a range of specific environmental quality issues, see CRS Videotape *Arctic Oil, Arctic Refuge*.)

Management of Support Services. Activities of the independent support service industry (repair, cleaning, laundry, aircraft supply, etc.) in the Prudhoe Bay area, particularly at Deadhorse, have been widely criticized. (Firms in this industry are generally employed by, rather than part of, major oil companies.) At Deadhorse, the state leases land for these independent services. Management and control of support facilities, while a complex subject, could be one of the areas where oil companies and environmentalists might reach common ground, if development were authorized by Congress.

Section 1003 of ANILCA does not cover the role the 1002 area might play as a land base for state or federal offshore activity. Both the United States and Alaska are proceeding with offshore leasing near the 1002 area. But despite occasional small flurries of interest, no well has been commercially developed offshore from the Refuge.

Long-Term Cleanup. Congress may consider various proposals on assuring the long-term environmental quality of the area. Central to any decision on these proposals is determining what the ultimate rehabilitation goal(s) should be. Environmentalists would want strong standards, but would simultaneously argue that complete recovery is nearly impossible. Development advocates would argue that existing and future ANS practices are adequate.

If Congress authorized development, but no commercial quantity of oil were found, the ecosystem is likely to recover substantially from exploratory activities (which often use roads and drill pads made of ice rather than more permanent gravel) in only a few years. If major quantities of oil were found, development would probably last for decades and, if production of associated natural gas became commercially feasible, perhaps even a century. Substantial recovery from the much higher level of disturbance might then take centuries in the harsh Arctic environment. Thus, Congress might be debating rehabilitation that would not begin until 2060 or 2090. Furthermore, some types of cleanup might not even be desirable or practical: deep gravel roads and drilling pads, for example, might be impossible to remove without creating further damage, and thus might necessarily become a permanent feature of the landscape. No existing federal laws (e.g., concerning performance bonds or fees) are known to cover such long terms in planning for a cleanup whose cause may never occur, and the exact nature of which is unknown.

Subsistence Use and Access

The village of Kaktovik (over 250 people) and the lands of the Kaktovik Inupiat Corporation (KIC) lie along the coast within the Refuge and mostly adjacent to the 1002 area. KIC owns significant land along the coast of the 1002 area, and even larger areas of subsurface rights. Current law prevents KIC from developing any energy resources that may underlie their lands. Natives of Kaktovik are the major users of the resources in the coastal plain, although they focus significantly on marine resources. Kaktovik Natives support leasing generally. However, they oppose both leasing in the primary caribou calving area in the east-central 1002 area and restrictions on discharging firearms. There is also a U.S. military Distant Early Warning (DEW) station near Kaktovik, with about a dozen employees. The DEW network has several unoccupied sites of former or uncompleted developments scattered in or near the 1002 area. Together with Kaktovik, the DEW site operates a garbage dump and a runway.

Subsistence hunters in the interior of Alaska and Canada (including especially the Gwich'in people who hunt the herd in its winter range) and the Canadian government oppose leasing in the calving area of the herd and support wilderness designation. If the area is opened to leasing, Congress may be asked to consider whether the current access or hunting rights of Native users should be restricted to protect pipeline safety; whether subsistence users should have a special voice in new regulations as 1002 exploration or development evolve, and what provision might be made to minimize any harmful impacts of development on Native culture among both north slope and interior Alaska groups.

Revenue Allocation

If oil is present, ANWR development revenues from bonuses, rents, and royalties, as well as from sales of gravel and water, could generate billions of dollars for the federal and native landowners, depending on the amount of oil that is found and on oil prices. However, 90% of the federal share of revenues would be paid to Alaska under current law. Peak annual royalties alone might range from $200 million to $2.5 billion, followed by declining revenues for 30-50 years. The allocation of these revenues between the state and the federal government could be one of the most contentious issues if development legislation were to proceed. Whatever the federal income, Congress would need to decide:

1. If development is permitted, should Alaska receive its current statutory 90% share of certain revenues from mineral leases on federal lands; and considering the terms of the Alaska Statehood Act, could Congress change Alaska's share? (See CRS Report 87-63 A.)

2. Should any federal revenues from ANWR be used for land acquisition in Alaska or elsewhere as part of the mitigation for reduced habitat values in a developed 1002 area as some have suggested? If so, how should the revenues be allocated, where might such mitigation lands be, and would opponents of drilling consider such acquisition to be a reasonable trade-off?

Legal Issues

For decades, the United States and Alaska disputed ownership of submerged lands within and offshore of ANWR. If Alaska had been found to own the lands beneath any navigable waters within the Refuge, this could have had serious consequences for protecting the area. In a very significant case, United States v. Alaska, 521 U.S. 1 (1997), the Supreme Court upheld the recommendations of the Special Master appointed in the case to the effect that: 1) certain areas along the coast of ANWR were not "inland waters" of Alaska for purposes of drawing the baseline from which to measure the state's territorial sea (a ruling that affects jurisdiction to develop minerals offshore); 2) a gravel and ice formation known as Dinkum Sands was not an island constituting part of Alaska's coastline; 3) the submerged lands beneath tidally influenced waters within the Refuge boundary did not pass to Alaska at statehood; and overruled the Special Master in order to hold that 4) certain of the tidelands offshore are within the Refuge boundaries and also did not pass to Alaska at statehood. To reach this result, the Court held that executive actions setting aside the lands before statehood were sufficient to preserve ownership in the United States, even under the difficult standard set for such actions in Utah v. United States, 482 U.S. 193 (1987).

A court held in a declaratory judgment in NRDC v. Lujan, 768 F. Supp. 870 (D.D.C. 1991), that DOI should have prepared a Supplemental Environmental Impact Statement (SEIS) encompassing new information about the 1002 area in connection with the Department's recommendation that Congress legislate to permit development. The last EIS was prepared in 1987 and it seems clear that, under current law, either an SEIS or a new EIS would have to precede development, unless Congress eliminates this requirement.

The bill also called for a 50/50 split of revenues from the development of ANWR. Alaska has indicated that the state will dispute any distribution of revenues from ANWR leases that deviates from the 90/10 share to which Alaska is entitled under a 1976 Act and, allegedly, under the Alaska Statehood Act. It can be argued, however, that that split was intended to put Alaska on a par with other states' share under the 1920 Mineral Leasing Act, which allows a 50/50 direct split and an additional 40% returned to the states indirectly through the Reclamation Fund, leaving 10% for the U.S. Treasury; and that Congress has at times prescribed other disposition of revenues, e.g., with respect to the Naval Petroleum Reserves. A federal court has agreed with the latter interpretation in Alaska v. United States, 35 Fed. Cl. 685, 701 (1996). That case also ruled for the United States on the issue of whether the provision in the Statehood Act resulted in any duty on the part of the United States to develop federal mineral lands in Alaska.

LEGISLATION

H.Con.Res. 290 (Kasich)
FY2001 budget resolution. Introduced March 20, 2000. Conference report (H.Rept. 106-577) agreed to by House and Senate, April 13, 2000.

H.R. 1239 (Vento)
Designates the 1002 area as the Morris K. Udall Wilderness. Introduced March 23, 1999; referred to the Committee on Resources.

H.R. 2250 (D. Young)
Repeals current prohibition against ANWR leasing; directs Secretary to establish competitive oil and gas leasing program; authorizes set-asides of Special Areas that restrict surface occupancy; sets minimum for bonus and royalty payments; and for other purposes. Introduced June 29, 1999; referred to Committee on Resources.

S.Con.Res. 101 (Domenici)
The accompanying report (p. 4) assumes leasing in ANWR will provide $1.2 billion in offsets for discretionary spending in FY2005. Introduced March 30, 2000; reported March 31, 2000 (S. Rept. 106-251). Amendment to delete report text tabled (51-49, roll call #58), April 6, 2000. For further action, see H.Con.Res. 290.

S. 867 (Roth)
Designates 1002 Area of ANWR as wilderness. Introduced April 22, 1999; referred to Committee on Environment and Public Works.

S. 2214 (Murkowski)
Repeals current prohibition against ANWR leasing; creates competitive oil and gas leasing program in 1002 area; and for other purposes. Introduced March 8, 2000; referred to Committee on Energy and Natural Resources.

S. 2557 (Lott)
Title V repeals current p prohibition against ANWR leasing; creates competitive oil and gas leasing program in 1002 area; and for other purposes. Introduced May 16, 2000. Placed on Senate Legislative Calendar under General Orders May 17, 2000.

FOR ADDITIONAL READING

ARCO Alaska, Inc. *Oil in the Arctic: The Environmental Record of Oil Development on Alaska's North Slope – Comments and Critique.* Natural Resources Defense Council, National Wildlife Federation, and Trustees for Alaska. 1988. 24 p.

Speer, Lisa, and Sue Libenson. *Oil in the Arctic: The Environmental Record of Oil Development on Alaska's North Slope.* Natural Resources Defense Council, Inc., 1988. 78 p.

Speer, Lisa. *Tracking Arctic Oil: The Environmental Price of Drilling in the Arctic National Wildlife Refuge.* Natural Resources Defense Council, National Wildlife Federation, and Trustees for Alaska. New York. 1991. 36 p.

U.S. Department of the Interior. Bureau of Land Management. *Overview of the 1991 Arctic National Wildlife Refuge Recoverable Petroleum Resource Update.* Washington, April 8, 1991. 8 p., 2 maps.

U.S. Department of the Interior. Fish and Wildlife Service. Arctic Refuge website. [http://www.r7.fws.gov/nwr/arctic]. Hypertext links to numerous other relevant sources, and maps and photographs from a variety of sources and viewpoints. Revised frequently.

U.S. Department of the Interior. Fish and Wildlife Service, Geological Survey, and Bureau of Land Management. *Arctic National Wildlife Refuge, Alaska, Coastal Plain Resource Assessment.* Report and Recommendation to the Congress of the United States and Final Legislative Environmental Impact Statement. Washington, 1987. 208 p.

U.S. Department of the Interior. Geological Survey. *Arctic National Wildlife Refuge, 1002 Area, Petroleum Assessment, 1998.* May 1998. 6 p.
   USGS Fact Sheet. FS-040-98.

U.S. General Accounting Office. *Arctic National Wildlife Refuge: An Assessment of Interior's Estimate of an Economically Viable Oil Field.* Washington, D.C. July, 1993. 31 p. GAO/RCED-93-130.

CRS Archived Issue Brief 95071. *The Arctic National Wildlife Refuge.* October 30, 1996. (For copies, please call the author.)

CRS Archived Issue Brief 91011. *Arctic Resources: Over a Barrel?* April 24, 1992. (For copies, please call the author.)

CRS Report RL30459. *Coping With High Oil Prices: A Summary of Options.* March 9, 2000.

CRS Report RS20487. *OPEC Oil Production - Facts and Figures.* March 8, 2000.

CRS Report RL30421. *Home Heating Oil: Price and Supply in the Winter of 1999-2000.* Feb. 4, 2000.

CRS Report RL30290. *Domestic Oil and Gas Producers: Public Policy When Oil Prices Are Volatile.* Nov. 12, 1999.

CRS Report 95-214 ENR. *West Coast Oil Exports.* Lawrence C. Kumins. 1995.

CRS Video. *Arctic Oil, Arctic Refuge.* Videotape by M. Lynne Corn, Robert Nickel, et al. 53 minutes. 1991. (Available to congressional requestors only.)

CRS Report 88-161 ENR. *The Arctic National Wildlife Refuge: Major Oil Development or Wilderness?* ed. by John E. Blodgett and John L. Moore. 1988. 162 p.

Natural Resources
Pages 109-126

ENDANGERED SPECIES:
CONTINUING CONTROVERSY

M. Lynne Corn

MOST RECENT DEVELOPMENTS

In the 106th Congress, only a few bills have been introduced to make significant changes in ESA. On February 2 and March 1, hearings were held on H.R. 3160, which would make extensive amendments in a number of provisions in current law. On July 28, 1999, the Senate Committee on Environment and Public Works reported S. 1100 (S.Rept. 106-126). The bill would change procedures for designation of critical habitat. Several bills have been introduced to provide funding from revenues from the Outer Continental Shelf oil and gas receipts to benefit land acquisition and other programs for the conservation of listed species. H.R. 701 reported by the House Resources Committee on February 16, 2000 (H.Rept. 106-499); it would provide permanent appropriations for new and certain existing programs that would benefit listed species. It was referred to the House Committees on Agriculture and Budget for a limited time. An Administration proposal to delist or downlist a number of species, including the threatened grizzly bears around Yellowstone National Park, may generate congressional oversight hearings. Proposals to revise Administration guidelines or regulations in the development of Critical Habitat, and new regulations for "no surprises" agreements and candidate conservation agreements may also spark congressional interest.

BACKGROUND AND ANALYSIS

What is the ESA? The 1973 ESA (16 U.S.C. 1531-1543; P.L. 93-205, as amended) began as a comprehensive attempt to protect all species and to consider habitat protection as an integral part of that effort. It is administered primarily by the Fish and Wildlife Service (FWS), but also by the National Marine Fisheries Service (NMFS) for certain marine species. Under the ESA, certain species of plants and animals (both vertebrate and invertebrate) are listed as either "endangered" or "threatened" according to assessments of the risk of their extinction. Once a species is listed, powerful legal tools are available to aid the recovery of the species and the protection of its habitat. As of Sept. 30, 1999, 1,775 species of animals and plants (of which 1,197 occur in the United States and its territories and the remainder only in other countries) had been listed as either endangered or threatened. Of the U.S. species, 886 were covered in 525 recovery plans. The authorization for funding under ESA expired on October 1, 1992, though Congress has appropriated funds in each succeeding fiscal year. (See the FWS website at [http://www.fws.gov/r9endspp.html].)

What is the Impact of the ESA? While the ESA plays an important role in the protection of species, it can also become a surrogate, at times, in quarrels whose primary focus is the allocation of scarce or diminishing lands or resources. Cases in which all economic interests line up squarely against those of a vanishing species are rare. Because other laws often lack the strict substantive provisions that Congress included in the ESA (see Major Provisions sections, below) regarding taking of species, critical habitat, and avoidance of jeopardy, the ESA often becomes the battleground by implication. Like the miners' canaries, declining species tend to flag larger controversies over resource scarcities and altered ecosystems. Examples of resource debates in which species were symptoms of larger controversies include the Tellico Dam (hydropower development and construction jobs versus farmland protection and tribal graves, as well as the snail darter); northwest timber harvest (protection of logging jobs and communities versus commercial and sport fishing, recreation, and ecosystem protection, as well as salmon and spotted owls); and the Edwards Aquifer (allocation of water among various users with differing short- and long-term interests, with a few spring-dependent species caught in the cross-fire).

In recent years, tensions over ESA have increased as species have been added to the protected list, and as the greater demands of a growing economy and human population have affected species' habitats. Both Congress and the Administration have sought to lessen these tensions by, among other things, tailoring application of the Act to special local circumstances. The Act's critics contend that the Administration's efforts do not go far enough; some feel that the same was true of the stalled efforts of the 105th Congress. The Act's defenders counter that it merely balances an inherent bias toward development in other governmental laws and policies, and that some of the current Administration's policies may go too far.

Debate, pro and con, on ESA splits largely along demographic lines. While most demographic groups support species conservation, that support is stronger among urban and suburban populations and less so in rural areas; and strong among those in the east and along the coasts and less so in central and mountain states. Sport hunters and anglers seem divided on the issue. It is also noteworthy that, while the debate often centers on jobs and biology, people on both sides claim ethical support for their positions, and some religious groups now participate in the debate. In addition, some industries (e.g., logging and land development) generally see ESA as a serious problem, while others (e.g., some commercial fishing and many recreation interests) see it as generally supporting their interests.

Has ESA Been Effective? The answer to this question depends very much on the choice of measurement. Since a major goal of the ESA is the recovery of species to the point at which the protection of the Act is no longer necessary, this seems a good starting point. If this is the only standard, the Act could be considered a failure, since only 11 species have been delisted due to recovery, as of July 31, 1997. Seven species have become extinct since their listing, and nine have been de-listed due to improved data. In the latter case, some of the nine species were originally listed to protect any last remaining few that might have been alive at the time of listing. It can be quite difficult to prove whether extraordinarily rare species are simply that, or in fact already extinct. For example, a rare shorebird thought by many to be extinct was re-discovered in a remote area of Canada a few years ago; it might just as easily have quietly gone extinct without being re-discovered. Rare species are, by definition, hard to find. In May 1998, Secretary Babbitt announced that FWS would study a number of species for delisting and downlisting. Like the pattern just noted, some would be delisted for reasons other than recovery. The announcement does not preclude the consideration of other species; the possible delisting of threatened grizzly bears around Yellowstone National Park, for example, was considered by FWS after this announcement.

Even so, since some scientific studies demonstrated that most species are listed only once they are very depleted (e.g., median population of 407 animals for endangered vertebrates according to one study), another measure of effectiveness might be the number of species that have stabilized or increased their populations, even if the species is not actually de-listed. If this is the only standard, the Act could be considered a success, since a large number (41% of listed species according to one study) have improved or stabilized their population levels. Other species (e.g., red wolves and California condors) might not exist at all without ESA protection, and this too might be considered a measure of success, even though the species are still rare. (See CRS Report 98-32, *Endangered Species Act List Revisions: A Summary of Delisting and Downlisting.*)

Leading Causes of Extinction. Until recent decades, the focus of the extinction debate was on losses due to over-exploitation, generally through hunting, trapping, or fishing. The poster species of the debate were passenger pigeons, tigers, wolves, and other well-known animals of today's ESA debate. But in the 20th century, a shift of focus and probably of fact has occurred. The vast majority of species now protected under the ESA reached that status due to habitat loss. Even those species for which direct taking was probably an early factor in their decline are generally also at risk due to habitat loss. Habitats reduced now to a small fraction of their former extent include tall-grass prairie, fresh and salt water wetlands, old growth forests of most types, free-flowing rivers, coral reefs, undisturbed sandy beaches, and others.

Another very high-ranking factor in the demise of many species is the introduction of non-native species. The non-natives can be diseases or parasites (e.g., avian malaria in Hawaii, or Asian long-horned beetles in North America), predators (brown tree snakes in Guam and Hawaii), or competitors (e.g., barred owls in the Pacific Northwest). The gradual homogenization of the world's flora and fauna has led to a demise of affected species. (See CRS Report RL30123, *Harmful Non-Native Species: Issues for Congress.*)

Is Extinction Normal? If extinction is normal, then one could argue that there is no need for government to intervene in a natural process. The vast majority of species that have ever lived on Earth are now extinct — an observation uncontested by paleontologists. But is the current rate of extinction different from background ("normal") extinction rates over time, and if so, by how much? Calculating current rates of extinction, much less making comparisons with the geologic past, is extremely difficult. Those who make the attempt generally base each step in their calculation on what they believe to be conservative assumptions, thus generating extinction rates that they consider low estimates. The estimates of numbers of species becoming extinct per year (17,000 species per year being a typical estimate) seem astonishingly large in part because laymen are generally unaware of the huge number of species in groups people pay little or no attention to (e.g., beetles, marine invertebrates, fish, etc.), and the large number of species estimated on Earth. Current estimates of total species range from 5 million to 100 million, with 10-30 million being commonly accepted numbers. If scientists are unsure of how many species exist, it is naturally difficult to estimate how fast they are going extinct.

Widely diverse methods all suggest that current rates of extinction exceed background rates, which are thought to be from one to ten species per 10 million per year. (That is, if there are 20 million species now, background levels would be about 2 to 20 species extinctions per year.) Common estimates of current extinction rates range from 100 to 10,000 times background rates — roughly comparable to the five great episodes of extinction in the geologic past. Critics most frequently question these calculations by stressing uncertainties, rather than citing specific factual errors. This criticism is not surprising, since no single step in these calculations can be 100% certain (e.g., estimating the number of existing species). A well-known critic, the late Julian Simon (Professor of Business Administration at the University of Maryland), called the calculations "statistical flummery." Most biologists counter by noting that similar numbers are generated in studies of widely different groups by scientists using not only different methods, but conservative assumptions.

Robust results (i.e., similar results from the testing of a hypothesis in a variety of ways) are usually considered scientifically sound.

Evolution continues, even in the face of high extinction rates, so perhaps new species will evolve that are better adapted to new conditions. If so, how long would evolutionary recovery (to an equal number albeit different species) take? Examining the geologic record after major extinction episodes, some scientists estimate that recovery to approximately equal numbers of species took up to 25 million years for the most severe extinction crises. Thus, if the current extinction rate and recovery rate are comparable, the return to species numbers of the pre-historic era would take several million years.

Issues in the 106th Congress

Some landowners fear that the presence of a listed species or the designation of their land as critical habitat will result in loss of some or all of their property rights. ("This is nothing but confiscation.... The government is stealing the property of citizens...," said John Silber, Chancellor of Boston University, regarding an ESA controversy near his property in Texas.) A more widespread concern is that there may be restrictions on new or current activities, thereby causing economic losses or reducing land values. At the other end of the spectrum, there are those who view the presence of a rare flower or frog on their land as an honor. The FWS claims that this attitude is common, particularly in the Northeast and Midwest, though rarely mentioned in the press.

Under the Constitution, no person's property can be taken without "just compensation," whether the taking occurs under ESA or any other federal law or whether the taking is done by FWS or any other agency. But "taking" has been interpreted strictly by the courts in the past and, according to current interpretations by the Supreme Court, does not include restrictions on permitted uses or a decrease in the value of the land unless the constraints are very severe, and the prohibited uses could not have been barred at the time the property was acquired.

Some critics of ESA have argued that the current standard is too strict when applied to ESA controversies, and would like to see the ESA amended to provide compensation in a broader range of circumstances than those required under the Constitution. (In general, such proposals target ESA, and sometimes the Clean Water Act; they do not typically change the threshold under the Constitution for compensation for taking of land by other agencies under other laws or for other purposes.) These critics generally propose compensation be offered for some specified percentage decrease in the value of their assets (including losses related to any loss of use of their land), since they feel that the property owner is otherwise forced to bear the cost of a public benefit.

Opponents of a new standard counter that they do not wish to see ESA singled out as having a different, more generous standard for payment of compensation from that required under current interpretation of the Constitution or for any other agency or law. They further state that the right of a property owner to use his or her land has never been absolute in any case. The cost to the federal government from changed thresholds for compensation and the constraints that would likely be placed on the operation of the ESA under a more lenient standard are among the contentious issues slowing action on reauthorization. (See also CRS Report 93-346A, *Endangered Species Act and Private Property Rights: A Legal Primer.*)

Funding for Land Conservation. A comparatively favorable federal budget estimate at the beginning of the 106th Congress led to interest in providing additional funds for the conservation of listed species, and one bill (H.R. 701), which would provide permanent appropriations for this and other purposes, was reported on February 16, 2000. The Administration has offered general support for such concepts through its Lands Legacy Initiative (see CRS Report RS20471, *The Administration's Lands Legacy Initiative in the FY2001 Budget Proposal – a Fact Sheet*) but has endorsed no particular bill of its own. Among other things, H.R. 701 would offer greater funding for land acquisition by the various federal land-managing agencies, including FWS, through the Land and Water Conservation Fund, and also provide incentives for conservation of listed species on private lands. It includes increased funding for measures to protect various species that are not listed; such programs could reduce the need for listing target species later. In the Senate, S. 25 is similar in many respects to H.R. 701 in its treatment of the LWCF. The recently introduced S. 2181 also shares many features of H.R. 701 in its sections dealing with the LWCF. A key feature of such proposals is that they would nearly all be permanently appropriated, and therefore offer a more secure funding source on which agencies and state governments could rely and plan. While such provisions would clearly be welcomed by the beneficiaries, they also augment the level of controversy surrounding the measures. (For a more information, see CRS Report RL30444, *Resource Protection: A Comparison of H.R. 701 (Amended)/S. 2123, S. 25 and S. 2181 with Current Law.*)

Salmon Conservation. NMFS officials listed nine salmon and steelhead populations in Washington and Oregon (March 1999) and two additional chinook salmon populations in California (September 1999), and proposed listing northern California steelhead trout (early February 2000). This completed most of the pending decisions on Pacific salmon, with a total of 26 populations now listed as either threatened or endangered. NMFS officials are working closely with state, local, and tribal officials, as well as the public, in developing a variety of recovery measures to address habitat restoration and other concerns. A critical decision will come on May 22, 2000 when NMFS will decide, in response to an Army Corps of Engineers review, whether to recommend to Congress that the four Lower Snake River hydroelectric dams be breached to benefit salmon recovery. NMFS is expected to announce that the four Lower Snake River dams should remain in place for at least 5 or 10 more years, to allow for a more complete assessment of progress toward recovering endangered salmon.

Making the ESA User-Friendly. As a result of the controversy over ESA and property rights, Interior Secretary Babbitt moved to decrease ESA conflict in several ways. New FWS policies relieve owners of small parcels of land of some of their responsibilities, and efforts were made to encourage landowners to increase the populations of listed species on their land. Under these "safe harbor agreements", the landowners receive, in return, promises that the presence of additional individuals of a listed population would not restrict their decisions to change the use of the land (see below). There has also been an Administration focus on listing species as threatened rather than endangered, to allow FWS to take advantage of the Act's more flexible provisions on the protection of threatened species.

The Administration also simplified some measures and requirements to address many of the concerns of private landowners. For example, as of February 1, 2000, 269 incidental take permits (ITPs) had been issued after permittees developed Habitat Conservation Plans (HCPs). FWS and NMFS have a simplified version for smaller projects with fewer impacts. HCPs have been criticized by industry as cumbersome, expensive, and unworkable (though this appears to be changing as industries gain more experience with them), while environmental groups have frequently denounced them as plans without serious protection, unmonitored and forgotten once signed, and most likely to be useful to large corporations. While these changes have been made within the framework of existing law, there is great interest among some groups in including many of them in an amended ESA.

No Surprises. Among the administrative changes of greatest interest is the "no surprises rule." Inclusion of this provision in an agreement with a landowner means that the owner properly carrying out a conservation agreement is assured that there will be no further costs or restrictions on the use of the property, except by mutual consent. In some cases, changes may be carried out provided that the costs are not borne by the landowner. While landowners like the increased certainty, the program has been criticized by conservationists as potentially locking in conservation measures that are inadequate or unable to respond to changing conditions. One conservation group sued over the agencies' failure to go through formal rule-making. The FWS and the National Oceanic and Atmospheric Administration jointly proposed a "no surprises" rule (62 FED. REG. 29091 (May 29, 1997)) in response to the March 21, 1997 settlement agreement in Spirit of the Sage v. Babbitt No. 1:96CV02503 (SS)(D.D.C.). A final rule was published at 63 FED. REG. 8859 (February 23, 1998). An attempt to enact this "no surprises" policy and regulation into law was a major impetus for Administration interest in ESA legislation in the 105th Congress.

The changes in the Federal Register of June 17, 1999 (see *Safe Harbor Agreements*, below) modified the no surprises policy, in part. Specifically, a condition of an incidental take permit is a finding that the permitted taking will not appreciably reduce the likelihood of the survival and recovery of the species. If continuation of permitted activities would be inconsistent with the finding, and the inconsistency is not remedied in a timely fashion, the new regulations provide for cancellation of the incidental take permits with no surprises agreements.

Safe Harbor Agreements. A safe harbor agreement is made between a landowner or other responsible party and FWS (or NMFS). The agreement is voluntary and unlike an HCP in that the agreement is not done as a condition of getting a permit. Rather, it is an attempt by the landowners to see that their "good deeds" in conserving listed species and habitat (beyond the requirements of the law) are not "punished" by increased restrictions based on the voluntary improvements. The landowners agree to carry out certain activities on the land that would tend to increase the numbers of the listed species. The agreement covers a specified number of years.

If, at the end of the agreement, the owner wishes to take actions that might reduce the resulting elevated population or the quality or quantity of the improved habitat, there will be no penalty under ESA for doing so, provided that the baseline conditions in the agreement continue to be met. (Provisions are included to require that the agency receive advanced warning so as to remove as many of the listed plants or animals as possible and take specified other steps to retain as much of the advantages gained during the terms of the agreement as possible.) Final rules for this program (including "No surprises" provisions similar to those discussed above) were published June 17, 1999 (64 FR 32706). Some property rights groups criticize the program as offering insufficient incentive to landowners; conservation groups are concerned that the standard for entering the agreements does not require that they support recovery, and in the end might harm recovery efforts if the landowner returns the property to baseline conditions.

Candidate Conservation Agreements. A landowner might enter such an agreement with FWS or NMFS to conserve a declining but unlisted species. If the landowner carries out the agreement as promised, she or he receives assurances from the agency that should the species be listed in the future no additional measures will be required beyond those specified. Landowners' efforts, singly and collectively, may stave off a listing. Criticism of these agreements on the one hand is that they do not offer sufficient incentive to landowners to stimulate their participation, and may indeed require them to carry out measures more strict than those that might have been necessary with a listed species. Environmentalists and others counter that the requirements on landowners may be minimal, and might stave off listing when such a decision is biologically unjustified. Final rules for this program were published June 17, 1999 (64 FR 32706).

Critical Habitat Designation. The Administration has supported restrictions on its own ability to designate critical habitat (CH) under ESA (*e.g.*, see proposed restrictions under appropriations process, below). In an announcement on Oct. 22, 1999, FWS placed designation of CH at the lowest priority in its listing budget, and stated that it could not comply with all of the demands of ESA under current budget constraints. Conservation groups saw a contradiction between that claim, and the agency's failure to request more funds for listing as well as its request in the last budget cycle to have Congress place a special cap on funding for designation of CH. (See *Appropriations Riders*, below.)

In the agency's view, CH offers little protection for a species beyond that already available under the listing process. Moreover, though the avoidance of adverse modification of CH is an obligation only for federal agencies and actions, it is frequently misunderstood by the public as a major restriction on a landowner's authority to manage land. While a landowner may feel some restrictions on management of land because of the presence of a listed species, the bulk of the restrictions, so this view holds, come as a result of the Act's prohibition on taking a listed species, and only occasionally due to the added strictures resulting from designated CH. Thus (according to some agency officials), the expense of CH designation, combined with the small margin of additional conservation benefit, make CH requirements a poor use of scarce budgetary resources, especially if the public views CH as the major regulatory impact of ESA, rather than as a supplement to the ESA's prohibition on "taking" a listed species. According to FWS, CH designation shows its greatest conservation benefit when it includes areas not currently occupied by the species; these areas may be important as connecting corridors between populations or as areas in which new populations may be re-introduced.

Under current law, the agency is obliged to designate CH at the time of listing. Two exceptions are provided. If the designation is not "prudent" (*e.g.* due to the threat of illegal collection or killing), it may be omitted. If it is not "determinable" due to insufficient data, it may be postponed up to one year after listing. In practice, FWS has designated CH for only about 10% of listed domestic species; in every case brought against the agency for failure to designate CH, the agency has lost. (At least 13 cases have been decided; others are pending.)

In a notice soliciting public comment, FWS proposes to "develop policy or guidance and/or revise regulations, if necessary, to clarify the role of habitat in endangered species conservation" (64 FR 31871-31874, June 14, 1999). The notice clarifies the agency's long-standing disaffection for this provision of the law and its view that its conservation benefit is low compared to its cost. Given the agency's stated position, the importance that the environmental community attaches to CH especially in some specific cases, and the distress its designation causes among many landowners, the issue has been the focus of at least one bill (S. 1100) in the 106th Congress. See CRS Report RS20263, *The Role of Designation of Critical Habitat under the Endangered Species Act.*

Convention on International Trade in Endangered Species. The 11th Conference of Parties to this treaty (CITES) will be held in Nairobi, Kenya in April 2000. U.S. draft proposals were published on July 8, 1999 (64 *FR* 36893), and are being finalized. To date, the likely issues at the meeting have not generated great controversy. For more information from FWS, see http://international.fws.gov/cop11/cop11.html.

Legislation in the 106th Congress. S. 1100 (Chafee, S.Rept. 106-126) would require, among other things, that CH be designated with the release of the final recovery plan for a species (due in 2½ years), or within 3 years of listing for species without a recovery plan. The change would lengthen the potential delay after listing from one year, as required in current law, to 3 years. As a practical matter, on the other hand, FWS has stated its negative view of CH designation generally, and (partly as a result) 90% of species have no designated CH. Therefore, if the change prompted FWS to revise its current practice and follow the proposed law, designation of CH might be shortened (i.e., from "nearly never, unless sued" to 3 years). CH could also be designated at the time of listing if necessary to avoid extinction.

In the House, Chairman Young introduced H.R. 3160 on Oct. 22, 1999; hearings were held on February 2 and March 1, 2000, and additional hearings are expected. The bill would reauthorize ESA, allow economic injury as grounds for a citizen lawsuit, increase the role of states in listing decisions, place a deadline on recovery plans, make data considered in listing decisions publicly available, permit federal agencies to go ahead with actions that may affect listed species if FWS or NMFS fail to meet deadlines for consultation, and make other changes. Hearings were held on February 2 and March 1, 2000; additional hearings are expected. H.R. 960 (Miller) is very similar to H.R. 2351 of the 105th Congress. It is a far-reaching reauthorization broadly supported by the environmental community.

Appropriations Issues. Appropriations bills continue to play an important role in the ESA debate in the 106th Congress. ESA funding over the last several years is shown in Figure 1 (below).

In a broader sense, the amount the federal government and others spend on ESA has been hotly debated. Even in an agency like NMFS, with major responsibilities for ESA, the amount of spending for endangered species cannot be reliably allocated to ESA alone. (NMFS's budget counts spending for both ESA and the Marine Mammal Protection Act under "Protected Species" and does not, for practical reasons, attempt to distinguish funds spent under one law or the other.) FWS itself funds some activities which benefit listed species through other programs, e.g., management of refuges which provide not only hunting, fishing, and bird-watching opportunities, but also habitat for listed species. Agencies with high probabilities of spending to benefit listed species include the Forest Service, National Park Service, and Bureau of Land Management. Agencies with responsibilities for dams and irrigation, soil erosion, pollution cleanup, etc., may also spend some fraction of their budget each year in ways that protect (or avoid deliberate harm to) listed species. Since some of the activities by these agencies might be done for more than just their ESA benefits (e.g., the re-routing of a trail to protect prime grizzly bear habitat may also benefit soil erosion control, bird habitat, and human safety), FWS spending might be viewed as the most readily measured part of federal spending.

In addition, state and local governments, business, and individuals may also spend in similarly complex ways. A FWS report estimated the "reasonably identifiable" expenditures of federal and certain state governments at $233 million for FY1993, with 18% of the amount used for land acquisition. One effort to take a more expansive view of this question was prepared by the Majority Staff of the House Resources Committee (Serial No. 104-65, p. 192-223). After discussion of many aspects of spending by various agencies and an attempt to develop estimates for many of them, the report noted "...it is probably impossible to quantify the costs of recovery since many costs may be indirect or hidden in other expenditures and the estimated costs found in recovery plans may bear no actual relationship to reality."

Figure 1. FWS Endangered Species Program Appropriations (Current dollars*)

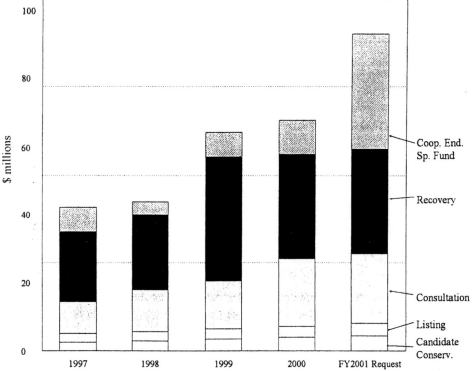

*Amounts for recovery in the FY2001 request include $4.98 million for the Landowner Incentive Program (LIP).

Sources: Annual FWS Budget Justifications.

Multinational Species Conservation Fund. The Multinational Species Conservation Fund, which benefits Asian and African elephants, tigers, and the six species of rhinoceroses, would increase from $2.4 million to $3.0 million (+25%) under the President's request for FY 2001. The Fund often works with efforts under the Convention on International Trade in Endangered Species (CITES), to which the United States is a Party. This program is authorized under three acts, described below. Table 1 shows funding levels for FY2000-2001. In the appropriations bill, the Fund is a separate line item from ESA funding.

Table 1. Funding for Multinational Species Conservation Fund, FY 2000-2001
(x $1000)

Multinational Species Conservation Fund	FY2000 Enacted	FY2001 Requested
African elephant	966	970
Tiger and Rhinos	676	970
Asian elephant	677	970
Administration	72	90
Total	**2,391**	**3,000**

Appropriations Riders, FY1998 — FY2000. In FY1998, Congress set a limit in the text of the Interior Appropriations bill on expenditures for the listing function (which, through FY1998, included listing, delisting, up-listing, downlisting, and designation of critical habitat). The effect is to limit the discretion of the agency to transfer funds for additional listings, e.g., if lawsuits mandate agency action on listing certain species. Without a cap, funding could have been transferred from other listing activities to meet the additional requirements of a lawsuit, or from other programs within the agency's Resources Management function. With the cap, a court order to carry forward a listing decision on particular species makes listing into a zero-sum game, at least at a fiscal level: the listing of some species or designation of their critical habitat would preclude the listing of others. FWS welcomed this change as a protection of other programs whose budgets it wishes to protect. (There are various lawsuits regarding listing pending in the courts, including one for a failure to list a number of plant species in southern California.)

For FY1999, Congress passed a variant of the previous year's language. The change exempts steps to delist or downlist a species from the cap on spending for Listing by transferring delisting and downlisting activities from the Listing function to the Recovery function, and listing of foreign species to the International Affairs program. The result of these changes leaves the Listing program managing only its most controversial functions: listing and uplisting of domestic species, plus critical habitat designation, and these functions would be subject to the cap.

For FY2000, the Administration proposed to add, within the cap for listing, a further restriction on designation of critical habitat, which is part of the listing function. Under the Administration's proposal, of the total amount for listing ($7.5 million proposed), no more than $1 million would have been allowed to be spent on designation of additional critical habitat. Since such designations are very costly, perhaps only one or two new areas may be able to be designated under this additional restriction. Congress accepted the restriction on the total amount available for listing, but did not include the restriction on designating critical habitat.

Major Provisions of the Current Law: Domestic

The ESA (16 U.S.C. 1531-1543) was passed in 1973, but was preceded by simpler acts in 1966 and 1969. It has been amended on numerous occasions since then: 1976, 1977, 1978, 1979, 1980, 1982, and 1988. The following are its major domestic provisions in the order they appear in the U.S. Code:

1. An **endangered species** is defined as "any species which is in danger of extinction throughout all or a significant portion of its range...." A **threatened species** is defined as "any species which is likely to become an endangered species within the foreseeable future throughout all or a significant portion of its range." The ESA does not rely on a numerical standard: such a standard would not reflect the wide variety of many species' biology. (For example, a population of 10,000 butterflies, all confined to one mountaintop, would clearly be at greater risk than 10,000 butterflies scattered over thousands of square miles.) The protection of the Act extends to all species and subspecies of animals (not just birds and mammals), although for vertebrates, further protection can be given even for distinct population segments within a species, and not just the species as a whole. More limited protection is available for plant species under the Act. (16 U.S.C. 1532)

2. The term "take" under the Act means to "harass, harm, pursue, hunt, shoot, wound, kill, trap, capture, or collect, or to attempt to engage in any such conduct" (16 U.S.C. 1532). (Harassment and harm are further defined in regulation at 50 C.F.R. 17.3.) Taking is prohibited under 16 U.S.C. 1538. There has been controversy over the extent to which the prohibition on taking may include habitat modification. A 1995 Supreme Court decision (*Sweet Home*) held that the inclusion of significant habitat modification was a reasonable interpretation of the term "harm" in the law. (See CRS Report 95-778 A.)

3. Most listed species are managed by the Secretary of the Interior through FWS. However, marine species, including some marine mammals, are the responsibility of the Secretary of Commerce, acting through the National Marine Fisheries Service (NMFS). The law assigns the major role to the Secretary of the Interior (all references to "Secretary" below are to the Secretary of the Interior unless otherwise stated) and provides in detail for the relationship of the two Secretaries and their respective powers. (16 U.S.C. 1533)

4. When the appropriate Secretary initiates or receives a substantive petition from a party (which may be a state or federal agency — including FWS or NMFS, an individual, or some other entity), the Secretary must decide whether to list the species, based only on the best scientific information and trade statistics, and after an extensive series of procedural steps to ensure public participation and the collection of information. The Secretary *may not take into account the economic effects that listing may have on the area* where the species occurs. This is the only place in the ESA where economic considerations are expressly forbidden. (See CRS Report 89-274 A, *Consideration of Economic Factors under the Endangered Species Act*, for an analysis of when the ESA does allow consideration of such factors.) Some steps may be skipped for emergency listings. Economic factors are not taken into account at this stage because Congress felt that listing was fundamentally a scientific question: is the continuation of the species threatened

or endangered? Through the 1982 amendments particularly, Congress clearly intended to separate this scientific question from subsequent decisions on appropriate protection. (16 U.S.C. 1533)

5. In the interval between a proposal and a listing decision, the Secretary must monitor the status of these "candidate" species and promptly list them to prevent sudden significant risks (16 U.S.C. 1533). Furthermore, federal agencies must confer with the appropriate Secretary on actions likely to jeopardize the continued existence of the species proposed to be listed. However, the agencies are not required, for candidate species, to avoid irretrievable commitments of resources. (16 U.S.C. 1536)

6. If a species is listed, the Secretary must designate critical habitat (either where the species is found or, if it is not found there, where there are features essential to its conservation) at the time of listing. However, if the publication of this information is not "prudent" because it would harm the species (e.g., by encouraging vandals or collectors), the Secretary may decide not to designate critical habitat. The Secretary may also postpone designation for up to one year if the information is not determinable. (16 U.S.C. 1533 etc.) As a practical matter, critical habitat has not been designated for many listed species. While any area, whether or not federally owned, may be designated as critical habitat, private land is affected by designation primarily if some federal action (e.g., license, loan, permit, etc.) is also involved. In either case, federal agencies must avoid "adverse modification" of critical habitat, either through their own actions or activities that are federally approved or funded.

7. The appropriate Secretary must develop recovery plans for the conservation and survival of listed species. Recovery plans to date tend to cover birds and mammals, but a 1988 amendment now forbids the Secretary to favor particular taxonomic groups. (16 U.S.C. 1533) The Act and regulations provide little detail on the requirements for recovery plans, nor are these plans binding on federal agencies or others.

8. Land may be acquired to conserve (recover) endangered and threatened species, and money from the Land and Water Conservation Fund may be appropriated for this acquisition. (16 U.S.C. 1534)

9. The appropriate Secretary must cooperate with the states in conserving protected species and must enter into cooperative agreements to assist states in their endangered species programs, if the programs meet certain specified standards. If there is a cooperative agreement, the states may receive federal funds to implement the program, but the states must normally provide a minimum 25% matching amount. Under the 1988 amendments, a fund was created to provide for the state grants. While the authorized size of the fund is determined according to a formula, money from the fund still requires annual appropriation. (16 U.S.C. 1535)

10. If their own actions or actions of non-federal parties that require the agencies' approval, permits, or funding may affect a listed species, federal agencies must ensure that those actions (including those affecting private actions such as funding, permit approval, etc.) are "not likely to jeopardize the continued existence" of any

endangered or threatened species, nor to adversely modify critical habitat. To be sure of the effects of their actions, they must consult with the appropriate Secretary. "Action" is quite broadly defined: it includes anything authorized, funded, or carried out by the agency, including permits and licenses. If the appropriate Secretary finds an action would jeopardize the species, he must suggest reasonable and prudent alternatives that would avoid harm to the species. Pending completion of the consultation process, agencies may not make irretrievable commitments of resources that would foreclose any of these alternatives. (16 U.S.C. 1536)

11. Proponents of federal action may apply for an exemption for that action (not for a species) from the Act. Under the ESA, a Committee of six specified federal officials and a representative of each affected state (commonly called the "God Squad") must decide whether to allow a project to proceed despite future harm to a species; at least five votes are required to pass an exemption. The law includes extensive rules and deadlines to be followed in applying for such an exemption and some stringent rules for the Committee in deciding whether to grant an exemption. The Committee must grant an exemption if the Secretary of Defense determines that an exemption is necessary for national security. (16 U.S.C. 1536) (For further discussion, see CRS Reports 89-274 A and 90-242 ENR.)

12. For actions without a federal nexus, the Secretary may also issue permits to allow incidental take of species for otherwise lawful actions that do not involve some federal nexus such as loans, permits, licenses, etc. The applicant for an "incidental take permit" must submit a habitat conservation plan (HCP) that shows the likely impact, the steps to minimize and mitigate the impact, the funding for the mitigation; the alternatives that were considered and rejected; and any other measures that the Secretary may require. Secretary Babbitt has vastly expanded use of this section and provided streamlined procedures for activities with minimal impacts. (16 U.S.C. 1539)

13. Other provisions specify certain exemptions for raptors; regulate subsistence activities by Alaskan natives; prohibit interstate transport and sale of listed species and parts; control trade in parts or products of an endangered species that were owned before the law went into effect; and specify rules for the establishment of experimental populations, among other specialized provisions. (Provisions of the Act referring to international activities are discussed below.) (16 U.S.C. 1539)

14. Prohibited actions are set out and criminal and civil penalties are specified, and provision is made for citizen suits to enforce the Act in certain respects. (16 U.S.C. 1538 and 1540)

Major Provisions of the Current Law: International

For the United States, the ESA implements the Convention on International Trade in Endangered Species of Wild Fauna and Flora ("CITES"; TIAS 8249; see CRS Report 94-675 ENR, *Convention on International Trade in Endangered Species: Its Past and Future*), signed by the United States on March 3, 1973; and the Convention on Nature Protection and Wildlife Preservation in the Western Hemisphere (the "Western Hemisphere Convention"; 50

Stat. 1354; TS 981), signed by the United States on October 12, 1940. CITES parallels the ESA by dividing its listed species into groups, according to the estimated risk of extinction, but uses three major categories, rather than two. In contrast to the ESA, however, CITES focuses exclusively on trade, and does not consider or attempt to control habitat loss. The following are the major international provisions of the ESA:

1. The Secretary may use foreign currencies (available under 7 U.S.C. 1691, the Food for Peace program) to provide financial assistance to other countries for conserving endangered species. (As a practical matter, however, very little money is currently available under this provision.) The Act also authorizes appropriations for this purpose. (16 U.S.C. 1537 and 1542)

2. The Act designates the Interior Secretary as the Endangered Species Scientific Authority (ESSA) under CITES. As the ESSA, the Secretary must determine that export from the United States and import from other countries of living or dead organisms, or their products, will not harm the species in question. The Secretary has authority to enforce these determinations. The Secretary is required to base export determinations upon "the best available biological information," although population estimates are not required. Certain other responsibilities are also spelled out in CITES. (16 U.S.C. 1537-1538)

3. The Interior Secretary is also named as the Management Authority for the United States under CITES. The Management Authority must assure that specimens are exported legally, that imported specimens left the country of origin legally, and that live specimens are shipped under suitable conditions. Certain other responsibilities are also spelled out in CITES. (16 U.S.C. 1537)

4. The ESA makes violations of CITES violations of U.S. law if committed within the jurisdiction of the United States. (16 U.S.C. 1538)

5. The ESA requires importers and exporters of controlled products to use certain ports and provides for exemptions for scientific purposes and for programs intended to assist the recovery of listed species. There are also certain exemptions for Alaska Natives and for products owned before December 28, 1973, including scrimshaw. (16 U.S.C. 1538-1539)

6. The 1988 amendments created a major program for the conservation of African elephants.

LEGISLATION

P.L. 106-113 (H.R. 3194, Istook)
Section 1001 (a)(3) contains appropriations for Interior and Related Agencies. Signed by President on November 29, 1999.

H.R. 701 (Don Young)

Creates a new program to benefit conservation of listed species on private lands and amends several existing programs, resulting in benefits to listed species or in reducing the risk of later species listings. These and other titles funded through permanent appropriations of receipts from leasing energy resources on Outer Continental Shelf. Introduced February 10, 1999; referred to Committee on Resources. Reported (amended) February 16, 2000 (H.Rept. 106-499, Part I). Referred sequentially to Committee on Agriculture until March 17, and to Committee on the Budget until March 31 for such provisions as fall within their respective jurisdictions.

H.R. 960 (Miller)

Reauthorizes and amends Act, adding several benefits in tax code for measures to conserve listed species on non-federal lands. Introduced March 4, 1999; referred to Committee on Resources.

H.R. 3160 (Don Young)

Reauthorizes ESA, allows economic injury as grounds for a citizen lawsuit, increases the role of states in listing decisions, places a deadline on recovery plans, makes data considered in listing decisions publicly available , permits federal agencies to go ahead with actions that may affect listed species if FWS or NMFS fail to meet deadlines for consultation, and makes other changes. Hearings held February 2 and March 1, 2000. Introduced October 27, 1999; referred to Committee on Resources.

S. 1100 (Chafee)

Amends ESA to require designation of critical habitat concurrent with recovery plan or within 3 years, whichever is first. Adds "military training and operations" to economic impacts as a factor to be considered in designation. Introduced May 20, 1999; referred to Committee on Environment and Public Works. Reported July 28, 1999 (amended), S. Rept. 106-126.

FOR ADDITIONAL READING

U.S. General Accounting Office. *Endangered Species Act: Types and Number of Implementing Actions.* [Washington] 1992. 40 p.
    GAO/RCED-92-131BR

U.S. House of Representatives. Committee on Resources. *Oversight Hearing on Examining the Expenditures of Agencies that Participate in Efforts to Save Endangered and Threatened Species.* Apr. 17, 1996. 350 p.
    Serial No. 104-65

CRS Products

CRS Report RS20263, *The Role of Designation of Critical Habitat under the Endangered Species Act.* Pamela Baldwin. 6 p.

CRS Report RL30444, *Resource Protection: A Comparison of H.R. 701 (Amended)/ S. 2123, S. 25 and S. 2181 with Current Law.* Jeffrey Zinn and M. Lynne Corn. 52 p.

CRS Report RL30123. *Harmful Non-Native Species: Issues for Congress*, by M. Lynne Corn, Eugene H. Buck, Jean Rawson, and Eric Fischer. 50 p.

CRS Report 98-178 A. *Endangered Species Act Amendments: Analysis of S. 1180 and H.R. 2351*, by Pamela Baldwin and M. Lynne Corn. 51 p.

CRS Report 98-32 ENR. *Endangered Species List Revisions: A Summary of Delisting and Downlisting*, by Robert J. Noecker. 19 p.

CRS Report 97-752 ENR. *African Elephant Issues: CITES and CAMPFIRE*, by M. Lynne Corn and Susan R. Fletcher. 6 p.

CRS Report 93-664 ENR. *The Clinton Administration's Forest Plan for the Pacific Northwest*, by Ross W. Gorte. 6 p.

CRS Report 94-675 ENR. *Convention on International Trade in Endangered Species: Its Past and Future*, by M. Lynne Corn. 17 p.

CRS Report 93-346 A. *Endangered Species Act and Private Property Rights: A Legal Primer*, by Robert Meltz.

CRS Report 90-242 ENR. *Endangered Species Act: The Listing and Exemption Processes*, by M. Lynne Corn and Pamela Baldwin. 29 p.

CRS Report 95-778 A. *Habitat Modification and the Endangered Species Act: The Sweet Home Decision*, by Pamela Baldwin. 2 p.

CRS Report 98-666 ENR. *Pacific Salmon — Anadromous Trout: Management Under the Endangered Species Act*, by John R. Dandelski and Eugene H. Buck. 6 p.

Natural Resources
Pages 127-132

THE LISTING OF A SPECIES:
LEGAL DEFINITIONS AND BIOLOGICAL REALITIES

M. Lynne Corn

INTRODUCTION

The 103d Congress will debate the reauthorization of the Endangered Species Act (ESA)[2] which expired on October 1, 1992. The Act has recently generated controversy, even though it passed in 1973 with virtually no opposition. Much of the debate concerns specific actions that would jeopardize particular species or populations. However, the controversy has been fueled by the discrepancies between two sets of legal definitions and the subtle biological realities that they approximate.

First, the ESA offers different levels of protection to vertebrates (fish, amphibians, reptiles, birds, and mammals), invertebrates (all other members of the Animal Kingdom), and plants. Some environmentalists have reacted against these differences by pressing for ecosystem protection in cases like the northern spotted owl, and arguing that recoveries could be more successful if all organisms were given equal protection.

Second, the Act defines populations and species without highlighting the subtleties of their distinctions or the difficulty of their determination. As a result, several complicated issues have arisen about the protection of organisms like the marbled murrelet and Florida panther. The distinctions among vertebrates, invertebrates, and plants, and between populations and species will be important issues in the ESA reauthorization debates.

LEGAL DISTINCTIONS

Without biological evidence to justify the distinction among vertebrates, invertebrates, and plants, each category receives different protection under the ESA. Individual vertebrate populations can be listed as well as whole species,

---

[1]Under the supervision of M. Lynne Corn, Joshua P. Nowlis, doctoral candidate at Cornell University, researched and wrote the final draft of the report.

[2]Act of December 28, 1973, Pub. L. No. 93-205 (as amended), 87 Stat. 884, codified at 16 U.S.C. 1531 *et seq.*

and listed vertebrates are protected on both public and private lands. For example, bald eagle populations in Washington, Oregon, Minnesota, Wisconsin, and Michigan are listed as threatened, and populations in the other contiguous 43 states are listed as endangered despite a healthy population in Alaska (bald eagles are not listed in Hawaii, an area outside of their natural range).

In contrast, although listed invertebrates are protected on both public and private lands, individual invertebrate populations cannot receive protection. For example, the monarch butterfly occurs in two populations: one migrating to California and the other to Mexico for winter. Although the Mexico-wintering population is declining due to habitat destruction, it cannot receive protection under the ESA as long as the California-wintering population is abundant. The bald eagle, on the other hand, receives protection in all contiguous 48 States despite its numbers in Alaska.

Listed plants receive the least protection, with no protection for populations or on private land without the landowner's consent. Historically, plants on private lands have been considered the property of landowners and therefore not controlled by government. In keeping with tradition, the ESA generally does not prohibit private landowners from damaging or destroying listed plants on their own property. Before its 1988 amendments, the ESA did not even protect listed plants from trespassers on private lands. The Virginia round-leaf birch was brought closer to extinction by trespassers, motivated by fear of government regulation, who purposefully destroyed trees on private lands. With the 1988 amendments, parties breaking other laws at the time they damaged or destroyed a listed plant can be charged using the ESA. However, landowners can still legally destroy listed plant species on their property if they are not breaking other national or state laws in the process.

In contrast to these legal distinctions, biological evidence would justify a *reverse* ranking in many cases - with plants receiving the most protection and vertebrates the least. Plants, which are less easily dispersed than most animals, supply energy for the rest of the ecosystem by converting the sun's light into a form accessible to animals. Invertebrates often assist in converting this plant energy into a form vertebrates can eat by digesting plant fibers and collecting the energy into concentrated bundles. Illustrating their importance, individual plant species have been found that house over 1,200 animal species, mostly invertebrates. This food chain can be symbolized by a house, with plants serving as the foundation, invertebrates as the walls, and vertebrates as the roof. Though the foundation and walls can stand without the roof, the roof cannot stand without the walls or foundation.

On the other hand, vertebrates can confer their enhanced protection on plants and invertebrates when the distribution of a vertebrate population overlaps significantly with that of a habitat type. Such a vertebrate species is called an indicator species. The northern spotted owl serves as an indicator for old growth forests of the Pacific Northwest. Therefore, protected spotted owl populations confer some of their protection on the other species occurring in old growth forests. This conferred protection may be particularly important because many species, especially invertebrates, have not been discovered or described yet.

Advocates of equal protection argue that even vertebrates would benefit from better protection of plants and invertebrates because many vertebrates, especially indicator species, suffer primarily from habitat destruction. To support their argument, these advocates list three gaps in the conferred protection that vertebrates can give. First, not all ecosystems have indicator vertebrates. Rocky intertidal ecosystems worldwide, for example, lack significant vertebrate presence. Second, conferred protection does not necessarily protect invertebrates or plant populations from targeted activities. Many cacti, for example, are threatened by plant collectors whose actions only damage the cactus population and not the surrounding desert. Therefore, the cacti cannot receive conferred protection from a listed vertebrate unless they are critical to its survival. Finally, conferred protection may under-represent the actual loss when certain actions are exempted, or permitted despite the ESA. For example, other species (both described and undescribed) may be harmed by the 13 Bureau of Land Management timber sales that were exempted from the ESA's protection of the northern spotted owl if these sales proceed.

Others use these gaps to argue for ecosystem protection, or an endangered ecosystem act. They argue that ecosystem protection would protect described and undescribed species in ecosystems with and without vertebrate indicators equally. In addition, they argue that ecosystem protection would be simpler for both developers and the Fish and Wildlife Service (or the National Marine Fisheries Service--NMFS) because they would only have to go through one listing or exempting process to determine the fate of an area, rather than a new process for each species in that area. However, ecosystems are even more difficult to describe and categorize than populations, subspecies, and species, although, as the next section will illustrate, the distinctions among populations, subspecies, and species are far from clear.

BIOLOGICAL DISTINCTIONS

The ESA treats populations, subspecies, and species as if they are neatly distinct categories. However, nature appears much blurrier to biologists. Populations, subspecies, and species are not static, but change with the ongoing processes of habitat modification and evolution. Therefore, biologists do not expect to always find distinct boundaries among these categories. Just as economists define terms like "poor," "middle income," and "rich," and then struggle to apply them, biologists find it easier to define a population, subspecies, and species than to assign these categories to actual groups in nature.

A population has been defined as "a group of organisms coexisting at the same time and place and capable for the most part of interbreeding"[3] and as

---

[3]Paul Colinvaux. *Ecology*. New York. John Wiley & Sons. 1986. p. 134.

a group of conspecific organisms that occupy a more or less well defined geographic region and exhibit reproductive continuity from generation to generation; it is generally presumed that ecological and reproductive interactions are more frequent among these individuals than between them and the members of other populations of the same species.[4]

The Fish and Wildlife Service (FWS) has classified populations in both contexts, e.g., by geographic areas (States) in the case of the bald eagle and by reproductive interactions (interbreeding) in the case of the marbled murrelet. Most biologists would agree that the second definition encompasses the concept of populations more fully than the first. In concurrence, the NMFS has recently decided to list Pacific Salmon populations only if they are evolutionarily significant units, defined as "substantially reproductively isolated" and "an important component in the evolutionary legacy of the species".[5] However the study of interbreeding requires greater sophistication and effort than the study of geographic distributions.

The difficulty in studying interbreeding highlights why some populations are hard to differentiate. Two groups of organisms can range from never interbreeding to nearly complete interbreeding. The marbled murrelet, a puffin-like bird, was proposed for listing as threatened in Washington, Oregon, and California. Its listing has been complicated by debate about whether the Washington State birds interbreed with more abundant populations in Canada and Alaska. It has been difficult to assess the degree of interbreeding because these birds move long distances and reproduce discretely high up in the canopy of old growth forests. Even when the degree of interbreeding is understood, it might be low but not trivial. In such a case, it could be a judgement call as to whether the birds from Washington, Canada, and Alaska were separate populations, and therefore, whether the Washington State birds could be listed.

Differentiating between subspecies also has led to controversy. The ESA defines a species as "any subspecies of fish or wildlife or plants."[6] In contrast, biologists consider subspecies and species to be separate categories. They divide a species into two or more sister subspecies if each occupies a distinct location in time and space, and varies in some important characteristic from its sisters.

When two distinct subspecies interbreed, their offspring is called a hybrid. Since the biological definition of species (see below) requires that each species is reproductively isolated, natural hybrids are not possible between *true* species (although they can occur between true species in certain artificial situations). Since sister subspecies are members of the same species, they are by definition

---

[4]Douglas J. Futuyma. *Evolutionary Biology.* Sunderland, Mass. Sinauer Associates, Inc. 1979. p. 506.

[5]56 FR 58612.

[6]ESA, Sec. 3 (15).

reproductively compatible and hybrids between them, though unusual, are natural. While artificial hybridization between true species can produce bizarre and unnatural mixes, hybridization between subspecies can be the only hope for some endangered subspecies. Groups of organisms require genetic variability to be able to respond to environmental changes, even over short time-scales. If a group becomes too small and does not receive genetic input from another source, its chances of recovery are significantly decreased. In these cases, hybridization can add genetic variability and increase the chances of recovery.

For example, today's Florida panther has descended from two subspecies, the remnants of a North American population and a small number of panthers from South America that were brought to Florida and released. The Florida panther population is quite small (under 50) and shows signs of low genetic variability, even with the two types of ancestors. As biologists would predict, the panthers that are most hybridized show the most vigor, while the panthers with little or no South American heritage have impaired ability to reproduce. The Florida panther will be more likely to recover because of the introduction of South American panthers, and other endangered subspecies may require increases in their genetic variability via intentional hybridization with sister subspecies in order to recover. Therefore, small subspecies with low genetic variability face the paradox of loss of protection if they are hybridized, and greater chances of extinction if they are not. Although the ESA definition protects unique subspecies, it is unclear whether hybrids should be granted the same protection; the FWS policy excluding hybrids from protection has been controversial.

Finally, biologists even have difficulty distinguishing between one true species and another. Definitions range from

> When populations of two kinds occur together without interbreeding, they are considered different species. When the populations do not occur together, the judgment of whether they belong to different species or are just geographic varieties of the same species can be arbitrary.[7]

to

> the members in aggregate of a group of populations that interbreed or potentially interbreed with each other under natural conditions; a complex concept.[8]

The definitions have two similarities: that a species is a group of organisms that actually or potentially interbreeds under natural conditions, and that the

---

[7]p. 631 in Paul R. Ehrlich and Jonathan Roughgarden, *The Science of Ecology*. Macmillan Publishing Co. New York. 1987. 710 p.

[8]p. 507 in Douglas J. Futuyma, *Evolutionary Biology*. Sinauer Associates, Inc. Sunderland, Mass. 1979. 565 p.

concept is difficult to define. How can it be so difficult to differentiate between two species?

First, surprisingly few species have been studied in nature. According to Malcolm Hunter, Jr., "It is only for a tiny portion of species that we have more than a vague notion of their abundance and distribution and ecological roles."[9] Given this constraint, it is difficult to assess whether two organisms can potentially or do actually interbreed.

Second, the boundaries between species, like populations, vary in their clarity. Some species, like African elephants, cannot produce viable offspring with any other. Other species, such as many ducks, can produce viable offspring with other species of duck in captivity, but do not do so in nature due to differences in courtship behavior. With these sometimes subtle barriers against interbreeding, it can be challenging to distinguish one species from another.

In sum, the ESA's preference for clear distinctions between populations, subspecies, and species clashes frequently with biology's *necessarily* blurry categories.

CONCLUSIONS

Living organisms are not treated equally in the ESA. Vertebrates are given first class status, invertebrates second class, and plants third class. These rankings, however, may be the reverse of their contributions to many ecosystems. Although indicator vertebrates can serve as umbrellas to both described and undescribed species, they leave several gaps in their protection of co-existing species. While some interests have used these gaps to support ecosystem protection, ecosystems would be even more difficult to define than populations, subspecies, and species.

Populations, subspecies, and species all describe regions on the spectrum of interbreeding, from nearly complete interbreeding (a single population) to never interbreeding (separate species). In contrast to legal definitions that draw clear boundaries between these categories, the actual boundaries are blurry and made even more hazy by the lack of information on most organisms. As a result, many proposed listings will continue to be complicated by debates over population structure and interbreeding. In addition, the use of hybridization as a conservation tool will undoubtedly continue to promote controversy. Therefore, it is crucial that Members of Congress understand the biological evidence both for and against current policy and the subtle distinctions that biologists must make.

---

[9]Malcolm L. Hunter, Jr. "Coping with ignorance: the coarse-filter strategy for maintaining biodiversity." In *Balancing on the Brink of Extinction*. Kathryn A. Kohm, ed. Washington. Island Press. 1991. p. 267.

Natural Resources
Pages 133-146

OUTER CONTINENTAL SHELF:
OIL AND GAS LEASING AND REVENUE

Lawrence Kumins

MOST RECENT DEVELOPMENTS

Owing to low oil and gas prices during 1998 and early 1999, revenue collection from the OCS has sharply declined from the record $5.2 billion in 1997 and $4.3 billion in 1998. Collections for fiscal 1999 were $3.3 billion. It is not apparent what effect lower revenues (which should recover in 2000) might have had on appropriations of OCS revenues and other legislative proposals.

Legislation introduced in the 106th Congress seeks to capture half of oil and gas revenues from the outer continental shelf (OCS) for coastal states. S. 25 was introduced early in the 106th with this general goal, earmarking half of OCS monies for an array of projects. Similar legislation, H.R. 701, was introduced in the House. In November, 1999 the Resources Committee reported a compromise bill. In addition, two identical bills were introduced (S. 446/H.R. 798) that closely follow the Administration's Lands Legacy Initiative proposal. This proposal provides for full $900 million funding of the Land and Water Conservation Fund (LWCF) in future budgets.

MMS promulgated a new proposal for both oil and gas valuation. It is scheduled to become effective on June 1. But the Independent Petroleum Association of America filed suit in the U.S. District Court for D.C. on behalf of gas producers seeking to overturn the proposal's treatment of gas marketing expense. At issue was the so-called duty to market principle, under which MMS asserted that marketing costs should be included in the computation of gas price for royalty assessment. This would have increased producer royalty payments. But in March, the court found in favor of the producers, raising questions about the validity of the duty to market principle. A suit on behalf of the oil producers seeking to invalidate the duty to market provisions in MMS proposed oil rules was initiated by the IPAA and the American Petroleum Institute in April.

Background and Analysis

As the technology for finding and producing underwater petroleum and natural gas developed after World War II, commercial interest arose in producing hydrocarbons on the outer continental shelf (OCS). The OCS is the federal portion of the continental shelf, extending outward from three nautical miles offshore to the 200-mile territorial limit. Offshore lands within three nautical miles belong to the states, except for western Florida and Texas, where state lands extend to the 9-nautical-mile line.

Responding to increasing interest in developing OCS oil and natural gas resources, Congress enacted the 1953 Outer Continental Shelf Lands Act (OCSLA). OCSLA as amended is intended to provide for orderly leasing of these lands, while affording protection for the environment and ensuring that the federal government received fair market value for both lands leased and the production that might result. The OCS program is carried out by the Minerals Management Service (MMS) of the Department of the Interior.

Between 1954 and 1998, bonuses (up-front cash payments to secure a lease tract) paid by successful OCS bidders have amounted to $60.9 billion. OCS lessors have paid an additional $1.5 billion in rents on leased tracts, and producers have paid the federal government royalties totaling $61.4 billion. Royalties are fixed at one-eighth or one-sixth of petroleum or natural gas value as it is removed from the lease. But because of concerns that MMS has been under collecting royalties, it has proposed a controversial method of determining the value of the resource upon which the royalty is computed. The Senate has attached a ban on implementing the new valuation program in the FY2000 Interior Department Appropriations bill.

There are a few royalty formula exceptions, including a handful of net-profit sharing and royalty-in-kind deals. In total, since the enactment of OCSLA, federal offshore lands have produced over $122 billion in government revenues.

In 1998, production on the federal OCS off Louisiana resulted in $2.2 billion (81%) of the $2.7 billion royalties received total for all of the OCS. The Texas offshore yielded $374 million. The bulk of OCS revenues have resulted from leases off Texas and Louisiana, which remain the interest center for future leasing, exploration and development. California and Alaska continue to be focal points of environmental concern, even though there is little current federal production in either locale. Prelease and leasing activity is banned in California until 2012; a few tracts on the Alaska OCS will be offered for sale in the current 5-year leasing plan.

Table 1 shows aggregate OCS hydrocarbon revenues from all sources during a recent 5-year period.

Table 1. OCS Revenues, 1994-98
($ in millions)

Year	Oil Royalties	Gas Royalties	Rents	Bonus Bids	Total
1994	779	1,545	40	331	2,715
1995	948	1,178	87	414	2,627
1996	1,220	1,866	159	878	4,123
1997	1,343	2,101	228	1,411	5,083
1998	909	1,795	258	1,320	4,305

Source: Federal Offshore Statistics, 1997 and Minerals Management Service website [http://www.mms.gov]

Prior to the softening in oil and gas prices in 1998, the data highlighted a doubling of total revenues from 1995-1997, larger oil revenues due to increasing production, greater gas revenues due to both increased output and higher prices, and larger bonus bid receipts due to greater interest in offshore drilling, resulting from improved deep-water technology and a deep water royalty rate reduction enacted in 1995 (P.L. 104-58). Lease sales into the winter of 1998 resulted in record amounts.

But prices declined to the $10 per barrel area in late 1998 and early 1999. As a result, OCS receipts for FY1999 declined by over one-third to $3.3 billion. But prices began to rebound in the latter half of the year, averaging in the $25 per barrel area at year-end. FY 2000 results were $3.55 billion. In FY 2001, DOI projects revenues of $5.08 billion, a figure which includes $1.8 billion in disputed lease sale revenues held in escrow for many years. This revenue–a one time event–stemmed from a court ruling settling a border dispute between the federal government and Alaska. Revenue flows are projected to decline in out years, reaching $2.1 billion in FY2010.

How the late 1999 and early 2000 oil pricing events–which saw prices touching $30 per barrel — will play out in the future is difficult to predict. A great deal hinges on the March 2000 OPEC meeting, where production levels will be reconsidered.

The Royalty Valuation Controversy

Debate has continued for several years regarding the way oil and natural gas produced from federal leases is valued for the purpose of determining the dollar amount of royalty owed by the producer. The royalty payment is computed as a percentage of the value of the resource as it leaves the lease. But under current market and regulatory conditions, even when sold in third-party transactions, the value is not always clearcut, because gathering and marketing costs are sometimes commingled and wrapped in a transaction where the commodity price may not be clearly visible.

Crude oil and natural gas royalty valuation issues have developed on different, although parallel, tracks. Historically, oil has been appraised at actual sale prices when crude is sold to third parties in arms-length transactions. Otherwise, it has been valued at posted prices. The posted price is a value established by oil producers in the field. The fact that producers set this price singlehandedly has led to a number of lawsuits wherein the fairness of posted prices as measures of the value of the oil in question have been disputed. Many of the disputes involved states suing for their share of royalties from production on state as well as federal lands. In recent years, a number of lawsuits were settled for amounts totaling $5 billion[1], including a $3.7 billion settlement in Alaska.

The history and current circumstances of natural gas valuation are a bit different than oil. Prior to the deregulation of both producer prices and pipeline rates, gas had been valued at the price paid the producer by the pipeline. But under regulation, nearly all gas was purchased by a pipeline for subsequent resale, so the sale price was easily determined (it was the price the producer received from the pipeline). This changed with deregulation. Pipelines no longer bought a significant share of natural gas production. In contrast, merchants and end users are the chief purchasers of gas from producers. Gathering and marketing costs, and each segment of transport cost, are itemized and billed separately in the deregulated format.

Critics of the current valuation system contend that the settlements in the royalty valuation suits are evidence that oil is being regularly undervalued in figuring royalty payments. They are especially vocal about situations where crude is sold to an affiliated party, and not in a third-party or true arms-length transaction. When there are no market

---

[1]See Senator Boxer at page S11323 of the *Congressional Record*, September 23, 1999.

transactions in a producing area to serve as a benchmark, current valuation rules do not provide objective pricing guides and the value of these crudes are determined by the producer alone.

The Minerals Management Service in the Department of Interior has been working on new valuation rules for oil and gas for several years. MMS proposed issuing final valuation regulations in 1998. The new regulations would value oil based on a series of benchmarks for each field. The benchmarks would be computed from oil traded on public markets, with transportation, location and quality differentials factored in. For gas, the rules would factor in marketing and gathering costs that producers had sought to exclude. The new rules would have likely resulted in higher royalty collections on both gas and oil. Their issuance was blocked until the end of FY1999 by last year's Interior Appropriations Bill.

Producer opposition to the new rules has been strong, and the debate over a legislative ban during consideration of the FY2000 Appropriations bill was lively. Senator Hutchison introduced an amendment to the FY2000 Interior Appropriations Bill extending the appropriation ban for another year. In debate, the proposed regulations were characterized as a tax increase imposed on producers. In fact, Senator Murkowski described the regulations as "another tax, a value-added tax, on oil produced in the United States on Federal leases."

Senators favoring a new valuations rule because of concerns about royalty under-collections mounted a filibuster led by Senator Boxer. Cloture was voted (60-39) on September 23. Senator Hutchison's amendment banning final regulation implementation was then passed by a 51-47 vote. On October 13, the Senate-passed version of H.R. 2466 was changed in House-Senate conference, and provision was made for a six-month GAO study, after which the new royalty plan can become effective.

The Administration opposed this plan and threatened to veto the original Interior and Related Agencies bill. A compromise–passed as H.R. 3194 in late November–was signed into law as P.L. 106-113 on November 29, 1999. It contained valuation rule language delaying the implementation of a rule until March 15, 2000. The GAO study was dropped from the legislative language.

The MMS moved forward proposing new rules for oil and gas which would become effective June 1, 2000. For gas, MMS called for a valuation based on prices at the lease which included aggregation, marketing fees, storage and transfer costs. There are two issues here: pricing in non-arms-length transactions and what is to be included in (or excluded from) valuation price. For valuation of gas sold in non-market transactions, MMS proposed a system of market-derived index prices which would vary based on location.

While the index pricing proved to be relatively non-controversial, determining what is included or excluded in that price for royalty calculation led to legal action by gas producers. The key principle at issue in the suit filed by the Independent Petroleum Producers of America (IPAA) in U.S. District Court for Washington DC is referred to as "duty to market." MMS has contended that leases by their very nature contain an implied duty to produce and sell resources, and that the leaseholder is obligated to deliver the resources to market at his own cost. For gas, the costs involved are clearly delineated since, as a condition of deregulation, gas ancillary and transport costs are "unbundled." Unbundling means that all cost elements are priced separately so gas buyers can tell the cost of each component, from wellhead to burner-tip.

On March 28, 2000, the court ruled in favor of the IPAA, finding that gas marketing and related costs were not part of the sale proceeds attributable to production. The court ruled these costs were deductible from sales prices in determination of the value upon which royalty is calculated. This has the effect of lowering producer royalty payments. The court also questioned the "duty to market" principle which MMS has asserted supports including marketing and ancillary costs in royalty value.

With duty to market called into question by the court, in April 2000 IPAA and the American Petroleum Institute (API) filed suit in the same court over the crude oil valuation proposal. At issue with the oil valuation rule is primarily what might be included in price for royalty computation. As far as prices themselves are concerned, the issue is less about the pricing mechanism and more about inclusion of marketing and related costs in the price for royalty valuation. Essentially, the proposed rules would value crude — other than that sold in arms-length transactions — at benchmark prices based on crudes traded on public exchanges, such as the NYMEX (the commodity exchange where oil is traded).

MMS valuation rules become effective on June 1, 2000, unless modified or delayed by the court.

Disbursement of OCS Revenue

Determining an acceptable division of revenue from the OCS between adjacent coastal states and the federal government has proven to be a difficult problem. Although the OCS is federal territory, coastal states argue that they bear the brunt of remediating environmental impact and infrastructure wear-and-tear accompanying OCS oil and gas activity. These states also harbor concern about rapid development in shore side communities possibly needed to support offshore activity.

As a result, various revenue-sharing methods have evolved over the years, including a higher state percentage of revenues to the closest areas of the OCS and the designation of a portion of OCS revenues to the Land and Water Conservation Fund (LWCF). However, coastal states contend that the current system is not operating as promised — due in part to Congress' unwillingness to appropriate funds — and have backed legislative changes.

Existing Revenue Disbursement Mechanisms. OCS revenue is a major source of funds for the Land and Water Conservation Fund and the National Historic Preservation Fund. The 1978 amendments to the LWCF Act of 1965 require the National Park Service to accumulate $900 million (at the end of each fiscal year) in the fund. While most of the $900 million comes from OCS revenues, additional monies are provided by surplus property sales, Treasury motorboat fuel tax collections, and recreation use fees collected by the Departments of Interior and Agriculture. State and federal entities use these funds to acquire park and recreational lands. (For additional information, see CRS Report 97-792 ENR, *Land and Water Conservation Fund: Current Status and Issues.*)

The National Historic Preservation Act of 1966 was amended in 1976 to establish the Historic Preservation Fund, to be funded annually with $150 million from OCS revenues through FY1997. These monies were intended for matching grants to the states and to the National Trust for Historic Preservation. Although Congress did not extend the $150 million annual authorization after it expired, unappropriated monies not expended remain available for future appropriation.

Table 2 shows both LWCF and NHPF appropriations for the past several years. In round numbers, appropriated monies have run roughly one-quarter of those authorized. Unappropriated monies for both funds nominally are accounted for in a Treasury reserve account, although, in reality, they have been used primarily for deficit reduction.

Both the LWCF and the NHPF recently received somewhat higher funding, although both funds still hold large unappropriated balances.

The unappropriated balance for the LWCF currently stands at $11.83 billion. The NHPF, whose $150 million annual authorization was not extended after the end of FY1997, held $2.3 billion in its unappropriated receipt account as recorded by Treasury in September 1998. Combined, both accounts — which are not "trust funds," but Treasury accounts that do not collect interest — recorded total balances exceeding $14 billion. Funds from those accounts cannot be spent unless they are appropriated. And any increase in annual appropriations requires a tradeoff with other programs, absent a Budget Enforcement Act waiver. Under current budget requirements, any effort to allow the funds to be expended without being appropriated would require Congress to mandate an equivalent spending offset.

Table 2. LWCF and NHPF Appropriations, FY1994-99
($ millions)

Fiscal Year	LWCF Approps.	NHPF Approps.
1994	255.6	40.0
1995	216.8	41.4
1996	138.1	36.2
1997	159.4	36.6
1998	969.1*	40.8
1999	328.7	72.4

Source: National Park Service Budget Office

* Includes $699.0 million from DOI Appropriation, Title V (P.L. 105-83) for priority land acquisition, exchanges and maintenance that was provided as part of the 1997 budget deal as a one-time item.

Another claim on OCS revenues results from state-federal sharing of resource rights on the so-called 8(g) lands. These lands — defined in the 1978 amendments to OCSLA — are submerged acreage lying outside the 3-nautical mile (nm) state-federal demarcation line (9 nm in the cases of western Florida and Texas), typically extending a total of 6 nm (or 12 nm) offshore. Section 8(g) provides for the "fair and equable" sharing of revenues from any of the zone's hydrocarbon resources that could be an extension of pools beneath federal and state waters.

A dispute over the meaning of "fair and equable" — dating back to 1979 — led to placing monies from 8(g) lands in escrow. The dispute was settled in the OCSLA amendments of 1985, which set the state share at 27% and called for disbursement of all the money held in escrow in FY1986-7. In addition to the $1.4 billion of escrow funds paid out in 1986-7, a total of $390 million in annual settlement payments to the states has been provided through 1997, with the annual payments to continue through 2001. The most recent settlement payment, for FY1997, was $65 million.

Going forward, recurring annual payments of 27% of royalties, rents and bonuses derived from the federal 8(g) zone drainage tracts are to continue for the life of production in the area.

A separate escrow account was established in a similar 1979 dispute involving Beaufort Sea, Alaska, monies. It was settled in 1988, when Congress passed further amendments (P.L. 100-202). This allowed a distribution of $323 million to Alaska in FY1988. Separate litigation (regarding another $1.4 billion from the Alaskan offshore) between the State of Alaska and the federal government involving disputes over the location of the 3-mile state-federal boundary was virtually settled in 1997. The state reportedly should receive roughly $300 million as the settlement is finalized, with the bulk of the disputed $1.4 billion being retained by the Treasury.

Revenue Sharing Legislation. The history of disputes between the federal government and states over OCS revenues — and the reluctance of Congress to appropriate authorized funds — led to the introduction of legislation in the 105th Congress to allocate half of OCS rents, royalties and bonuses to coastal states. This allocation has a parallel in the on-shore revenue program for production from federal lands. With on-shore revenues, 50% is allocated to the state in which the lease is located, and 40% is earmarked for the Reclamation Fund. Only 10% goes to the Treasury.

Legislative debate over the allocation of OCS revenues to projects in coastal states began to intensify with bill introductions late in the 105th Congress. With start of the 106th and the introduction of H.R. 701 and S. 25, the OCS revenue expenditure discussion was continued.

During 1999, H.R. 701 moved though the legislative process further. Several hearings were held in the Resources Committee. On November 10, 1999, the committee the original language was recast into a broad-based compromise. The new language was voted out of committee by a 37 to 12 vote. As reported by the Resources Committee, H.R. 701 calls for annual dedicated funding at specified levels for a variety of programs. This funding would be distributed among the 50 states, so that even states not adjacent to producing areas would receive a share of OCS revenues. Programs would be funded at these amounts:

1.   Coastal Impact Assistance and Conservation–$1 billion
2.   Land & Waste Conservation Fund Revitalization–$900 million
3.   Wildlife Conservation and Restoration Fund–$350 million
4.   Urban Park & Restoration Fund–$125 million

5.   Historic Preservation Fund–$100 million
6.   Federal & Indian Lands Restoration–$200
7.   Conservation Easements & Species Recovery–$150 million
8.   Payments- in-Lieu of Taxes & Refuge Revenue Sharing–$200 million

In the Senate, the 3-title S.25 remains in the hearing stage; 5 hearings were held during the 1999. S. 25–as it currently stands--proposes a permanent appropriation of one -half of OCS revenues to 30 coastal states for coastal impact assistance, land and water conservation and wildlife programs. Major titles provide for:

- OCS Impact Assistance — 27% of revenues to be distributed by formula among 30 states for such projects as air and water quality, wetlands and coastline restoration, infrastructure, and public service needs. Distribution formula based on production, coastline miles, and population. Minimum state share set at 0.5%. Recipient states would be required to distribute 60% of funds to local governments.

- LWCF — 16% of revenues to be used for federal land acquisition, state matching grant programs, and urban park and recreation programs; funding to be split 45%-45%-10% respectively. Federal land purchases (authorized by Act of Congress) from willing sellers only.

- Wildlife Conservation Programs — 7% of revenues made available to state fish and game departments for conservation programs.

It is not clear if S.25 will progress in the Senate Energy Committee, and how House action might influence its direction. S. 25 might evolve on its own, or it could shift toward the H.R. 701 approach.

Other parallel bills were also introduced in the first session of the 106th Congress. Hearings have been held on S.446 and H.R. 798, which would provide $900 million as a permanent appropriation. (For more details, see CRS Report RL30133, *Resource Protection and Recreation: A Comparison of Bills to Increase Funding.*)

Proponents of increased funding cite benefits to infrastructure and other shoreside amenities. Those favoring the status quo generally wish to keep OCS revenues for deficit reduction. Other proponents of current law — including those concerned about increased drilling activity — view new funding as an incentive for state support for leasing in areas now off-limits. The latter may be moot, because leasing is controlled by the 1997-2002 Plan, which itself incorporates a long history of congressional moratoria and leasing bans imposed by the Administration.

Economics comes into play here too. The decision to bid on an available lease or produce oil is a corporate decision governed by the price of oil and the economics of its production. It is difficult to envision a grant to a state overwhelming the energy economics intrinsic in a given lease tract. Environmental opponents of legislation to give more OCS monies to states are concerned about creating financial incentives for states to support leasing they might otherwise oppose for environmental reasons. But no state has given any indication that it would seek new production in environmentally sensitive areas just to get a fractional interest in royalty revenue.

Those favoring legislative proposals which permanently allocate funding from OCS revenues focus on the consistent appropriation to the LWCF well below the level of OCS revenues designated to the fund. They also seek funding to mitigate shore-side infrastructure wear and tear from production-related activities and their impact on wetlands and other environmental assets. And it is contend further that consumers of underwater minerals should fund the protection and enhancement of other environmental amenities.

An additional consideration regarding permanent fixed funding based on a given level of OCS cash flow is the current instability of the revenue stream. Because oil and gas prices can be extremely volatile–and they have been during 1999–it may be risky to provide for permanent funding levels under the assumption the OCS revenues will directly or indirectly provide the cash flow.

OCS Leasing: Limitations, Moratoria and the 5-Year Leasing Plan

After the much-publicized oil spill off the coast of Santa Barbara, CA, in 1968, OCS activities have become subject to essentially three types of restrictions:

- administrative restrictions imposed by Presidents Bush and Clinton, currently in force through 2012;

- leasing moratoria imposed by Congress in annual appropriations bills; and

- restrictions embedded in a sequence of MMS 5-year leasing plans, most recently for 1997-2002.

Congressional leasing moratoria were included in annual Interior Department appropriations bills beginning with FY1982. The annual moratoria started with California offshore areas and were eventually expanded to include New England and the Georges Bank, the mid-Atlantic, and later a 50-mile-wide band off the Atlantic coast. Also included was the Pacific Northwest, much of Alaska, and the Eastern Gulf of Mexico off northwestern Florida.

In FY1999 appropriations legislation, both Houses incorporated the moratoria of past years' appropriations legislation by reference. But the Omnibus Appropriations Legislation containing the Interior Department funding questioned the need for further annual congressional moratoria in light of substantial administrative bans.

However, not all are convinced. Legislation has been introduced in the House (H.R. 33) that would establish a joint federal and state task force to study the OCS region off of Florida and evaluate what areas could safely support future oil and gas development. The Administration testified before a House Resources subcommittee in early August 1999 that the bill would duplicate functions presently carried out by MMS, and that current law and regulation provide adequately for such assessments. Representative Porter Goss (R.-Fla.), who introduced the bill, argues that there is a need to review current studies and to determine whether additional studies need to be made so that a decision regarding the Florida OCS can be made with more precision and certainty.

The current OCS leasing program is embodied in the MMS *Final Outer Continental Shelf Oil & Gas Leasing Program, 1997 to 2002*. This plan identifies all the individual tracts to be offered for sale during the period. It was formulated with extensive comment from virtually all stakeholders, and it includes the moratoria from the annual appropriations bills. Additionally, in 1990 President Bush issued a directive that the executive branch conduct no leasing or preleasing work on lands under legislative moratoria until the year 2000; in June 1998 President Clinton extended that ban until 2012.

The 1997-2002 leasing plan was designed to accommodate the sensitivities of as many major interest groups as possible. As a result, only lands in the Central and Western Gulf of Mexico and a few selected places off Alaska will be offered for lease. Oil and gas producers have expressed general satisfaction with the plan, because the Central and Western Gulf is the location of nearly all OCS hydrocarbon activity — both active and prospective — as well as the needed infrastructure. Beyond the appeal of looking for hydrocarbons in known oil- and gas-prone areas, producers seek to avoid environmentally controversial areas for reasons of public relations as well as economics.

OCS Lease Buybacks

The Department of the Interior halted the process of developing certain leases in environmentally critical areas. These include 23 tracts in Bristol Bay, AK, 53 off the coast of North Carolina, and 73 in South Florida, below 26 degrees N. Latitude. The leaseholders initiated litigation, demanding compensation from MMS, contending that the Government's development halt constituted breach of contract, and a taking of leaseholders' (purchased) property rights.

In August 1995, litigation was settled with regard to the Alaska and Florida leases in two agreements covering all remaining claimants. In one suit's settlement, Conoco was paid $23 million from the Justice Department's Claims and Judgments Fund. This circumvented the barrier to buybacks posed by a of lack of appropriated funds in DOI's budget.

In the second settlement, regarding leases in South Florida, seven other claimants will be paid a total of $175 million from the Judgment Fund. A claim by Shell had been settled several years earlier as part of a deal involving an offsetting claim on disputed royalty payments owed the federal government.

The leases off the North Carolina coast are currently in litigation. In March 1996, a U.S. Court of Federal Claims ruled that the government illegally barred seven oil companies holding leases from developing their tracts. The court determined that leaseholders should be paid fair market value for the tracts or be reimbursed for lost revenues from the tracts. The federal government brought the case to the Court of Appeals, which ruled 2 to 1 against the firms on a technicality. Further appeal is possible.

Development bans, and the process that ultimately resulted in the buybacks, introduced an element of uncertainty in the leasing process and led to litigation. The current leasing framework includes well-established moratoria and a comprehensive 5-year leasing plan that avoids tracts where development might encounter roadblocks. Thus, future bans on the development of leased tracts, and the litigation that has resulted, are much less likely.

LEGISLATION

H.R. 33 (Goss)
Imposes certain restrictions and requirements on the leasing under the Outer Continental Shelf Lands Act of lands offshore Florida, and for other purposes. Introduced January 6, 1999; referred to Committee on Resources and the Subcommittee on Energy and Mineral Resources. Hearings held August 5, 1999.

H.R. 701 (Young)
Conservation and Reinvestment Act of 1999. Provides OCS impact assistance to state and local governments. Introduced February 10, 1999; referred to the Committee on Resources. Hearing held March 10, 1999.

S. 25 (Landrieu)
Conservation and Reinvestment Act of 1999. Amends OCSLA, the Land and Water Conservation Fund Act of 1968, and the Federal Aid in Wildlife Restoration Act to provide funding of half the receipts of revenues from the outer continental shelf. Introduced January 19, 1999; referred to Committee on Energy and Natural Resources. Hearings held April 19, 20, April 27, May 4 and May 11, 1999.

S. 446 (Boxer)/H.R. 798 (Miller)
Resources 2000 Act. Provides permanent protection of the resources of the United States. Introduced February 23, 1999; Senate bill referred to the Committee on Energy and Natural Resources, and House bill referred to Committee on Resources. Hearings on S. 446 held by the Senate Committee on Energy and Natural Resources April 27, May 4, and May 11, 1999. Hearings on H.R. 798 held by the House Committee on Resources March 10, 1999.

FOR ADDITIONAL READING

U.S. Department of the Interior, Minerals Management Service. *Proposed Final Outer Continental Shelf Oil & Gas Leasing Program — 1997 to 2002.* Decision Document. August 1996.

——. *Mineral Revenues 1997: Report on Receipts from Federal and Indian Leases.*

——. *Federal Offshore Statistics: 1997 Leasing, Exploration, Production and Revenue as of December 31, 1997.*

——. Minerals Management Service Web Site: [http://www.mms.gov]

CRS Products

CRS Issue Brief IB10015. *Conserving Land Resources: The Clinton Administration Initiatives and Legislative Action.* Updated regularly.

CRS Report RL30133. *Resource Protection and Recreation: A Comparison of Bills to Increase Funding.* April 9, 1999.

Natural Resources
Pages 147-168

Natural Resources: Assessing Nonmarket Values through Contingent Valuation

Joseph Breedlove

Introduction

Contingent valuation is a survey method used to estimate the nonuse value of public goods — generally defined as the value people place on certain goods simply because those goods exist. Contingent valuation is becoming more widely used in appraising natural resource damages and in decisionmaking. Critics object to its use, arguing that such surveys of existence values are not comparable to the traditional measures of utilitarian values, because resource use generates economic and social benefits beyond those measured by price and quantity (the traditional measures of utilitarian value). This issue is of interest to Congress, because the regulations to implement Superfund allow the use of contingent valuation for measuring nonuse values in damage assessment. The Superfund tax has recently expired and its re-authorization may be debated in the 106th Congress. Other laws allow for nonuse values in damage appraisals and cost recovery, and federal resource management agencies are often required to balance values provided. Ultimately, Congress may be asked to decide whether and how nonuse values are to be included and balanced with use values in damage assessments and in resource management.

This report describes the use of contingent valuation surveys for estimating nonuse values. It contains a brief legislative background on the use of contingent valuation surveys under Superfund and other statutes providing for cost recovery for resource damages. That is followed by an overview of the economic theory behind measuring nonuse values, and then a brief discussion of three cases where contingent valuation surveys were used. The remainder of the report describes the contingent valuation method — survey design, reliability and measurement error, validity and bias, and three empirical critiques.

Legislative Background

Federal Resource Decisionmaking

As described in the following section, governments that own natural resources manage them for a number of purposes. Their actions are sometimes justified by the real or perceived failures or limitations in the markets for many of the goods and services provided by lands and resources. For example, the Reclamation Act of 1902 authorized the Secretary of the Interior to provide water to irrigate agricultural lands in the arid west when private developers were unable or unwilling to finance water development. The purposes for building and operating large water projects have been expanded over the years to include municipal and other water supplies, down-stream flood control, recreational use, and fish and wildlife habitat. The Bureau of Reclamation and the Army Corps of Engineers, which constructs and operates dams mainly in the east and midwest, are required to allocate costs among the various beneficiaries, and thus implicitly to value the goods and services that the projects provide and that are not sold in markets.[1]

Similarly, management decisions for federal lands often address goods and services that are not sold in markets. The national forests managed by the Forest Service and the public lands managed by the Bureau of Land Management are to be administered for sustained yields of multiple uses: high regular or periodic outputs ("for outdoor recreation, range, timber, watershed, and wildlife and fish purposes") while maintaining the productivity of the land. The Federal Land Policy and Management Act of 1976 also specifies that the federal government should "receive fair market value of the use of the public lands and their resources unless otherwise provided for by statute." Because the level and mix of uses are mainly determined in public planning and by the annual congressional budget process, some analysts believe comparable valuation measures for the marketed commodities and the non-marketed goods and services could prove useful for approximating a socially efficient mix of outputs; this could include more astute use of markets and market signals, as well as nonmarket valuation techniques.

To date, contingent valuation has apparently not been used by the agencies for valuing the unmarketed goods and services in either of these contexts. The statutes and regulations governing these decisionmaking processes do not specify how to value the unmarketed goods and services, or to balance these values with marketed goods and services. However, the necessary allocations — explicit for water projects and implicit for land management — require some comparable valuation. Contingent valuation is a technique that might prove useful in some situations

Damage Assessment

In contrast to federal resource decisionmaking, federal damage assessment laws and regulations have been more explicit, with respect to assessing nonuse values that have been damaged. Legislative issues have focused on resource damage assessment under Superfund — the Comprehensive Environmental Response, Compensation, and Liability Act (CERCLA) of 1980[2] — authorizing federal cleanup of waste sites and recovery of damages. Damage measurement was delegated to the Department of the Interior, with little guidance in the act. The regulations allow some damages to be

---

[1] See, for example, the Water Resources Development Act of 1986 (WRDA; P.L. 99-662), which altered cost-sharing formulas for many Corps projects. Typically, authorizing legislation for water projects specify which costs are to be at least partly reimbursed by users (such as for irrigation and for municipal and industrial use) and which are to be borne by the federal government (such as for recreation use and fish and wildlife habitat); these cost shares are allocated based on the relative benefits produced. For more, see CRS Report 98-980 ENR, *Federal Sales of Natural Resources: Pricing and Allocation Mechanisms*.

[2] P.L. 96-510, 94 Stat. 2767, as amended. 42 U.S.C. 9601 *et seq.*

determined using "simplified assessments requiring minimal field observation." More complicated damages are determined using "alternative methodologies for conducting assessments in individual cases to determine the type and extent of short and long-term injury and damages." The regulations allow measuring option and existence values only if no use values can be determined, and contingent valuation can only be used in such circumstances.[3] (The distinction between use and existence value is discussed below.) This effectively created a hierarchy, in which use values and market methods were preferred to nonuse values and nonmarket methods.[4]

Critics argue that these regulations underestimate damages, and the regulations have been challenged. In *State of Ohio v. U.S. Department of the Interior*, 10 states (including Ohio) and 3 environmental organizations challenged the regulations, claiming that resource damages would be underestimated using those procedures.[5] The court found that

> regulation prescribing hierarchy of methodologies by which lost use value of natural resources could be measured, that focuses exclusively on market values for such resources when market values are available, was not reasonable inter-pretation of CERCLA.

A utility, a manufacturing company, and a chemical trade organization also challenged the regulations, arguing that contingent valuation could not be labeled a "best available procedure," as required by §301(c)(2) of CERCLA. The court upheld this part of the regulations, stating that

> Department of the Interior's inclusion of contingent valuation as method-ology to be employed in assessing damages resulting from harm to natural resources ... was proper; contingent valuation process includes techniques of setting up hypothetical markets to elicit individual's economic valuation of natural resource, and the methodology qualified as best available procedure for determining damages flowing from destruction of or injury to natural resources if properly applied and structured to eliminate undue upward biases.

Other federal laws also provide for damage recovery, and thus may implicitly authorize contingent valuation for some values.[6] The Clean Water Act authorizes the government to act as a natural resources trustee to recover damages (originally equal to restoration or replacement costs) or hazardous discharges into navigable waters or

---

[3] 43 *C.F.R.* Part 11.

[4] Robert F. Copple, "NOAA's Latest Attempt at Natural Resource Damage Regulation: Simpler ... But Better?" *Environmental Law Reporter: News & Analysis*, v. 25, no. 12 (Dec. 1995): 10671-10677; and Erik D. Olson, "Natural Resource Damages in the Wake of the Ohio and Colorado Decisions: Where Do We Go From Here?" *Environmental Law Re-porter: News & Analysis*, v. 19, no. 12 (Dec. 1989): 10551-10557.

[5] *State of Ohio v. United States Department of the Interior*, 880 F.2d 432 (D.C. Cir. 1989).

[6] Frank B. Cross, "Natural Resource Damage Valuation," *Vanderbilt Law Review*, v. 42, no. 2 (March 1989): 269-341.

near the coastline.[7] Other federal legislation — such as the Deepwater Port Act of 1974, the Trans-Alaska Pipeline Act, and the Outer Continental Shelf Lands Act — also provide for recovery of damages, but also typically fail to specify which methods can and should be used for calculating damages.[8] Some state laws also allow damage recovery and provide various types and levels of coverage.

In 1990, Congress enacted the Oil Pollution Act, delegating natural resource damage assessment for oil discharges into navigable waters, adjoining shorelines, or the Exclusive Economic Zone to the Department of Commerce, National Oceanic and Atmospheric Administration (NOAA).[9] To assist in developing the regulations, NOAA commissioned a panel of economic experts, co-chaired by Nobel laureate economists Kenneth Arrow and Robert Solow, to evaluate the use of contingent valuation in determining nonuse values for natural resource damage assessment. The panel concluded that contingent valuation could be used for such a purpose, subject to numerous conditions; the final report was published in the *Federal Register* on January 15, 1993.[10]

Economic Theory of Measuring Values

The capitalist economic system of the United States generally relies on transactions between producers and consumers in free markets to determine the outputs of goods and services. Prices established within this private exchange system are the basis for allocating land, labor, and capital among producers, and goods and services among consumers; prices are also the standard measure of value for such privately traded goods and services.

Governments often intervene in private transactions — by regulating private actions, by altering incentives, or by owning factors of production — to alter market results that are deemed socially or politically unacceptable. Reasons cited for government intervention include two classical market limitations (also called market failures): externalities and public goods. *Externalities* occur when private transactions between producers and consumers affect third parties (those not involved in the exchange), and those effects are not taken into account in the exchange.[11] For example, timber sales are exchanges between landowners and timber processors, but

---

[7] P.L. 92-500, 86 Stat. 816, as amended. 33 U.S.C. 1321(f).

[8] Respectively: P.L. 93-627, 88 Stat. 2126 (33 U.S.C. 1501, *et seq.*); P.L. 93-153, 87 Stat. 576 (43 U.S.C. 1651, *et seq.*); and P.L. 95-372, 92 Stat. 629 (43 U.S.C. 1301, *et seq.*).

[9] P.L. 101-380, 104 Stat. 484. 33 U.S.C. 2701, *et seq.*

[10] U.S. Dept. of Commerce, National Oceanic and Atmospheric Admin., "Natural Resource Damage Assessments Under the Oil Pollution Act of 1990," *Federal Register*, v. 58, no. 10 (Jan. 15, 1993): 4601-4614. (Hereafter referred to as the NOAA Panel.)

[11] Some mechanisms, such as litigation, can force producers and consumers to consider third-party effects. Markets respond to such mechanisms by internalizing at least some of the costs; for example, safety devices to protect consumers from unsafe automobiles have at least partly resulted from insurance litigation (as well as from government regulation), and the cost of these devices are now internal to the private transaction between producers and buyers. When third-party costs are fully internalized, no externalities occur.

sales can affect other people by altering animal habitats, the quantity and quality of water flows, and other land and resource conditions. Externalities are considered market limitations, because the exchanges ignore some of the costs (or benefits) they impose on society, and thus may result in more (or less) production than is socially desirable.

The second classical market problem is *public goods*: goods and services which can be used by one person without affecting the amount available for others and which are provided to all, because individuals cannot be excluded from the benefits. (Such goods are also called nondepletable or nonrival goods.) If the good is provided at all, it is not possible to exclude anyone from obtaining the benefits; for example, if we have national defense, all citizens have the same amount available to them, no matter how great a demand they have for it or how much they pay. Two additional aspects are common (but not required) in public goods: indivisibility and high transaction costs. Indivisibility results when the good or service cannot be divided among users; for example, individually owned pieces of the Statue of Liberty would not make much sense, because its value is in its entirety, not in its constituent pieces. High transaction costs occur when the owner or producer has difficulty controlling (and therefore charging for) the use or enjoyment; for example, the sheer size and accessibility of many lakes would prevent effective private control and access fees. In the most extreme forms, individuals *cannot* be excluded from receiving benefits. Private transactions in public goods may result in market "failures," because the possibility of simultaneous use, the indivisibility, and the difficulty or impossibility of controlling benefits make profitable private exchange ineffective, and thus, fewer public goods would be provided by private markets than are considered socially desirable.

Nonuse Values

As discussed above, public goods (*e.g.*, the Statue of Liberty) provided by the government are often used (*e.g.*, for recreation). Many public goods also have nonuse values — the value individuals place on goods or services, which they do not consume directly, often because an amenity or resource simply exists (known as existence value). It appears to have been first described by John Krutilla in 1967.[12] Evidence of such values is illustrated by voluntary contributions to a multitude of efforts and organizations; people are often willing to contribute time and money for things they feel have social value (*e.g.*, public television). For individuals, existence value can be inherent (valued solely because it exists) or for the future (valued because future generations will have it available, even if it is never used; this is sometimes known as bequest value).[13]

When uncertainty is considered, another form of existence value may result. People may be willing to pay for the option of using a good or service in the future,

[12] John V. Krutilla, "Conservation Reconsidered," *American Economic Review*, v. 56 (1967): 777-786.

[13] Robert Cameron Mitchell and Richard T. Carson, *Using Surveys To Value Public Goods: The Contingent Valuation Method* (Washington, DC: Resources for the Future, 1989), p. 62. (Hereafter referred to as Mitchell and Carson.)

typically at a particular price; for example, although you may not currently want to visit a recreational site, you may be willing to pay to have the option to visit it later. (This is often known as option value.) People may also be willing to pay for delays until better information is available; for example, an individual may be willing to pay to delay a project that may cause some irreversible effects that are not fully under-stood, if further information is likely to eliminate or to clarify those effects.[14] On the other hand, markets exist for option values of depletable goods and services, and are generally considered an efficient means of valuing future options and compensating the owner for maintaining that option.

Measuring Value

In a market economy, private goods and services are exchanged between pro-ducers and consumers. The standard measure of value for such goods and services is the price at which the exchange occurs willingly. Many government-provided goods, however, cannot be valued so readily, because they are not traded in markets and thus have no market price as a sign of the willingness of users to pay for the good.[15] Nonetheless, having values for such government-provided goods to approx-imate market prices can be useful for comparing alternative government programs that provide goods, both to improve government efficiency and to achieve a balance when the production of various goods conflict (*e.g.*, in situations where timber pro-duction compromises production of clean water from federal lands).

When market prices do not exist for government-provided goods, alternative methods must be used if one is to estimate the benefits of the public project, and to encompass total value: both use and nonuse values. One common approach — physical linkages — uses damage functions to estimate changes in direct use values, but it does not yield a complete measure of benefits, because it does not measure existence values. The second general approach — behavioral linkages — aggregates individual be-haviors to estimate values. Several approaches are possible, based on whether some relevant market behavior can be observed (observed *v.* hypothetical markets) and on how individual preferences for the good in question can be revealed (direct *v.* indirect measures). Table 1 shows these possibilities.

Observed/direct methods examine market behavior to estimate the value of a particular good directly. Referenda can measure popular support for a particular public project using a voting format. Simulated markets can determine a market price for a good by setting up an experimental market, such as a simulated market for hunting permits. If parallel private markets exist (*e.g.*, hunting clubs with exclusive hunting rights on certain lands), they can be used to estimate the value of a govern-ment-provided good. These methods are most effective when the value of the good

---

[14] Mitchell and Carson, pp. 69-74.

[15] This is not to say that markets cannot exist for many government-provided goods, but rather that society has chosen not to use markets for allocating those resources and for determining efficient production levels. Livestock grazing on federal lands, for example, is not allocated among ranchers by market decision, and is priced at an administratively determined fee, not at a rate set by a market for such grazing.

Table 1. Behavior-Based Methods of Valuing Unmarketed Goods

	Direct Measures	Indirect Measures
Observed behavior	Referenda Simulated markets Parallel private markets	Household production Hedonic pricing Actions of bureaucrats or politicians
Hypothetical markets	Contingent valuation Allocation game with tax refund Spend more-same-less survey question	Contingent ranking Willingness-to-pay (or -to-accept-compensation) Allocation games Priority evaluation technique Conjoint analysis Indifference curve mapping

Source: Mitchell and Carson, p. 75.

in question is primarily derived from its use (including the option for future use), but may be inadequate for goods with substantial nonuse values.

Observed/indirect methods examine market behavior for other, related goods to infer the value of the government-provided good. One commonly used household production function is the travel-cost method, which measures recreational benefits by calculating how much people are apparently willing to pay to visit a site (based on how far they travel to the site). Another technique is hedonic pricing, which includes property value and wage studies, to measure the value of certain character-istics of a location or a job, such as environmental amenities or health risks, which are capitalized in the property value or wage respectively. As with observed/direct methods, these methods may be inadequate for goods with substantial nonuse values. In addition, the severe data requirements and complex methodological considerations make implementation difficult.

Hypothetical/direct methods attempt to directly estimate the benefit of a good or service using a hypothetical situation. Contingent valuation is one such technique. It surveys the affected population to elicit the willingness-to-pay (or willingness-to-accept-compensation) for a change in the amount of a good provided (or available). Another technique is to survey citizen opinions concerning the adequacy of current spending levels for public projects. Such methods are useful, because they measure both use and existence values for public goods, and they can support the estimation of demand curves, and thus be more comparable to market prices for private goods. However, the rigorous data and methodological requirements make these techniques difficult to use fairly.

Hypothetical/indirect methods rely on hypothetical markets to indirectly obtain values for the public good in question. Examples include contingent ranking or the hypothetical travel-cost method. Contingent ranking generates a list of sites in order of preference, which are then translated into values. Some researchers claim that contingent ranking is easier for respondents than attempting to assign values to commodities, but the technique yields results that are less readily comparable to market prices for private goods and services.

Property Rights and Value

Private markets work because the owners of the various goods have the right to deny use of the good to those who don't pay. (Thus, private goods are also called excludable goods.) In contrast, public goods are characterized partly by the inability of owners to exclude beneficiaries who do not pay. The rights of individuals to use a particular public good (or to have it exist) are often ill-defined. This lack of clarity leads to two different questions that can be asked to elicit the value of a particular public good: how much would you be willing to pay to acquire the proposed change (willingness-to-pay); or how much would you be willing to accept for the loss (of use, of quality, *etc.*) associated with the proposed change (willingness-to-accept-compensation). Willingness-to-pay essentially presumes that respondents do not have rights to the good in question, and must buy it. Willingness-to-accept presumes that respondents do hold property rights to the good in question, and that the right to change current conditions must be bought from them.[16]

Researchers have found differences between willingness-to-pay and willingness-to-accept amounts for the same public good, with the willingness-to-accept amount sometimes being substantially larger. Willingness-to-accept is likely to be higher for those goods that do not have close substitutes, and/or where people refuse to sell the good in question or want very high compensation for it because of some personal attachment. Furthermore, uncertainty and aversion to risk may lower responses of willingness-to-pay. Other theoretical explanations exist, such as that losses in utility (well-being) are valued differently than equivalent gains in utility.[17] The choice between willingness-to-pay and willingness-to-accept depends essentially on who has the right to the good in question. Since those rights are often not clearly established statutorily, the choice may not be obvious or indisputable.

Applications of Contingent Valuation

Contingent valuation is a survey technique to estimate nonuse values by asking respondents how much they are willing to pay or to accept for a change in the good in a hypothetical market framework. The first identified description of contingent valuation was in 1947 in an article by S. V. Ciriacy-Wantrup about measuring the benefits of preventing soil erosion.[18] Its first use was apparently by Robert Davis in his Ph.D dissertation in 1963, to measure the value of a recreation area to hunters and

---

[16] Daniel S. Levy, James K. Hammitt, Naihua Duan, Theo Downes-LeGuin, and David Friedman, *Conceptual and Statistical Issues in Contingent Valuation: Estimating the Value of Altered Visibility in the Grand Canyon*, MR-344-RC (Santa Monica, CA: Rand, 1995). (Hereafter cited as RAND Study.)

[17] Mitchell and Carson, pp. 30-41.

[18] Paul R. Portney, "The Contingent Valuation Debate: Why Economists Should Care," *Journal of Economic Perspectives*, v. 8, no. 4 (Fall 1994): 3-17.

wilderness advocates.[19] Since then, many studies have been conducted on a wide range of commodities, including environmental amenities and natural resources. Three significant studies are summarized here to illustrate several of the possible categories of nonuse values: altering visibility at the Grand Canyon; the *Exxon Valdez* oil spill; and changing the operating system at Glen Canyon Dam.

To improve visibility at the Grand Canyon, the U.S. Environmental Protection Agency (EPA) in 1991 required the Navajo Generating Station in Page, Arizona, to install scrubbers to reduce haze caused by sulfur dioxide emissions, at a cost of about $100 million annually. EPA was required to value the benefits, and chose to use a contingent valuation survey that estimated total annual benefits of $130-$250 mil-lion. The utility company responded with its own contingent valuation survey that estimated a benefit of only $50 million. Because of a long-standing interest in valuing public goods, RAND evaluated both studies and found several problems.[20] First, RAND asserted that willingness-to-accept should have been used (rather than willingness-to-pay), because the United States public allegedly holds property rights to Grand Canyon visibility. Second, RAND stated that the EPA study had incorrectly used visibility changes that were much larger than the actual changes. Finally, neither study was found to have used a large enough sample of respondents to be representative of the population of the United States.

Another significant use of contingent valuation was to measure lost existence values caused by the *Exxon Valdez* oil spill in 1989. Eleven million gallons of oil were spilled into Alaska's Prince William Sound, damaging surface waters, coastal land (including beaches and wetlands), marine plants, birds, fish, and marine mam-mals. A study for the State of Alaska[21] used willingness-to-pay; the authors argued that this was because of concerns about respondent beliefs about their rights, and because willingness-to-pay yields conservative estimates (compared to willingness-to-accept). A hypothetical scenario — another spill occurring again within the next 10 years if nothing was done to prevent it — asked how much respondents would be willing to pay to prevent similar damages. The result was a median willingness-to-pay of $31 per household, resulting in total damages of $2.8 billion ($31 each for an adjusted number of U.S. households), and was asserted to represent the lower bound of damages because conservative procedures were followed. An alternative study calculated recreation losses using the travel cost method.[22] It estimated a loss of $3.8 million for 1989, with no losses in 1990 and beyond. The authors of this second study expressed skepticism about contingent valuation results showing losses of several billion dollars, given such low values for recreation use losses.

---

[19] Portney, p 4.

[20] RAND Study.

[21] Richard T. Carson, Robert C. Mitchell, W. Michael Hanemann, Raymond J. Kopp, Stanley Presser, and Paul A. Ruud, *A Contingent Valuation Study of Lost Passive Use Values Resulting from the Exxon Valdez Oil Spill*, A Report to the Attorney General of the State of Alaska (Nov. 10, 1992).

[22] Jerry A. Hausman, Gregory K. Leonard, and Daniel McFadden, "Assessing Use Value Losses Caused by Natural Resource Injury," in *Contingent Valuation A Critical Assessment*, ed. James A. Hausman (Amsterdam: North-Holland, 1993), pp. 341-359.

The third example is the reoperation of Glen Canyon Dam on the Colorado River in Arizona. Environmental impact statements were ordered from the Bureau of Reclamation by the Secretary of the Interior in 1989, to determine methods for operating the dam to protect downstream resources and Native American resources, on the belief that then-current operations were damaging those values. Altering operations to better approximate natural ecological conditions below the dam would, however, reduce power production, which was the principal purpose of the dam. Different operations — including varying the maximum and minimum flows, the variation in daily flow, and the rate of variation — were considered for improving resource conditions.[23] The Bureau contracted for a contingent valuation study to estimate the benefits of protecting downstream resources.[24] A mail survey was used to compare moderate flow fluctuation, low flow fluctuation, and seasonally adjusted steady flow with the baseline (no change). For the national sample, the aggregate annual values were $2.3 billion for the moderate flow fluctuation, $3.4 billion for the low flow fluctuation, and $3.4 billion for the seasonally-adjusted steady flow. For power users surveyed, the values were substantially lower: $62 million for the moderate flow fluctuation, $61 million for the low flow fluctuation, and $81 million for the seasonally adjusted steady flow.

The U. S. General Accounting Office (GAO) evaluated the contingent valuation study.[25] GAO reported that the recommendations from the NOAA panel of experts and Dillman's mail survey procedures (a standard for mail surveys) were generally followed, with two major exceptions: (1) in-person surveys are significantly better than the mail surveys used, and (2) the survey was six to eight pages longer than recommended. An unpublished rebuttal to the study by C.V. Jones (Economic Data Resources, Boulder, CO) and Mark Graham (Tri-State Generation and Transmission Association, Denver, CO) also had numerous criticisms, including that the national sample was not representative of the U.S. population and that the function used to estimate mean willingness-to-pay did not match the sample responses.[26] Others have suggested that the survey questions implied a significantly greater change in downstream environmental quality than was likely to result, at least for the first several years.[27]

---

[23] U.S. Dept. of the Interior, Bureau of Reclamation, Colorado River Studies Office, *Operation of Glen Canyon Dam: Draft Environmental Impact Statement. Summary* (Salt Lake City, UT: 1993), 65 pp.

[24] M.P. Welsh, R.C. Bishop, M.L. Phillips, and R.M. Baumgartner, *GCES Non-Use Value Study Final Report* (Madison, WI: Hagler Bailly Consulting. Sept. 8, 1995).

[25] U.S. General Accounting Office, *Bureau of Reclamation: An Assessment of the Environmental Impact Statement on the Operations of the Glen Canyon Dam*, GAO/RCED-97-12 (Washington, DC: U.S. Govt. Print. Off., Oct. 1996), 213 pp.

[26] C.V. Jones and Mark Graham, *Rebuttal to the GCES Non-Use Value Study Final Report,* unpublished report (June 4, 1996).

[27] Personal communication with John E. Schefter, Chief, Office of External Research, Water Resources Division, U.S. Geological Survey, Dept. of the Interior, on May 21, 1997.

The Contingent Valuation Method

Survey Design

A contingent valuation survey usually includes several parts: (1) an indication of property rights; (2) an emphasis on disposable income; (3) a description of the good to be valued; (4) the anticipated effects on the prices of other goods; (5) the payment mechanism; (6) the questions; and (7) data about the respondent.[28] But contingent valuation surveys differ from conventional surveys in several important ways. First, contingent valuation surveys usually value goods with which respond-ents have little experience. Second, contingent valuation surveys use hypothetical markets that must be believed and understood by respondents. Third, extra effort is required by respondents to determine which goods they prefer and how much they would pay to obtain them. These are some of the tests researchers face in designing valid and reliable contingent valuation surveys.

The NOAA panel of scientific experts[29] recommended in-person interviews over telephone surveys, which were, in turn, preferred to mail surveys. In-person surveys are more expensive than the other forms, but more complicated scenarios can be explained better using visual aids under this format. In contrast, telephone surveys are relatively inexpensive, but it may be difficult to explain the scenario in detail because phone calls are typically time-constrained. Mail surveys avoid interviewer bias, but are not subject to the same control that an in-person survey would generate.

The survey can simulate a private goods market or a political goods market. In a private market, people choose to buy varying amounts of the good at "market" prices. The average consumer is defined as the consumer who purchases the *mean* quantity of the good. In a political goods market, people vote as in a referendum on a public project, with payment coming through increased taxes. The average voter is the one who votes for the *median* quantity of the good. Potential problems exist for both formats. In the private goods model, a small number of individuals with high valuations can influence decisions and make everyone pay for the public good (suggesting that the *mode* might be preferable to the *mean* or *median*).[30] However, in a political goods market a majority can influence the decision to provide the good and not bear its full costs. The NOAA panel advocated the political goods market model, because it more closely resembles the way people already make decisions about government-provided goods.

---

[28] Mitchell and Carson, pp. 50-52.

[29] The panel was established by NOAA under the Oil Pollution Act of 1990 (P.L. 101-380); their report was printed in the *Federal Register*, v. 58, no. 10 (Jan. 15, 1993): 4601-4614.

[30] The *mean* is the average response, with the total (quantity or value) divided by the number of respondents. The *median* is the middle amount, with an equal number of higher and lower responses. The *mode* is the most common response (*i.e.*, the response given by the largest number of respondents).

Table 2 shows the choice of elicitation mechanisms (methods of asking about values) that are available. The methods can be separated depending on whether one or several questions are asked, and on whether the actual maximum willingness-to-pay (WTP) amount or a discrete approximation (a yes-or-no from each respondent to a specific amount) is received.

Table 2. Elicitation Mechanisms Available for Valuing Public Goods

	Actual WTP amount	Discrete indicator of WTP
Single question	Direct/open-ended question Payment card Sealed bid auction	Take-it-or-leave-it offer Spending question offer Interval checklist
Iterated series of questions	Bidding game Oral auction	Take-it-or-leave-it offer (with follow-up)

Source: Mitchell and Carson, p. 98.

Open-ended/direct questions do not give respondents an amount to consider; rather, they must come up with an amount on their own.[31] The payment card asks respondents to circle the value or specify a value that represents their maximum willingness-to-pay for the good, given a range of numbers listed on the survey form. It is not subject to starting-point biases from which some auction techniques suffer, but the range of numbers may bias responses.

Bidding games and auctions can also be used. In English auctions, bids are increased until the highest valuation is reached. In Dutch auctions, the initial price is set high and lowered until someone chooses to buy at that price.[32] Although these methods allow bidders to more carefully consider different prices, they may be subject to starting-point biases and may be expensive and time-consuming to implement.

The take-it-or-leave-it offer asks respondents to answer whether they would be willing to pay a set amount for a good. Although this format is likely to provide a more truthful valuation, it requires substantially more data than do other methods. Follow-up questions can improve the efficiency of this method, but they add their own statistical complications and potential biases.[33]

Additional criteria were suggested by the NOAA panel to cover other aspects of the survey instrument, including
- the willingness-to-pay question should correspond to a potential future event, not one that has already occurred;

---

[31] W. Michael Hanemann, "Valuing the Environment Through Contingent Valuation," *Journal of Economic Perspectives*, v. 8, no 4 (1994): 19-43.

[32] R.G. Cummings, D.S Brookshire, and W.D. Schulze, *Valuing Public Goods: An Assessment of the Contingent Valuation Method* (Totowa, NJ: Rowman and Allanhead Publishers, 1986), p. 39.

[33] Mitchell and Carson, pp. 99-104.

- the implications of any decision should be described in detail;
- respondents should be reminded of their budget constraints (that spending for a good means a reduction in other kinds of goods that can be purchased);
- respondents should also be made aware of possible substitutes for the good they are valuing; and
- follow-up questions should test how well respondents understood the scenario and to try to determine the motivation behind the different responses.[34]

The goal of contingent valuation researchers is to elicit responses that are both reliable and valid. A variety of techniques, such as pretesting tools and training interviewers, can reduce or minimize measurement error and bias. Texts on how to conduct good surveys exist (see, *e.g.*, Mitchell and Carson), and the techniques are not described here.

Reliability and Measurement Error

Reliability measures the variability among responses; valuations with relatively low variation among responses are considered more reliable estimates of value. Reliability measures whether the responses are consistent with each other, and thus is comparable to precision in statistics; it does *not* measure whether the responses accurately estimate the true value of the good. (The latter measure is called validity, and is discussed below.) Reliability contains a deterministic component (the normal variation in values among individuals) and random error due to imperfections in the survey instrument and/or sampling variance.

Sampling procedures, which are controlled by the researcher, influence reliability. Two approaches can improve the reliability of responses: (1) larger sample sizes, and (2) robust statistical techniques to handle "outliers" (responses that are considered too extreme, relative to the presumed distribution). Robust statistical techniques adjust responses that do not represent the true value (*e.g.*, a response of "99" to "number of dependents in the household") and would significantly influence the total valuation. Average willingness-to-pay, for example, can be significantly influenced by very high responses. Using robust techniques, such as the median value or a trimmed value (eliminating a percentage of responses from both ends of the distribution), generally improves the statistical reliability of contingent value surveys.[35]

Validity and Bias

Validity measures how accurately the contingent valuation of the good estimates the good's true value to society. This is comparable to accuracy in statistics, and bias is the term for the difference between the estimated value and the true value. Four categories of validity can be used to assess whether the responses are biased: (1) content validity; (2) criterion validity; (3) construct validity; and (4) theoretical validity. Contents are typically deemed valid, if the survey questionnaire is unambiguous and accurate, and closely matches the theoretical concept to be

---

[34] Portney, p. 8.

[35] Mitchell and Carson, pp. 211-229.

measured. Since questionnaire surveys are necessarily subjective, content validity is always a concern with such surveys.

Criterion validity requires comparison with some other method that is closer to being theoretically accurate, such as an estimate based on a derived demand curve. For goods where use is the majority of the value, prices from simulated markets can be used for comparison; an example would be a simulated market for hunting permits. For goods where nonuse accounts for the majority of the value, hypothetical values can be compared to actual referenda results.

Construct validity compares different measures for consistency. One form is to compare two methods, such as contingent valuation and the travel cost method, to see if the results are reasonably consistent; this, in essence, assesses the correlation between two or more measures. Significant differences, such as were found for the *Exxon Valdez*, raise questions about the construct validity of the contingent valuation survey.[36]

Theoretical validity evaluates whether the results are consistent with theoretical expectations; this typically involves a regression of the willingness-to-pay with other, independent variables to check whether the direction, magnitude, and strength of the relationships among variables are consistent with what would be expected under economic theory. The lack of criteria and truly comparable methods makes some of these tests of the validity of contingent valuation difficult, but surveys can usually be evaluated for their content and theoretical validity.[37]

Certain aspects of contingent valuation surveys could influence responses and lead to biased results. Biases can arise in numerous ways, because individuals be-have differently in various settings. Respondents may interpret the questionnaire differently, may be motivated by different aspects of the scenario when making decisions, may respond based on inferences about the use of their answers, or may use different cost-minimizing procedures or rules-of-thumb to make decisions when they know little about the good. Mitchell and Carson describe four types of biases:[38] (1) incentives to misrepresent responses; (2) implied value cues; (3) scenario misspecification; and (4) sampling design and benefit aggregation biases.

Incentives to Misrepresent Responses. Compliant and strategic behaviors may lead respondents to inaccurately represent their preferences, because there are no incentives to tell the truth when the constructed market is hypothetical. Com-pliance

---

[36] On the other hand, in the case of the *Exxon Valdez*, the contingent valuation survey tried to measure the total value of the losses caused by the oil spill, while the travel cost method tried to measure the lost recreational value. One might anticipate that the total value would greatly exceed the recreational value, because: (1) the beauty and uniqueness of the Alaskan coast are well known, but the distance to Alaska inhibits recreational use, thus making nonuse values substantial, relative to use values; and (2) the recreation increase in the second year might be attributable to "rubbernecking" that occurs with many disasters, and does not necessarily offset the nonuse value losses of the disaster.

[37] Mitchell and Carson, pp. 189-209.

[38] Mitchell and Carson, pp. 231-293.

bias occurs when respondents give answers that they feel the interviewer wants. Surveying by a neutral party can usually correct for such bias, but respondents may still feel the need to give a "right" or "normal" (*i.e.*, compliant) answer.

Strategic bias arises when respondents intentionally misrepresent their preferences, because they believe it will influence the amount of the good provided, the amount or system for collecting money to provide it, or in damage appraisals, the compensation. Table 3 shows the types of strategic behavior, depending on the likelihood of the good being provided and the perceived obligation to pay for the good.

Table 3. Strategic Behavior in Valuing Public Goods

	Obligation to pay perceived as the amount offered	Obligation to pay perceived as being uncertain	Obligation to pay perceived as being fixed
Provision of good perceived as contingent on revealed preference	True preference (reveals true value)	Variable (true value might be overstated or understated)	Overpledge (overstates true value)
Provision of good perceived as likely, regardless of revealed preference	Free ride (understates true value)	Free ride (understates true value)	Nonstrategic minimum effort (answers that minimize time/ effort)

Source: Mitchell and Carson, p. 144.

The table describes predictions of how individuals would act under different payment and provision characterizations. A contingent valuation survey is intended to identify true values. True values are most likely to be revealed when both the fees charged and the amount provided will be based on the response (*i.e.*, on the stated willingness-to-pay). On the other extreme is minimal effort, where respondents feel they will have to pay a fixed amount and the good will be provided regardless of what they say. The other categories contain different types of strategic behavior that will cause respondents to "bid" inaccurately. Free-riding (underbidding) is more likely to occur when respondents feel that the good will be provided irrespective of their response. Overpledging (overbidding) is more likely to occur when respondents believe that the good is more likely to be provided with higher bids, but the bidders expect to pay a fixed amount, regardless of the bids. Most contingent valuation studies fall into the variable category because the payment amount is typically uncertain and provision is usually believed to depend on stated amounts; in this situation, free-riding and overpledging are both possible outcomes.

Other individual behaviors may mitigate strategic behavior, including altruistic motives, personal honesty and integrity (interest in telling the truth), the belief that many people are being interviewed in the survey, consideration of one's budget constraint when offering a bid, and the possibility that the good may not be provided at all. Nonetheless, if respondents have beliefs about the likelihood of the good being provided or about the obligation to pay, or if they infer such information from the survey, strategic behavior can bias the valuation.

Implied Value Cues. Another type of bias arises when respondents decide on a valuation based on some particular aspect of the survey. This characteristic of the survey appears to give them a clue as to the "right" answer even if it were not intended to do so. *Starting point bias*, which typically occurs when using a bidding game format, can result when respondents feel that the starting bid is intended to approximate the correct value. A related problem — "yea-saying" — can occur when respondents simply accept a bid, even if it doesn't match their true valuation. The payment card approach was developed to correct the starting point bias of bidding games.

Respondents also infer values from other aspects of the survey. For example, some respondents give high valuations, because they feel that a study would not be conducted unless the resource or project being valued was important. Some methods, such as payment cards, include a range of values and typically benchmarks to suggest how much is spent on other (presumably similar) commodities. *Range bias* can occur when respondents' valuations are higher or lower than the highest or lowest amounts listed, when the amounts listed influence the bids, or when respondents do not find their valuations listed on the card. *Relational bias* can occur when respond-ents focus on benchmarks (particularly benchmarks related or similar to the good in question) to help determine their valuation. Finally, if several items are being valued, respondents may infer an indication of their values from their order in the list; typically, items listed first are perceived as being "more valuable" than items listed later. Thus, *position bias* could lead to invalid results. Altering the order in different interviews can overcome this bias, but it substantially increases the number of interviews needed.

Scenario Misspecification. A third type of bias, scenario misspecification, can arise when the scenario is either not specified properly according to theoretical or policy information (*theoretical bias*) or it is interpreted incorrectly by the respondents (*methodological bias*). Theoretical misspecification occurs when part of the survey is incorrectly specified, based on theoretical knowledge or policy information; this bias can usually be minimized with sufficient research beforehand to check the survey's consistency with theoretical and policy guidelines.

Methodological biases can occur in numerous ways, including[39]
- when respondents value the symbolic nature of a good, rather than the amount (resulting in the same willingness-to-pay for different levels of the good);
- when respondents include items beyond the level of the good in question, such as items outside of the specified location and benefits often associated with (but not part of) the good in question;
- when respondents use a different measurement scale (*e.g.*, general qualitative terms rather than exact numerical changes) than the researcher intended;

---

[39] Mitchell and Carson, pp. 231-259.

- when respondents are skeptical that the good will be provided, that adequate funding exists, or that the project will achieve the desired goals after completion;
- when respondents value the good differently based on how it is funded or who provides it;
- if respondents fail to adequately reconcile purchases with their income constraints;
- when respondents give an amount that they think the project will cost, feeling that if they bid their higher valuation, a portion will be wasted;
- when respondents use other materials in the survey (such as general questions in the opening part of an interview) to help come to a decision; or
- if respondents don't treat unrelated valuations as independent (similar to position bias, discussed above).

The need to devise a realistic scenario leads to three criteria to assess the survey instrument: familiarity, understandability, and plausibility. Particularly important survey elements include: the description of the good, the quantity produced, the market, the payment vehicle, and the elicitation method. The scenario may be familiar to respondents, if they have previous information; if not, it must be easy to understand and must convey new information effectively. The scenario must convey the expected change and consequences accurately; the studies of Grand Canyon air quality and Glen Canyon Dam re-operation were criticized for presenting excessive quality improvements. The scenario must also seem plausible or responses may not be meaningful. The researcher faces a realism-bias tradeoff, because more informa-tion makes the scenario more realistic but may cause strategically biased responses. When respondents feel that the survey is unrealistic, they typically give "don't-know" responses, guess randomly, or respond to other cues. This is particularly a problem for assessing damages after a disaster (such as the *Exxon Valdez* oil spill), since the scenario for a contingent valuation cannot be an event that has already occurred.

Sampling Design and Inference Biases. The other principal type of bias arises when sampling design or benefit aggregation is not performed properly. The sample used for the contingent valuation survey must be designed so that the appropriate population is sampled and the sample fully represents that population. Determining the appropriate population (of individuals or households) can be difficult when the people who pay differ from those who benefit from the proposed change. This is further complicated by affected private property owners and individuals with existence values for the good who live at substantial distances from the affected site. A sufficiently large population is needed to capture all of these values. Furthermore, the portion of the population that is sampled must accurately represent the values of the entire population, or the results could be biased. Inadequate or unrepresentative samples were criticisms of all three of the applications discussed earlier.

Nonresponse (to the survey in general or to specific questions) can also lead to biased results. Nonresponse to questions can include: don't know; refusal to answer; protest zeros (obviously erroneous answers, usually of zero, to register objection to the survey or the issue); and responses that are not internally consistent. Follow-up questions are usually necessary to distinguish between protest zeros (where respondents do not agree with the survey procedure) and actual zeros (where respondents would pay nothing for the good). Internally inconsistent responses (*e.g.*, responses that are improbable or infeasible, given the identified income) can also bias results. Other outliers can be eliminated by statistical techniques or judgment, but arbitrary or biased decisions could affect the validity of the survey. Stratified sampling procedures can moderate nonresponse biases among distinguishable groups (where the individuals value the good differently) within the population, but cannot account for nonresponse biases among people with similar characteristics who have different nonresponse rates and value the good differently.

Inference biases may occur when the results from one particular contingent valuation study are used to estimate the value of a different good.[40] *Temporal selection bias* may occur when data from one study are used for a different time period, because public preferences for the good may change. However, evidence from two sources — public opinion polls and other contingent valuation studies — indicate that valuation results are fairly stable over time; valuations are also likely to be more stable for a good with which respondents are familiar than for one with which they have little experience.[41]

Sequence aggregation bias may occur when data from independent studies are aggregated over additional locations or goods. For example, if several areas are to be cleaned up, the valuations of each area measured in a particular sequence may differ from the valuations of each area measured independently or in a different sequence, because of income and substitution effects. Money "spent" on the first area in the survey typically reduces the amount identified as being "spent" on other areas (income effect) and the first area may act as a substitute to some of the features of additional areas to be valued (substitution effect). Items reached at a later point in a sequence thus are likely to be valued less than if they were valued independently or earlier in the sequence. Bias arises when values from these kinds of surveys are aggregated without considering the sequence of valuations.

Empirical Criticisms

Several studies have attempted to empirically assess the reliability and validity of contingent valuation surveys. One should be aware, however, that such studies typically use existing contingent valuation surveys or conduct new ones, and thus are subject to all of the errors and biases of the contingent valuation surveys being evaluated. Therefore, their conclusions may be no more reliable or valid than the results of the surveys they critique.

Diamond, *et al.*[42] Four researchers used their own contingent valuation studies to determine whether economic preferences are actually being measured. They focused on a criticism called the embedding effect — that willingness-to-pay is the

---

[40] Mitchell and Carson, pp. 261-287.

[41] Mitchell and Carson, pp. 261-287.

[42] Peter A. Diamond, Jerry A. Hausman, Gregory K. Leonard, and Mike A. Denning, "Does Contingent Valuation Measure Preferences? Experimental Evidence," in *Contingent Valuation: A Critical Assessment*, ed. J.A. Hausman (Amsterdam: North-Holland, 1993), pp. 41-62.

same whether one item is valued or several items are valued. This is similar to symbolic and sequence aggregation biases, discussed above (under Scenario Misspecification and Sampling Design and Inference Biases, respectively). The example presented by Diamond *et al.* is that similar valuations resulted from different num-bers of wilderness areas protected. Proponents of contingent valuation argue that income and substitution effects explain the discrepancy in values. Diamond *et al.* counter that this effect is insufficient to explain the large variation in values observed in contingent valuation studies. Because the portion of income lost in valuing a sequence of goods is typically small, relative to average income, they conclude that income effects are insignificant.

Diamond *et al.* conducted several tests to determine whether substitution effects could explain differences in valuations. Other researchers have noted that, in a sequence of valuations, the valuation of goods later in the sequence will be lower than the valuation obtained independently, if some items can be substituted for others. Diamond *et al.* designed a survey to test the hypothesis that respondents would be willing to pay higher income taxes to prevent the development of more wilderness areas. They posited that, as more areas are developed, fewer substitute wilderness areas exist for recreation, so the current area being considered should be valued more highly. Their results led them to reject the hypothesis, implying that the substitution effect is not large, at least in this case. Further tests were conducted to examine whether alternative means of measuring the same quantity yielded the same answer. For example, they compared the value assigned to two areas (with seven already developed) to the sum of the value of one of the areas (with seven already developed) plus the value of the other area (with eight already developed). Using parametric tests, which put less weight on outliers, they conclude that such different ways of measuring the same quantity fail to give similar results, and thus violate one of the validity standards described above. Diamond *et al.* argue that these results arise from a "warm glow" effect, where respondents feel a sense of improved well-being by contributing to a good cause, and that contingent valuation does not measure true economic preferences.

Desvousges *et al.*[43] A study by six researchers was conducted to determine if contingent valuation surveys yield valid and reliable results. The authors used three hypotheses to test for validity and reliability. Data on willingness-to-pay to protect different numbers of migratory waterfowl by improving response services for oil spills were used to test these hypotheses. Based on a statistical analysis of the respondents, the researchers concluded that responses to different levels of protection were taken from the same population.

The first hypothesis was that higher levels of a good would elicit higher values. To test this hypothesis, the authors used an open-ended question to measure the value of protecting 2 thousand, 20 thousand, and 200 thousand migratory waterfowl from small and all oil spills. The results showed similar valuations across the changes in

---

[43] William H. Desvousges, F. Reed Johnson, Richard W. Dunford, Sara P. Hudson, and K. Nicole Wilson, "Measuring Natural Resource Damages with Contingent Valuation: Tests of Validity and Reliability," in *Contingent Valuation: A Critical Assessment*, ed. J.A. Hausman (Amsterdam: North-Holland, 1993), pp. 91-114.

quantities, leading the authors to reject the hypothesis and conclude that contingent valuation surveys were not valid.

The second hypothesis was that open-ended and dichotomous-choice questions would yield similar results when used to value the same quantity. To test this hypothesis, the two formats were used to measure the difference in the value associated with differing levels of response service for oil spills. The authors found that the dichotomous-choice format yielded a significantly larger number of high bids and generally yielded higher results than did the open-ended questions. Since the questions were measuring the same quantity but yielded different results, they rejected the hypothesis and again concluded that contingent valuation does not yield valid results.

The third hypothesis was that the results would not be affected by the procedures used to handle the data (such as functional forms or the bid structure), to assess the reliability of contingent valuation results. The first test compared total values calculated using linear and nonlinear functional forms for responses. The second compared total values from a survey using a high bid of $250 versus another survey using a high bid of $1000. The authors found that results varied significantly, leading them to reject the hypothesis and conclude that estimates from contingent valuation surveys are not reliable, as well as not valid.

Kahneman and Knetsch.[44] These two researchers concluded that responses to contingent valuation questions represent people's willingness-to-pay for moral satisfaction rather than for the good in question. They also concluded that people derive more benefits when they contribute more to a good cause, rather than when they consume more. The authors found that a ranking of projects based on moral satisfaction predicts the ranking by different willingness-to-pay amounts with a high degree of correlation. Willingness-to-pay, as an index of moral satisfaction, also helps to explain the embedding effect discussed by Diamond *et al.*, because addi-tional amounts of the good may add little to moral satisfaction. The second point made by the authors is that many individuals have a portion of their budget already devoted to purchasing moral satisfaction. They found that measured willingness-to-pay for additional moral satisfaction reduced discretionary spending, rather than reducing (substituting for) current purchases of moral satisfaction.

Conclusion

Contingent valuation is becoming more widely used in natural resource damage appraisal and in decisionmaking. It is and will likely remain controversial, however, because it is a complicated and imperfect device. Its application is an expensive and time-consuming research project, and a host of potential problems make the results of contingent valuation surveys suspect. However, the relevance or magnitude of the many types of errors and biases described in this report can only be assessed for each

---

[44] Daniel Kahneman and Jack L. Knetsch, "Valuing Public Goods: The Purchase of Moral Satisfaction," *Journal of Environmental Economics and Management*, v. 22 (1992): 57-70.

survey; it is impossible to reach an unqualified conclusion as to the reliability and validity of such surveys generally.

When attempting to assess public preferences, nonuse values are real, and at times significant, possibly exceeding use values substantially. Proponents contend that excluding nonuse values in calculating damages and in decisionmaking would understate total values affected, and that contingent valuation is a theoretically valid way to estimate nonuse values. Opponents argue that the methodology is weak and the measures are not comparable to traditional measures of utilitarian values (because resource use generates economic and social benefits beyond those measured by price and volume), and thus can lead to arbitrary assessments of damage. Congress has recognized such values in directing federal land management agencies to "balance" values produced and protected. Congress has more explicitly acknowledged nonuse values in damage recovery programs, and may debate methods for measuring such values, including contingent valuation, particularly in any consideration of reauthorization of Superfund.

Natural Resources
Pages 169-210

WETLANDS REGULATION AND THE LAW OF PROPERTY RIGHTS "TAKINGS"

Robert Meltz

Talk about wetlands preservation today and you may soon be talking about private property and takings. The reason is simple enough: while the need for wetlands preservation is widely conceded, many are privately owned — in the case of the federal wetlands permitting program, almost 75% of the covered acreage in the lower 48. When a wetland owner is denied a permit to develop property (or offered a permit with very burdensome conditions), its value may drop substantially. Even when a permit is granted, permit processing time or agency errors may on occasion impose costly development delays. Accounts of land owners aggrieved by wetlands regulation have been widely circulated by the property rights movement, and challenged by environmentalists.

The conflict, as viewed by some, is straightforward. The benefits of wetlands preservation, they argue — water filtration, wildlife habitat, protection against flooding and erosion — inure to the public. By contrast, the burdens of wetlands preservation, in terms of development denied, fall on the wetland owner. (The burden is enhanced because coastal regions, lake fronts, and riversides are especially coveted areas in which to build.) The public receives the benefits of wetlands without having to compensate the wetland owner.

Others, however, assert that not only the public, but the restricted wetland owner too, receives benefit from the regulatory scheme (e.g., prevention of flooding), through the comparable restrictions placed on other wetland owners. These benefits should be regarded as "offsetting" the burdens imposed. Moreover, they contend, wetlands regulation should not be viewed as creation of a public benefit, but rather as avoidance of a societal harm — from the loss of the above wetlands functions. It is bad public policy, they argue, to compensate landowners for not inflicting injury.[1]

---

[1] Wetlands regulation is hardly unique among land-use-oriented government programs in posing this public benefits/private burdens quandary. Consider, for example, protection of endangered species habitat and historic landmarks.

A prime example of the "offsetting benefits" debate is in one of the leading Supreme Court "takings" decisions, Penn Central Transportation Co. v. New York City, 438 U.S. 104 (1978). The 6-justice majority opinion found that the city's historic landmark ordinance conferred benefits on the plaintiff-landmark owner, as well as burdens, through its preservation of hundreds of other buildings citywide. The 3-justice dissent, to the contrary, asserted that "no such reciprocity exists." *Id.* at 140.

In the courts, wetlands regulation continues to generate "takings" lawsuits by landowners.[2] Such a suit alleges that by severely curtailing the economic uses to which a wetland can be put, the government has permanently "taken" the wetland. Or that administrative delays and errors have brought about a temporary taking. Accordingly, plaintiffs seek compensation under the Fifth Amendment Takings Clause: "[N]or shall private property be taken for public use, without just compensation."

In Congress, the "property rights issue" has played out with particular force in the area of wetlands regulation. Many property rights bills have targeted wetlands regulation. Congressional efforts to amend the wetlands permitting program's charter[3] — section 404 of the Clean Water Act[4] — have been stymied for years now, in part because of polarized views on how private property rights should be accommodated. The result is that the wetlands permitting program remains what it has long been: a major environmental initiative built upon statutory language that only awkwardly accommodates it, and that gives the administering agencies (the Army Corps of Engineers and Environmental Protection Agency) little in the way of clear guidance.

As background for continuing congressional efforts to give the federal wetlands permitting program an explicit legislative charter, this report reviews the takings cases involving wetlands regulation. We include not only federal wetlands program cases, but state and local ones as well. The inclusion of non-federal wetlands cases seems particularly appropriate with regard to the long-simmering debate as to whether states should be given a larger role in implementing the federal permitting program, and the specter of state and local liability for takings that such proposals arguably raise.

A final prefatory note. As the title of this report makes clear, our concern is exclusively with government wetlands programs of a *regulatory* nature. The reason: non-regulatory approaches generally do not spawn takings claims. The reader should be aware, nonetheless, that non-regulatory approaches are in wide use alongside regulatory ones. Non-regulatory approaches include the federal "swampbuster"

---

[2] There are more takings challenges to the federal wetlands program than to any other federal environmental program. *See generally* U.S. General Accounting Office, *Clean Water Act: Private Property Takings Claims as a Result of the Section 404 Program* (RCED-93-176FS 1993); Richard C. Ausness, *Regulatory Takings and Wetlands Protection in the Post-Lucas Era,* 30 Land and Water L. Rev. 349 (1995). As a matter of perspective, however, it should be noted that environmental programs are involved in only a minority of takings actions against the United States, the bulk of such cases dealing with a diverse assortment of other matters.

[3] *See generally* Jeffrey A. Zinn and Claudia Copeland, *Wetland Issues*, CRS Issue Brief IB97014.

[4] 33 U.S.C. § 1344 (implementing regulations at 33 C.F.R. part 323). Under Clean Water Act section 301, 33 U.S.C. § 1311, discharge of dredged or fill materials into "navigable waters," broadly defined by the Act as "waters of the United States," is forbidden unless authorized by a Corps of Engineers permit pursuant to section 404.

program for agricultural wetlands,[5] as well as various federal and state approaches such as real estate tax incentives, technical assistance and grants, and land acquisition from voluntary sellers.[6]

I. Brief overview of takings law

Takings law is the body of principles courts have articulated in interpreting the Takings Clause of the U.S. Constitution (and similar clauses in state constitutions). While complex and often vague, its precepts share a simple goal: to ascertain when government so severely interferes with private property rights that it should compensate the property owner for the taken value.

Before a court can reach a property owner's taking claim, however, several threshold hurdles have to be surmounted. Has the statute of limitations expired? Is the taking claim ripe — for example, has the government agency rendered a "final decision"? Should a federal court facing a challenge to state or local land-use regulation abstain, deferring to a state tribunal? Was the plaintiff the owner of the tract when the alleged taking occurred?

Once these (and other) matters are resolved in plaintiff's favor – and only then – the court can proceed to the taking issue in the case. There are at least two types of takings: physical and regulatory. Physical takings may occur when the government effects a physical invasion of private land, as by back-up waters from a government dam. Regulatory takings may occur when government severely restricts the use to which property may be put. Many observers, recognizing the distinct body of law the Supreme Court has developed, would define a third type of taking: when an exaction condition on issuance of a development permit is unrelated, in its goal or degree of burden imposed, to the impact of the proposed development.

When a government regulation of private wetlands raises a taking issue, it almost always will be of the regulatory taking variety.[7] The Supreme Court canon for recognizing regulatory takings divides into two approaches. First, there are *per se* rules, defining circumstances that constitute automatic takings (if exceptions do not apply). In the wetlands context, the only important *per se* rule has been the "total taking" rule of *Lucas v. South Carolina Coastal Council.*[8] The *Lucas* total taking rule holds that government action eliminating *all* economic use of land is necessarily a taking — *if* the barred use was not prohibitable under "background principles" of

---

[5] 16 U.S.C. §§ 3821-3823.

[6] Association of State Wetlands Managers, State Wetlands Regulation: Status of Programs and Emerging Trends 31-34 (1994).

[7] Explicitly noting the appropriateness of the regulatory taking framework for takings challenges to the federal wetlands permitting program, and the inappropriateness of a physical takings approach, are Forest Properties, Inc. v. United States, 177 F.3d 1360, 1364 (Fed. Cir.), *cert. denied*, 120 S. Ct. 373 (1999), and Plantation Landing Resort, Inc. v. United States, 30 Fed. Cl. 63, 69 (1993).

[8] 505 U.S. 1003 (1992).

law existing when the property was acquired.[9] An earlier formulation of *Lucas*, in
Agins v. City of Tiburon, is often cited by state courts in lieu of *Lucas*.[10]

The second approach applies when the government action does not come under
a *per se* rule — for present purposes, when its impact falls short of a *Lucas* total
taking. This approach consists of a multi-factor balancing test, first announced by the
Court in *Penn Central Transportation Co. v. City of New York*.[11] The factors in this
test are the economic impact of the government action, the extent to which it
interferes with reasonable investment-backed expectations, and its "character."
Application of these factors is fact-intensive and *ad hoc;* critics say unprincipled.

By definition, a plaintiff able to fit the challenged government action within a *per
se* rule wins his/her case (if no exceptions apply), and is generally compensated. Thus,
wetlands owners often assert a *Lucas* "total taking" as their opening salvo. Plaintiffs
relegated to the *Penn Central* balancing test typically lose — though recent
developments in a prominent federal wetlands/taking case portend change here.[12]

II. The historic pendulum in wetlands/takings case law

Comparing the history of regulatory takings decisions involving state and local
wetlands programs with that of case law on the federal program, one discovers a
common feature. Each displays a distinct point in time when the relevant courts
shifted sharply in how they balanced the benefits and burdens of wetlands
preservation. As a crude generalization, not without exception, state-program cases
shifted toward greater deference toward government; federal-program cases, toward
less.

Cases involving state and local wetlands programs

1960s and early 1970s. This first generation of wetlands/takings cases saw state
courts respond sympathetically to the aggrieved wetlands owner, probably because
the public goals of the new wetlands statutes were contrary to prevailing attitudes
about such ecosystems. Typical of the period is *Morris County Land Improvement*

---

[9] Another *per se* rule of takings law has never been exclusively relied on to find a wetlands
taking, in the rare case where it has been invoked and found violated. This is the due-process-
like rule of Agins v. City of Tiburon, 447 U.S. 255, 260 (1980), declaring that government
action effects a taking if, among other things, it fails to substantially advance a legitimate
government interest.

[10] 447 U.S. 255, 260 (1980). The Court there stated that a land use regulation effects a
taking if it "denies an owner economically viable use of his land." No explanation was
provided by the Court as to how this test related to the multifactor *Penn Central* test
announced just two years before.

[11] 438 U.S. 104 (1978).

[12] *See* text accompanying notes 81-84.

Co. v. Township of Parsippany-Troy Hills,[13] addressing a township zoning ordinance. The court found "[o]f the highest legal significance" that the prime object of the zoning was to retain plaintiff's land substantially in its natural state — that is, in the court's view, to secure a public benefit rather than prevent a harm. Hence, the zoning restriction was seen as likely compensable.[14]

Early 1970s to the present. This era began with a judicial pendulum swing from suspicion to acceptance of wetlands regulation. Few *final* decisions during this period find takings, even though more states have wetlands protection regimes in place. *Just v. Marinette County* represents an early high water mark of judicial sensitivity to wetlands.[15] States well represented in the case law of this period are Connecticut, Florida, Massachusetts, Michigan, New Hampshire, and New York.[16] These courts appeared to accept the special status of wetlands, and often stretched to find noncompensable even the strictest of regulations. Even after the landowner-friendly takings decisions since the late 1980s from the Supreme Court, Federal Circuit, and Court of Federal Claims, state-court final decisions show little willingness to find takings as the result of wetlands regulation.[17]

The restriction of the above discussion to *final* state-court decisions is important. Several of the wetlands/takings cases during this period initially produced trial court and/or intermediate appellate decisions for the property owner, only to be reversed by the state high court. A recent decision by the intermediate appellate court of South

---

[13] 40 N.J. 539, 193 A.2d 232 (1963).

[14] Other takings holdings in favor of wetland owners during this period include Commissioner of Natural Resources v. S. Volpe & Co., 349 Mass. 104, 206 N.E.2d 666 (1965) (on remand, lower court found taking); State v. Johnson, 265 A.2d 711 (Me. 1970); and Bartlett v. Town of Old Lyme, 161 Conn. 24, 282 A.2d 907 (1971)

[15] 56 Wis. 2d 7, 201 N.W.2d 761 (1972).

[16] The parade of cases from New Hampshire is illustrative. All of them find no taking. Sibson v. State, 115 N.H. 124, 336 A.2d 239 (1975); Claridge v. New Hampshire Wetlands Bd., 125 N.H. 745, 485 A.2d 287 (1984); New Hampshire Wetlands Bd. v. Marshall, 127 N.H. 240, 500 A.2d 685 (1985), and Rowe v. Town of North Hampton, 131 N.H. 424, 553 A.2d 1331 (1989).

[17] Final, reported state wetlands decisions during the 1990s finding no taking include Brotherton v. DEC, 252 A.D.2d 499, 675 N.Y.S.2d 121 (1998); Volkema v. DNR, 542 N.W.2d 282 (Mich. App. 1995), *aff'd*, 457 Mich. 884, 586 N.W.2d 231, *cert. denied*, 119 S. Ct. 590 (1998); Alegria v. Keeney, 687 A.2d 1249 (R.I. 1997); Gazza v. New York State, 89 N.Y.2d 603, 679 N.E.2d 1035, *cert. denied*, 118 S. Ct. 58 (1997); FIC Homes of Blackstone, Inc. v. Conservation Comm'n, 673 N.E.2d 61 (Mass. App. 1996), *rev. denied*, 424 Mass. 1104, 676 N.E.2d 55 (1997); Zealy v. City of Waukesha, 201 Wis. 2d 365, 548 N.W.2d 528 (1996); and Mock v. DER, 154 Pa. Commw. 380, 623 A.2d 940 (1993), *aff'd*, 542 Pa. 357, 667 A.2d 212 (1995), *cert. denied*, 517 U.S. 1216 (1996). In Gardner v. New Jersey Pinelands Comm'n, 125 N.J. 193, 593 A.2d 251 (1990), the vitality of a 1960s state-court decision finding a wetlands taking was said to have eroded due to the subsequent rise in societal environmental awareness.

Research reveals only one final, reported state wetlands decision during the 1990s that found a taking: Vatalaro v. DER, 601 So.2d 1223 (Fla. App. 1992).

Carolina, finding a taking of a wetland, may provide the next test of this pattern when the state supreme court rules.[18]

Cases involving the federal wetlands program

1970s and early 1980s. The first takings decision involving the federal wetlands program was *Zabel v. Tabb*,[19] decided in 1970. This case, and the few others during the period, found no takings[20] — paralleling the new resistance to takings in contemporaneous state challenges. Court decisions cited the Supreme Court's tendency to uphold land-use restrictions if soundly based on public interest, even where landowners suffer dramatic value loss. Also, the challenged permit denials were held not to deny all reasonable uses of the landowner's property *as a whole* (see section VIII)— either because the property included unregulated uplands, or because a permit had been granted for the filling in of some, even if not all, of the wetlands on the parcel.

Mid-1980s to the present. By the mid-1980s, the winds of change were blowing — possibly because the federal wetlands program had now taken hold and confronted a more conservative federal bench. In 1983, a federal wetlands permit denial was judicially deemed a taking for the first time.[21] Then followed two important interim rulings favorable to the wetland owner. In 1986, in *Florida Rock Industries v. United States*, the U.S. Court of Appeals for the Federal Circuit again weighed the public interest in wetlands preservation against the landowner's loss, as it had above in the early 1980s. But this time it tipped toward the landowner.[22] Two years later, a key ruling on the "property as a whole" issue went against the United States in another wetlands/taking case: *Loveladies Harbor, Inc. v. United States*.[23] When the trial-level U.S. Claims Court reached the takings question in these two cases, it found takings in both.[24]

(A word about court names. Trial jurisdiction over most takings claims against the United States is vested in the U.S. Court of Federal Claims, with appeals to the U.S. Court of Appeals for the Federal Circuit, and thence to the Supreme Court. It was not always so, however. Prior to 1982, both trial and appellate jurisdiction over such claims were vested in a U.S. Court of Claims. In 1982, Congress split the two

---

[18] McQueen v. South Carolina Coastal Council, 329 S.C. 588, 496 S.E.2d 643 (Ct. App. 1998), *appeal pending*.

[19] 430 F.2d 199 (5th Cir. 1970). Being pre-section 404, this case involves permitting under only the Rivers and Harbors Act of 1899.

[20] The leading decisions of this period are Deltona Corp. v. United States, 657 F.2d 1184 (Ct. Cl. 1981), *cert. denied*, 455 U.S. 1017 (1982), and Jentgen v. United States, 657 F.2d 1210 (Ct. Cl. 1981), *cert. denied*, 455 U.S. 1017 (1982).

[21] 1902 Atlantic Limited v. Hudson, 574 F. Supp. 1381 (E.D. Va. 1983) (dictum).

[22] 791 F.2d 893 (Fed. Cir. 1986), *cert. denied*, 479 U.S. 1053 (1987). Notwithstanding the rebalancing, the court on other grounds vacated the holding below in favor of the landowner.

[23] 15 Cl. Ct. 381 (1988).

[24] *Florida Rock*, 21 Cl. Ct. 161 (1990); *Loveladies Harbor*, 21 Cl. Ct. 153 (1990).

jurisdictions, placing the trial jurisdiction in a U.S. Claims Court and the appellate responsibility in a newly created U.S. Court of Appeals for the Federal Circuit. In 1992, Congress gave the U.S. Claims Court its current name: the U.S. Court of Federal Claims.)

These decisions, and other claims court rulings of the time, embodied an unmistakably different balancing of the equities in wetlands/takings cases than did earlier federal decisions. *Florida Rock* and *Loveladies Harbor* in particular decided key unresolved issues of takings law against the government. In the following round, in 1994, the Federal Circuit affirmed *Loveladies*[25] and remanded *Florida Rock*[26] with guidance to the Court of Federal Claims (CFC) that led that court in 1999 to find a taking once again.[27]

Since 1994, and despite the 1999 CFC decision in *Florida Rock*, this swing of the judicial pendulum toward the property owner has been less clear. Indeed, a review of final, reported federal wetlands/takings decisions shows that the United States has won every one since the 1994 decision in *Loveladies Harbor*. (At this writing, the 1999 CFC decision in *Florida Rock* is still appealable.) One recent case in particular, *Good v. United States*, generated no-taking holdings on difficult facts that easily could have produced contrary rulings.[28] Still, we remain in a period where the United States must offer a convincing defense; its almost-six-year winning streak may stem more from an increased willingness at the Department of Justice to settle the difficult cases than from any substantial judicial pendulum shift back to the government side.

With so few wetland-owner wins, why this report?

The discussion above reveals that particularly recently, there have been precious few final, reported takings decisions in which the wetland owner won. Notwithstanding, the application of takings law to wetlands protection repays attention, for several reasons. Most important, takings law and the potential of government liability influence how wetlands agencies implement and enforce their regulatory programs. One may speculate whether the significant recent reduction in the annual number of permit denials by the Corps of Engineers was influenced by the greater vulnerability of outright denials, as opposed to conditioned approvals, to takings actions.[29] Nor, in this regard, does it take more than an occasional adverse court decision to maintain the hot breath of taking liability on the regulator's neck. Today, state and federal wetlands regulators know how far they can go before a

---

[25] 28 F.3d 1171 (Fed. Cir. 1994).

[26] 18 F.3d 1560 (Fed. Cir. 1994), *cert. denied*, 513 U.S. 1109 (1995).

[27] 45 Fed. Cl. 21 (1999).

[28] 38 Fed. Cl. 81 (1997), *aff'd*, 179 F.3d 1355 (Fed. Cir. 1999)

[29] The Corps denied 393 individual-permit applications in FY 1992 (8.8% of applications), as compared to 158 in FY 1998 (3.2% of applications). See web site of Public Employees for Environmental Responsibility, www.peer.org/corps (visited on Aug. 30, 1999).

property owner's threats of a taking action must be taken seriously, and often act accordingly.

In addition, state wetlands managers report that in fact there *are* final court decisions in favor of the landowner. However, they are unreported state trial-court decisions that do not get appealed[30] — often because the wetlands agency reaches a compromise with the landowner.

Finally, the property-owner complaints and government counter-arguments that crop up in wetlands takings litigation may shape future legislative efforts in the wetlands protection area.

III. Ripeness

Ripeness doctrine is concerned with the timing of litigation. It seeks to ensure that disputes are not brought to the courts too early, involving them in issues that are not yet clearly defined or that may yet resolve themselves without judicial intervention. The Supreme Court has been particularly attentive to the demands of ripeness doctrine in the context of takings litigation.

"Final decision"

For a claim of permanent taking of land to be ripe, the government generally must have reached a "final decision" as to the nature and extent of development permitted on the property.[31] "Final decision" is a legal term of art, with much case law gloss. To get a final decision, the Supreme Court says, it may be necessary for the property owner, after his/her initial proposal is rejected, to reapply with scaled-down or reconfigured proposals. Also, variance opportunities have to be exhausted.

Typically, the final-decision prerequisite means that the wetland owner's taking claim is not ripe until at least one application for a development permit has been submitted and ruled upon, based on the merits.[32] An agency's mere designation of a

---

[30] One such decision, following the Massachusetts high court's remand in Lopes v. City of Peabody, is described in a later high court ruling in the case at 430 Mass. 305, 718 N.E.2d 846, 849 (1999).

[31] Williamson County Regional Planning Comm'n v. Hamilton Bank, 473 U.S. 172 (1985). Though this decision addressed takings-ripeness in the federal courts, many state-court cases as well have adopted its insistence on a final decision.

[32] Discussed later are two exceptions to the need for a permit denial: (1) the futility exemption (this section) and (2) claims of *temporary taking* based on unreasonable delay in an agency's processing of the permit application (section VII). A third exception, more specialized, was enunciated in Robbins v. United States, 40 Fed. Cl. 381, *aff'd without op.*, 178 F.3d 1310 (Fed. Cir. 1998), *cert. denied*, 119 S. Ct. 2400 (1999). *Robbins* held that events need not reach the permit denial stage when the claimed taking is not of land, but rather of a land purchase contract cancelled by the buyer upon learning that the Corps had found jurisdictional

(continued...)

parcel as within its wetlands permit jurisdiction cannot by itself be a taking, since it leaves open the possibility that the permit, if applied for, will be granted.[33] The same holds true when the government orders construction on a wetland to cease and desist until the owner secures a permit.[34] Little better is the incomplete permit application; Corps of Engineers rejection of an incomplete application through a "denial without prejudice" confers no ripeness, unless in actual fact rejection was based on the merits of the application.[35]

The CFC and Federal Circuit have looked at whether administrative, judicial, and political efforts to overturn a wetlands permit denial negate its status as "final" — in the context of determining whether takings claims were filed within the statute of limitations. (The limitations period begins to run only when the taking claim becomes ripe. See section IV.) *Creppel v. United States* held that such post-permit-denial skirmishing, resulting in the Corps' reversing its initial position, ended any temporary taking that might have been caused by the initial decision and allowed a second, completely new alleged taking to begin when EPA exercised its permit veto authority.[36] Thus, while the temporary taking claim was untimely, the permanent taking claim based on the later EPA veto was timely.

More recent decisions seek to limit *Creppel*. They suggest that post-decision efforts to overturn a denial, *where unsuccessful*, do not undermine the "final" status of an agency decision for ripeness purposes.[37] When such efforts take the form of an administrative appeal of a permit denial, however, the new Corps administrative appeals rule may have preempted this case law (see page 11).

---

[32] (...continued)
wetlands on the property. (The claim was rejected on the merits.)

[33] United States v. Riverside Bayview Homes, Inc., 474 U.S. 121 (1985). *Accord, Robbins,* 40 Fed. Cl. 381; Marcantonio v. Russo, 684 N.Y.S.2d 567 (Supr. Ct. App. Div. 1999); Carabell v. DNR, 478 N.W.2d 675 (Mich. App. 1991); Wedinger v. Goldberger, 71 N.Y.2d 488, 522 N.E.2d 25 (1988).
The fact that agency jurisdictional determinations do not ripen takings claims is particularly important because at least at the Corps of Engineers, their number vastly exceeds that of permit denials.

[34] Tabb Lakes, Ltd. v. United States, 10 F.3d 796, 800-801 (Fed. Cir. 1993).

[35] *Compare* City National Bank v. United States, 33 Fed. Cl. 759 (1995) (ripeness found notwithstanding Corps' describing permit denial as "without prejudice," since denial actually was merits based) with Heck v. United States, 134 F.3d 1468 (Fed. Cir. 1998) (ripeness lacking, since denial without prejudice was based, as Corps asserted, solely on application's incompleteness). *See* 33 C.F.R. § 320.4(j)(1) (Corps of Engineers' definition of permit denials without prejudice).

[36] 41 F.3d 627 (Fed. Cir. 1994).

[37] Bayou des Familles Devpmt. Corp. v. United States, 130 F.3d 1034 (Fed. Cir. 1997); Cristina Investment Corp. v. United States, 40 Fed. Cl. 571 (1998). *Bayou des Familles* does not reject post-decision developments as decisively as *Cristina*, since it seems to allow that on the facts presented, finality may have been established not upon permit denial, but when that denial was upheld by the district court some years later. Using either date, plaintiff's taking claim was untimely.

Other finality ripeness issues: For how long must a wetlands permit applicant wrangle with the government over what permit conditions (e.g., for compensatory mitigation) are mutually acceptable?[38] Can a claim that the government has taken plaintiff's *entire* wetland be ripe if based on the denial of a permit to fill only a fraction thereof?[39]

"Final decision": reapplications, variances, appeals

In the state courts, wetlands/takings plaintiffs have been denied finality ripeness owing to their failure, following first permit denial, to reapply with modified proposals.[40] On occasion, this duty of the wetland owner to reapply has led courts to express impatience with state agencies that issue permit denials without any indication of what they *would* accept.[41] The issue is a pervasive one in takings law, pitting the needs of the landowner against the limited resources government can commit to developing alternatives to submitted proposals. If variance and appeal mechanisms are available, the landowner may have to exhaust them, too.

In the CFC, by contrast, reapplications and variances have not been a problem for plaintiffs. As for reapplications, the CFC consistently has read the Corps' language accompanying the initial permit denial as precluding its approval of *any*

---

[38] In Plantation Landing Resort, Inc. v. United States, 30 Fed. Cl. 63 (1993), *aff'd without pub. op.*, 39 F.3d 1197 (Fed. Cir. 1994), *cert. denied*, 514 U.S. 1095 (1995), the court said it could not view a Corps permit denial as a taking when the denial was the result of a failure to reach agreement with the landowner on mitigation requirements. Though the decision was not couched in the language of ripeness, since the permit was denied, it nonetheless highlights the duty of the wetland owner to pursue reasonable negotiations as to permit conditions before claiming a taking.

[39] *Compare* Florida Rock Industries, Inc. v. United States, 791 F.2d 893 (Fed. Cir. 1986) (claim that entire parcel was taken by denial of permit for portion is premature), *cert. denied*, 479 U.S. 1053 (1987) *with* Formanek v. United States, 18 Cl. Ct. 42 (1988) (claim that entire parcel was taken is ripe). In the most recent Florida Rock opinion, the CFC addressed wetlands acreage not covered by the permit denial by requesting the parties to come up with a compensation plan for submission to the court. 45 Fed. Cl. 21 (1999).

[40] *See, e.g.*, Hoffman v. Town of Avon, 28 Conn. App. 262, 610 A.2d 185 (1982) (no taking where plaintiff submitted only one application). One court held that four denials of permit applications to build a home (three on the merits) was insufficient for ripeness. Gil v. Town of Greenwich, 219 Conn. 404, 593 A.2d 1368 (1991). Though the lot was zoned residential, its wetland classification should have warned the buyer, said the court, that development would be difficult. Moreover, the four applications were similar to each other and out of keeping with other homes in the neighborhood.
Failure to reapply has also been analyzed by state courts in a non-ripeness context — as showing in the merits analysis that the wetland owner failed to establish the requisite economic impact for a taking. See, e.g., Emond v. DEM, Civ. No. PM96-4584 (R.I. Super. Ct. Oct. 5, 1999); Alegria v. Keeney, 687 A.2d 1249 (R.I. 1997); Carabell v. DNR, 191 Mich. App. 610, 478 N.W.2d 675 (1991).

[41] *See. e.g., Emond.*

development on the parcel.[42] Thus, the initial permit denial made the taking claim ripe. Nor have section 404 takings plaintiffs been required to exhaust variance possibilities, since Corps procedures offer none.

A new development is the March, 1999 promulgation by the Corps of Engineers of an administrative appeal process.[43] Under it, applicants for 404 permits may appeal within the Corps a denial with prejudice by the district engineer, or a declined proffer by the Corps of an individual permit. Important here, the new regulations assert that no federal-court action based on such denials or declined permits may be filed until the applicant "has exhausted all applicable administrative remedies ...."[44]

Absent this exhaustion provision, it is unclear whether appeal within the Corps is a ripeness prerequisite to a taking action against the agency. Courts are divided on whether finality ripeness can be established without exhausting such "vertical" appeals to a higher administrative authority. The sounder position under Supreme Court precedent is that vertical exhaustion is required when challenging the *validity* of a government act, but not when compensation is sought per the Takings Clause. Rather, takings claims are subject only to "horizontal" reapplication and variance-seeking requirements.[45]

Futility exemption

The key exception to these ripeness requirements of permit application, negotiation, reapplication, and variance pursuit is futility doctrine: a landowner should not have to pursue government procedures when doing so would be pointless. Courts have often invoked this "futility exemption" to ripeness prerequisites where the government's conduct, or its rationale for denying the permit, indicates that no development of economically viable extent would be allowed on the wetland. Recall the just-discussed CFC cases finding no reapplication necessary.

---

[42] *See, e.g.*, Cristina Investment Corp. v. United States, 40 Fed. Cl. 571 (1998); Formanek v. United States, 18 Cl. Ct. 785, 792-793 (1989); Beure-Co. v. United States, 16 Cl. Ct. 42, 47-51 (1988); Loveladies Harbor, Inc. v. United States, 15 Cl. Ct. 381, 385-386 (1988).

[43] 64 Fed. Reg. 11708 (March 9, 1999); codified at 33 C.F.R. part 331.

[44] 33 C.F.R. § 331.12.

[45] *See, e.g., Cristina Investment Corp.*, 40 Fed. Cl. 571; Good v. United States, 38 Fed. Cl. 81, 101-102 (1997), *aff'd*, 179 F.3d 1355 (Fed. Cir. 1999), *pet. for cert. filed. Contra*, Bayou des Familles Devpmt. Corp. v. United States, 130 F.3d 1034, 1040 (Fed. Cir. 1997) (suggesting prophetically that if Corps allowed agency appeals of section 404 permit denials, applicants would have to pursue them to establish ripeness). *Cristina and Good* take their cue from the leading takings/ripeness decision, Williamson County Regional Planning Comm'n v. Hamilton Bank, 473 U.S. 172 (1985), in which the Supreme Court was at pains to distinguish between avenues for adjusting the scope of the land-use agency's initial decision, such as variances, and challenges to the validity of that decision, such as appeals to a higher administrative body. Unless futile, it said, the former must be pursued for finality ripeness; the latter need not.

On the other hand, the wetlands owner cannot plead futility "whenever faced with long odds or demanding procedural requirements"[46] — absent a more definitive indication from the government that the permit cannot be obtained. The permit application process must be pursued to the end even when several federal agencies have recommended to the Corps that the permit be denied, since the Corps in the past has not always followed such recommendations.[47] Similarly, the fact that section 404's presumptions against development that is not water-dependent reduce the probability of receiving a permit does not support a futility argument.[48]

Moreover, use of the futility exemption to excuse making the *initial* permit application, has been rejected by some courts;[49] it is generally applied to soften the requirement for later, scaled-down or reconfigured proposals.[50] To be sure, confining the futility exemption to reapplications runs counter to CFC cases holding that in some instances, the administrative process itself may be so burdensome as to deprive the property of value.[51] In the two wetlands/takings cases where this unduly-burdensome-process argument was pressed, however, it has been rejected.[52] One case held, unsurprisingly, that a permit applicant cannot claim futility based solely on unsupported allegations that analysis of the environmental impacts of development at alternative sites, required by section 404 regulations, would be overly burdensome.[53]

The Corps of Engineers reports that some section 404 permit applicants are now seeking "wall to wall" development of their wetlands parcels, and seem uninterested in negotiation with the Corps over compromise possibilities. For such applicants, the Corps has issued a permit for a portion of the proposed project even though the applicant has not sought it. This strategy may permit the Corps to avoid argument by the applicant-turned-plaintiff that scaled-down proposals would be futile, and to defend the case based on the more government-friendly ground of residual economic value.[54]

---

[46] Heck v. United States, 37 Fed. Cl. 245, 252 (1997), *aff'd*, 134 F.3d 1468 (Fed. Cir. 1998).

[47] *Id.*

[48] *Id.*

[49] *Heck*, 134 F.3d at 1472 (Fed. Cir. 1998), *citing* Southern Pac. Transp. Co. v. City of Los Angeles, 922 F.2d 498, 504 (9th Cir. 1990).

[50] *See, e.g.*, Marks v. United States, 34 Fed. Cl. 387 (1995), *aff'd without pub. op.*, 116 F.3d 1496 (Fed. Cir. 1997), *cert. denied*, 118 S. Ct. 852 (1998); Loveladies Harbor, Inc. v. United States, 21 Cl. Ct. 153, 157 (1990), *aff'd*, 28 F.3d 1171 (Fed. Cir. 1994); Formanek v. United States, 18 Cl. Ct. 785, 792-793 (1989); Orion Corp. v. State, 109 Wash. 2d 621, 747 P.2d 1062, 1068 (1987) (en banc), *cert. denied*, 486 U.S. 1022 (1988).

[51] *See, e.g.*, Hage v. United States, 35 Fed. Cl. 147, 164 (1996).

[52] Robbins v. United States, 40 Fed. Cl. 381, *aff'd without op.*, 178 F.3d 1310 (Fed. Cir. 1998), *cert. denied*, 119 S. Ct. 2400 (1999); Lakewood Assocs. v. United States, 45 Fed. Cl. 320 (1999).

[53] *Lakewood Assocs.*

[54] *See, e.g.*, Walcek v. United States, No. 94-315 L (Fed. Cl., filed May 13, 1994). Plaintiff
(continued...)

The usual insistence of ripeness doctrine on at least one agency decision might, one suspects, tempt an agency to attempt forestalling a ripe claim by simply refusing to deny the permit application. To circumvent this, ripeness may be found, lack of a permit denial notwithstanding, where the agency's position on the necessary mitigation conditions seems final and non-negotiable and plaintiff asserts that such conditions are overly restrictive.[55] Contrariwise, refusal to deny is perfectly acceptable, and does not confer ripeness, when the application lacks adequate information and the agency has yet to take a final position.[56]

Role of statutes

Statutes may affect the ripeness determination by adding procedures that must be utilized by the wetland owner before filing suit. In New Jersey, a "safety valve" provision in the state's wetlands statute was judicially interpreted to mean that the state and the land developer must confer whenever the state takes an initial position that would be a taking.[57] Because the process leading to permit denial was thus seen to be incomplete until the state decides whether its opening-shot restrictions might be relaxed, the taking claim was held not ripe until that reconsideration and subsequent denial.

But while statutes may add procedures, they may not always subtract them. The Massachusetts high court rejected use of a state statute to authorize the filing of takings suits based on individual land-use decisions regardless of whether they constitute final determinations.[58]

---

[54] (...continued)
applied for a section 404 permit for a subdivision occupying the full extent of a 14.5 acre property, including 13.2 acres of jurisdictional wetland. Later he offered to reduce the proposal to 8 acres, though this may have been simply a recognition that the state was unlikely to issue a permit for the 5 acres of tidal wetlands. The Corps ultimately issued a permit for 1.3 acres of the jurisdictional wetland, a "lesser included" element of one of the development scenarios then under discussion. The Corps is now seeking summary judgment on the parcel's remaining value, which it contends leaves the plaintiff with at least a quarter million dollar profit.

In *Walcek*, the unilateral permit offer was made during litigation. Reportedly the Corps is now making such offers purely as an administrative matter.

[55] *See, e.g.*, Taylor v. United States, No. 99-131L (Fed. Cl. Aug. 18, 1999) (where agency refused to process endangered species permit application or deny permit until plaintiff agreed to mitigation conditions it proposed, ripe taking claim exists).

[56] *See, e.g., Lakewood Assocs.*

[57] East Cape May Assoc. v. State of New Jersey, 300 N.J. Super. 325, 693 A.2d 114 (1997).

[58] Daddario v. Cape Cod Comm'n, 425 Mass. 411, 681 N.E.2d 833, *cert. denied*, 522 U.S. 1036 (1997). *Daddario* arose from an effort to mine sand and gravel, and apparently did not involve wetlands.

IV. Statutes of limitations

Ripeness (section III) dictates that takings claims not be filed too early. Statutes of limitations dictate they not be filed too late. Several wetlands/takings cases in the CFC, some noted in section III, have foundered on that court's statute of limitations.[59] Under it, takings cases must be filed within six years after the date of the taking.

The date of taking occurs, and the limitations period begins to run, when the taking claim becomes ripe.[60] Usually, this is the date when the wetlands permit is denied on the merits. This is particularly true in the CFC and Federal Circuit, which, as noted in section III, have yet to require a rebuffed section 404 permit applicant to submit subsequent, scaled-down proposals. Recall, however, the several exceptions noted in section III, where events other than permit denial defined the moment of ripeness.

Interestingly, the linkage between ripeness and when to start the limitations period creates two opposing classes of property owners. A ruling favorable to the plaintiff with a statute of limitations problem, picking a trigger date occurring *late* in his/her dealings with regulators, is a ruling that is unfavorable to future plaintiffs lacking statute of limitations problems, who want takings claims to ripen at an *early* stage of developments.

> *Note: sections V through VII show how the general takings tests in section I have been applied in the specific context of wetlands regulation. Some important cross-cutting issues are broken out for separate treatment in sections VIII through XI.*

V. Regulatory takings test: permission to fill denied

The landowner is in the clearest position to assert a taking claim when he/she has been formally denied a permit on the merits.

Cases involving state and local wetlands programs

Overview. As noted, final, reported state-court decisions in recent decades have been less likely to find takings based on wetlands regulations than their CFC and Federal Circuit counterparts. Perhaps the reason is that such state-court decisions more often speak of the public benefit (or public trust) in wetlands, generally finding it to outweigh even substantial detriments to the wetland owner. Then, too, many state courts insist outright that for a regulatory taking to be discerned, plaintiff must

---

[59] 28 U.S.C. § 2501.

[60] Bayou des Familles Devpmt. Corp. v. United States, 130 F.3d 1034 (Fed. Cir. 1997); Cristina Investment Corp. v. United States, 40 Fed. Cl. 571 (1998).

have lost *all or nearly all* economic use of the parcel[61] — seemingly rejecting, or narrowly confining, the *Penn Central* test for less-than-total takings.

Other reasons exist, too. For one, state appellate courts have accepted rather modest post-permit-denial uses of wetlands properties as sufficient to deflect the land owner's taking argument — e.g., seasonal placement of a trailer,[62] camping,[63] a single family home,[64] and agricultural/open space use.[65] (State trial courts have not always agreed, however.[66]) For another, state courts have not placed as much importance as the CFC and Federal Circuit on whether the plaintiff is able to recover its initial investment following permit denial.[67]

Harm/benefit. Interwoven with the prevailing state test is the classic distinction in regulatory takings law between government curtailment of property use to prevent harm, generally held not to be takings, and use constraints that secure public benefits, often held to be takings. Many state courts have long embraced this dichotomy to find wetlands preservation efforts noncompensable as a prevention of public harm.[68] For example, one court explained that the wetlands restriction before it was not to be thought of as securing a benefit by maintaining land in its natural state; rather, it prevented harm from the change in the natural character of the land that, given its location on a lake, would pollute water and degrade fishing and scenic beauty.[69]

---

[61] State wetlands cases requiring elimination of all or nearly all economic use in order to find a taking include Mock v. DER, 154 Pa. Commw. 380, 623 A.2d 940 (1993), *aff'd*, 542 Pa. 357, 667 A.2d 212 (1995), *cert. denied*, 517 U.S. 1216 (1996); Vatalaro v. DER, 601 So. 2d 1223 (Fla. Ct. App. 1992); Wedinger v. Goldberger, 71 N.Y.2d 488, 522 N.E.2d 25 (1988); State v. Capuano Bros., Inc., 120 R.I. 58, 384 A.2d 610 (1978); Brecciaroli v. Comm'r of Envtl. Protection, 168 Conn. 349, 362 A.2d 948 (1975).

[62] Hall v. Board of Envtl. Prot., 528 A.2d 453 (Me. 1987).

[63] Claridge v. New Hampshire Wetlands Bd., 125 N.H. 745, 485 A.2d 287 (1984).

[64] Moskow v. Comm'r, 384 Mass. 530, 427 N.E.2d 750 (1981).

[65] April v. City of Broken Arrow, 775 P.2d 1347 (Okla. 1989).

[66] *See, e.g.*, East Cape May Assoc. v. State of New Jersey, 300 N.J. Super. 325, 693 A.2d 114 (1997) ("minimal uses" insufficient to undermine taking claim, citing *Lucas*).

[67] *See, e.g.*, Alegria v. Keeney, 687 A.2d 1249, 1253 (R.I. 1997).

[68] *See, e.g.*, Tahoe Sierra Preservation Council, Inc. v. Tahoe Regional Planning Agency, 638 F. Supp. 126, 135 (D. Nev. 1986), *aff'd in part, rev'd in part on other grounds*, 911 F.2d 1331 (9th Cir. 1990), *cert. denied*, 499 U.S. 943 (1991); Graham v. Estuary Properties, 399 So. 2d 1374 (Fla.) (conceding that harm/benefit dichotomy unclear), *cert. denied*, 454 U.S. 1083 (1981); Moskow v. Comm'r, 384 Mass. 530, 427 N.E.2d 753 (1981); Sibson v. State, 115 N.H. 124, 336 A.2d 239 (1975); Just v. Marinette Cty., 56 Wis. 2d 7, 201 N.W.2d 761 (1972).

[69] *Just*, 201 N.W.2d at 768.

The harm/benefit distinction was undercut in 1992 by the Supreme Court's rejection of it as manipulable and value-laden.[70] Many government actions, said the Court, can plausibly be characterized as *either* harm preventer or benefit securer, citing wetlands protection as an example.

"Background principles". If a proposed property use is prohibitable under "background principles of the state's law of nuisance or property" existing when the property was acquired, it cannot under *Lucas* be a taking. The scope of the "background principles" concept, however, has been debated since its introduction. The *Lucas* majority opinion, in discussing the concept, focusses on common-law nuisance doctrine and pre-existing easements.[71] The concurring and dissenting opinions in the case read the majority opinion as precluding outright the inclusion of pre-existing *statutes* as background principles. Subsequently, however, considerable case law has endorsed statute eligibility (see section IX). Bringing state statutes in as background principles is a crucial development, since it allows states and localities to defend taking actions on the ground that the wetland was acquired after the state wetlands statute was enacted — regardless of whether the proposed wetland use constitutes a nuisance.

A recent Rhode Island decision may be the first instance of a wetlands fill proposal being held a nuisance in a *Lucas*-based taking analysis.[72] Based on its nuisance status, the court held, the state's thwarting of the proposal could not under *Lucas* be a taking, even if it eliminated all economic use of the property.

Public trust doctrine. Under this amorphous, much-debated concept, there *is* no right to use property impressed with the trust in a manner that impairs trust interests, however one defines them. Plainly, viewing the waters of a state as natural resources infused with a public trust serves to bolster wetlands regulation against takings challenges.[73]

One variant of the public trust doctrine is in *Just v. Marinette County*: "[a]n owner of land has no absolute and unlimited right to change the essential natural character of his land so as to use it for a purpose for which it was unsuited in its natural state and which injures the rights of others."[74] Relying on this principle, the court found no taking in a county requirement that a permit be secured to fill in wetlands along a pristine lake, where such fill might harm water quality and recreational values. At the same time, the court explained that it would not find the requisite harm to the rights of others in *all* instances of wetlands destruction, as in the

---

[70] Lucas v. South Carolina Coastal Council, 505 U.S. 1003, 1024-1026 (1992).

[71] 505 U.S. at 1028-1029.

[72] Palazzolo v. Coastal Resources Mgmt. Council, No. 88-0297 (R.I. Super. Ct. Oct. 24, 1997) (unpublished).

[73] *See, e.g.*, Orion Corp v. State, 109 Wash. 2d 621, 747 P.2d 1062 (1987) (en banc), *cert. denied*, 486 U.S. 1022 (1988).

[74] 201 N.W.2d at 768.

case of an "isolated swamp unrelated to a navigable lake or stream."[75] The *Just* rule is the pinnacle of judicial protection of wetlands, and has been adopted in a handful of states.[76]

A tantalizing question is whether the public trust doctrine in any of its incarnations will be accepted by courts as the kind of "background principle of property ... law" referred to in *Lucas*. At least in those states in which the doctrine is well-established, it would seem to qualify.[77]

Cases involving the federal wetlands program

Overview. In the CFC/Federal Circuit, two elements of the *Penn Central* test, economic impact and interference with investment-backed expectations, have eclipsed the third, the "character" of the government action. The character factor, where it is mentioned at all,[78] appears to function mainly as a buttress to takings determinations reached on the basis of the other two factors.[79]

---

[75] *Id.* at 769.

[76] Rowe v. Town of North Hampton, 553 A.2d 1331, 1335 (N.H. 1989); Graham v. Estuary Properties, Inc., 399 So. 2d 1374, 1382 (Fla.), *cert. denied*, 454 U.S. 1083 (1981); American Dredging Co. v. DEP, 391 A.2d 1265, 1271 (N.J. Super. Ct. Ch. Div. 1978), *aff'd*, 404 A.2d 42 (N.J. Super. Ct. App. Div. 1979). *Just* has also been reaffirmed recently in its state of origin. Zealy v. City of Waukesha, 201 Wis. 2d 365, 548 N.W.2d 528 (1996) (clarifying that *Just* rule goes beyond geographic limits of traditional public trust doctrine).

[77] Agreeing with the text proposition are Hope M. Babcock, The Impact of Lucas v. South Carolina Coastal Council on *Wetlands and Coastal Barrier Beaches*, 19 Harv. Envtl. L. Rev. 1 (1995), and Paul Sarahan, *Wetlands Protection Post-Lucas: Implications of the Public Trust Doctrine on Takings Analysis*, 13 Va. Envtl. L.J. 537 (1994). Mr. Sarahan argues that owing to interrelated hydrology, the doctrine may even be applicable to wetlands adjacent to public trust waters. He suggests that when imposing development restrictions on wetlands, states develop data as to the probable impact of the proposed development on those waters.

A pre-Lucas view of the public trust concept is Mary K. McCurdy, *Public Trust Protection for Wetlands*, 19 Envtl. L. 683 (1989).

[78] The Federal Circuit recently admonished the CFC (in a wetlands case) to address all *three* of the *Penn Central* factors when deciding a regulatory taking case, including the character of the government action. Broadwater Farms Joint Venture v. United States, 121 F.3d 727 (Fed. Cir. 1997) (unpublished). The CFC had looked at only the economic impact of the government action.

It remains to be seen whether the Circuit's directive will result in more than perfunctory consideration of the character factor. On remand, the CFC noted with understatement that "[c]ourts do not always examine the character of the Government action in a partial takings analysis." 45 Fed. Cl. 154 (1999). And in Good v. United States, 189 F.3d 1355 (Fed. Cir. 1999), *petition for cert. filed*, the Federal Circuit itself said that where there is a complete absence of reasonable development expectations, no other *Penn Central* factors need be scrutinized.

[79] To some extent, this uncertain role for the character factor results from the Supreme Court's failure to give it much content beyond saying that it refers to the fact that takings are more likely to result from physical invasions than from purely regulatory interference. Adding

(continued...)

Economic impact. While state courts generally translate the economic impact factor of the regulatory takings test into an examination of the property's remaining economic *uses,* the CFC and Federal Circuit focus heavily on the property's remaining economic *value.* These latter courts typically do detailed analyses of the parcel's fair market value before and after the permit denial.[80] Typically, the CFC will figure the value diminution as a percentage, and then, if it is great enough, look for other circumstances (almost always found) supporting a taking.

Until 1994, the value diminutions in section 404 permit denial cases held great enough to constitute a taking ranged upwards of 88%.[81]   In that year, a Federal Circuit ruling in *Florida Rock* asked, in discussing the concept of a "partial regulatory taking," whether a value diminution of only 62% might be sufficient to take.[82] On remand, this query bore fruit when the CFC found a partial regulatory taking based on a 73.1% value loss.[83] Though the courts have never explicitly established any particular percentage of value loss as necessary to establish a taking, these developments in *Florida Rock* suggest an easing of the quantum of economic impact

---

[79] (...continued)
to the confusion, some Federal Circuit decisions have defined "character" to mean that if the regulation prevents a nuisance, no taking occurred. *See, e.g.,* Creppel v. United States, 41 F.3d 627, 631 (Fed. Cir. 1994). This seems highly redundant, since the nuisance status of the proscribed landowner activity is already part of the takings analysis through the "background principles" and "reasonable investment-backed expectations" concepts.

[80] *Florida Rock,* 18 F.3d at 1567. The most frequently used method of ascertaining fair market value is through comparable sales, where they exist.

[81] Loveladies Harbor, Inc. v. United States, 28 F.3d 1171 (Fed. Cir. 1994) (99% value loss); Florida Rock Industries, Inc. v. United States, 21 Cl. Ct. 161 (1990), *vacated and remanded,* 18 F.3d 1560 (Fed. Cir. 1994) (holding that trial court used improperly low "after value," but not disputing that such value warranted finding a taking), *cert. denied,* 513 U.S. 1109 (1995) (95% value loss); Bowles v. United States, 31 Fed. Cl. 37 (1994) (finding 100% value loss, but holding that even if government estimate of 92% value loss was correct, there was a taking); Formanek v. United States, 26 Cl. Ct. 332 (1992) (88% value loss). *See also* 1902 Atlantic Limited v. United States, 26 Cl. Ct. 575, 579 (1992) (88% value loss from permit denial satisfies economic impact factor in *Penn Central* test, though no taking found).

[82] 18 F.3d at 1567. The underlying issue is what function the Supreme Court-invented concept of regulatory takings should serve. If regulatory takings doctrine only seeks to compensate when the regulatory restriction is so total as to be the functional equivalent of a physical ouster of the land owner, as some decisions suggest, diminutions in value much below 100% should not be compensated. If a broader view of the doctrine is contemplated, compensation for regulatory losses well short of 100% may be perfectly proper.

[83] 45 Fed. Cl. 21 (1999).

needed to support a regulatory taking.[84]   Moreover, if the CFC ruling becomes final, it will establish a clear difference between federal and state takings jurisprudence.

At the opposite end of the value-loss spectrum, losing the use of only 15% of one's land while still able to turn a profit on the entire parcel is plainly not a taking,[85] nor is a 25% loss in value where the remaining value far exceeds plaintiff's cost basis.[86]   Given the general canon that takings law requires severe impact on the property owner, these no-taking holdings at the low end of the value-loss spectrum are unsurprising. The battle right now is for the high middle ground of value loss.

Other ingredients of the economic-impact stew tend, as mentioned, to be secondary to the value-loss calculation. One, as just noted, is whether a wetland owner, following permit denial, can recoup his/her cost basis in the parcel.[87] For example, the CFC rejected a taking attack on a 404-permit denial in part because plaintiffs had previously sold the upland portion of the parcel for more than twice the original cost of the parcel as a whole (deemed to include the upland portion).[88]

A second economic-impact factor is "average reciprocity of advantage" — an inquiry into whether the burdens imposed on the property owner by the challenged regulatory regime have been offset by benefits accruing to the owner from the very same regime. In finding a taking, the CFC in *Florida Rock* found that plaintiff's "disproportionately heavy burden was not offset by any reciprocity of advantage."[89] There is some ambiguity in Federal Circuit opinions as to just how completely the burdens on the landowner have to be offset by such benefits.[90]

---

[84] Partial regulatory takings also raise issues of remedy. Previous wetlands/takings cases in the CFC, based as they were on near-total value losses, were compensated by requiring the United States to buy fee simple title. With 26.9% of its value remaining, however, the CFC in *Florida Rock* could not require the United States to buy the acreage outright — the government cannot be required to buy what it has not taken. Thus, the CFC required the United States to pay for only the right to use the property, not the right to sell to speculators that accounted for the remaining value. 45 Fed. Cl. at 43.

Of course, the United States has acquired less-than-fee interests in the past as part of *settlements* in its wetlands/takings litigation.

[85] Forest Properties, Inc. v. United States, 177 F.3d 1360 (Fed. Cir.), *cert. denied*, 120 S. Ct. 373 (1999).

[86] Ciampitti v. United States, 22 Cl.Ct. 310, 320 n.5 (1991).

[87] The canonical statement of this factor is in Florida Rock Industries, Inc. v. United States, 791 F.2d 893, 905 (Fed. Cir. 1986), *cert. denied*, 479 U.S. 1053 (1987): "In determining the severity of economic impact, the owner's opportunity to recoup its investment or better, subject to the regulation, cannot be ignored." *Accord*, Ciampitti v. United States, 22 Cl. Ct. 310, 320 n.5 (1991), Walcek v. United States, 44 Fed. Cl. 462, 466 n.5 (1999).

[88] Palm Beach Isles Assocs. v. United States, 42 Fed. Cl. 340, 364 (1998), *appeal pending*. Cost basis is not limited to the original purchase price, but may include other capital expenditures on the property. Walcek, 44 Fed. Cl. at 466 n.5.

[89] *Florida Rock*, 45 Fed. Cl. 21, 37 (1999).

[90] The second Federal Circuit opinion in *Florida Rock* can be read to mean that the

(continued...)

A third factor is the availability of transferrable development rights (TDRs) that may soften the economic impact of permit denial. TDRs are a widely used land use planning mechanism that seeks to direct development away from environmentally sensitive areas such as wetlands and toward land more suitable for development. TDRs do this by granting the owner of restricted property the right to build on another property he/she owns at a density greater than otherwise allowed, or to sell such development rights to other property owners. Thus, the availability of TDRs to a wetland owner may confer value on a development-prohibited wetland that otherwise would have little. Whether such TDR-conferred value may be used to deflect a taking claim (rather than being confined to the calculation of compensation, where a taking occurs) is a lively issue in takings law today. A majority of the current Supreme Court appears disposed to answer the question in the affirmative.[91] And a recent wetlands case so held.[92]

As in land valuation generally, where the government seeks to support its valuation of a permit-denied wetland by alleging remaining uses, they must meet a "showing of reasonable probability that the land is both physically adaptable for such use *and* that there is a demand for such use in the reasonably near future."[93] In similar fashion, plaintiff cannot base pre-permit-denial value on projects that fail this test.[94]

Investment-backed expectations. This *Penn Central* factor has come to be the vehicle in the Federal Circuit for defeating wetlands takings claims when the plaintiff acquired the wetland after the section 404 program was put into place (or some related date). A fuller treatment of this "notice rule" is in section IX.

When the land was acquired *before* there was a 404 program (or related date), interference with investment-backed expectations may or may not cut in favor of

---

[90] (...continued)

landowner's burden must be *fully* offset — a powerful principle for landowners, if followed. See 18 F.3d at 1570.

[91] *See* Suitum v. Tahoe Regional Planning Agency, 520 U.S. 725 (1997). The underlying issue, widely debated since *Lucas* in 1992, is whether the regulatory taking determination hinges on a property's remaining *use* — in the sense of immediate development potential — or remaining value. If remaining use (as defined), TDRs are plainly not part of the takings analysis, and the Court's explicit endorsement of TDRs in *Penn Central* as part of that analysis, 438 U.S. at 137, is no longer good law. If remaining value, the endorsement of *Penn Central* still stands. Significantly, the majority's rationale in *Suitum*, a post-*Lucas* decision, presumes the relevance of TDRs to the takings analysis.

[92] Good v. United States, 39 Fed. Cl. 81, 108 (Fed. Cl. 1997), *aff'd*, 189 F.3d 1355 (Fed. Cir. 1999), *pet. for cert. filed. Good* rejects the argument that *Suitum* somehow undercuts the relevance of TDRs to the takings determination. An early wetlands decision supporting use of TDRs in takings analysis is Deltona v. United States, 657 F.2d 1184, 1192 n.14 (1981), *cert. denied*, 455 U.S. 1017 (1982).

[93] *Loveladies Harbor*, 21 Cl. Ct. 153, 158 (1990) (emphasis in original), *aff'd*, 28 F.3d 1171 (Fed. Cir. 1994).

[94] *Palm Beach Isles*, 42 Fed. Cl. at 364.

finding a taking. The CFC in *Florida Rock* recently explicated this circumstance.[95] Such interference points more strongly towards a taking, it said, when the plaintiff's "primary" expectations for the site were thwarted. (Plaintiff bought the wetland solely to mine the underlying limestone; that objective was entirely thwarted.) Also significant is how much of the parcel has been burdened by the regulation. (The limestone underlay the entire parcel.) And finally, the investment-backed expectations factor may include a look at plaintiff's ability to earn a reasonable return on his/her investment — similar to the recoupment of cost basis noted above under economic impact.

Elsewhere, the CFC has noted that state and local restrictions must be considered in determining the presence or absence of reasonable investment-backed expectations to engage in the proscribed use.

"Background principles". Usually, the CFC/Federal Circuit take a narrow view of the *Lucas* "background principles" concept. Most of their decisions addressing the issue accept as a source of background principles only the state's common law of nuisance,[96] or the state's common law of nuisance and property, or the latter plus state statutes rooted in the state's common law of nuisance and property.[97] Generally, federal statutes have been excluded from "background principles"[98] — though, importantly, they are very much a part of the subsequent *Penn Central* analysis of investment-backed expectations (see section IX).

In the same vein, and unlike some state courts, the CFC/Federal Circuit have shown no disposition to embrace anything resembling a public trust doctrine.[99] Nor has the CFC/Federal Circuit ever accepted the United States' argument that the proposed wetlands fill would constitute a nuisance.[100]

A big exception to the CFC/Federal Circuit's usual emphasis on state law as the source of background principles is their post-*Lucas* endorsement of the federal navigation servitude as an absolute defense to takings, where the wetlands are within

---

[95] 45 Fed. Cl. 21.

[96] The chief affirmation of the state-common-law-of-nuisance view is in the plurality opinion in Preseault v. United States, 100 F.3d 1525, 1538 (Fed. Cir. 1996) (en banc), a rails-to-trails case. Wetlands cases endorsing the view are *Loveladies Harbor*, 28 F.3d at 1179, and Bayou des Familles Devpmt. Corp. v. United States, 130 F.3d 1034, 1038 (Fed. Cir. 1997). All three opinions are by Judge Jay Plager.

[97] *Good*, 39 Fed. Cl. at 105.

[98] *Contra*, M&J Coal Co. v. United States, 47 F.3d 1148, 1153 (Fed. Cir.) (background principles "may also stem from federal law"), *cert. denied*, 516 U.S. 808 (1995).

[99] *See, e.g., Loveladies Harbor*, 15 Cl. Ct. 381, 395 (1988).

[100] *See, e.g.,* Florida Rock Industries, Inc. v. United States, 45 Fed. Cl. 21 (1999); Forest Properties, Inc. v. United States, 39 Fed. Cl. 56, 70-71 (1997), *aff'd*, 177 F.3d 1360 (Fed. Cir.), *cert. denied*, 120 S. Ct. 373 (1999).

the servitude's shoreward reach.[101] The servitude, noted the CFC in language intended to invoke *Lucas*, "inheres in a private landowner's title."[102] To be sure, *Lucas* virtually dictates this conclusion, its emphasis on state law notwithstanding. In that decision, the Court stated that no compensation is owed when government merely "assert[s] a permanent easement that was a pre-existing limitation on the landowner's title," citing as illustrative one of the Court's federal navigation servitude decisions.[103]

Harm/benefit. Both before and after *Lucas*' rejection of this dichotomy, the CFC and Federal Circuit have viewed wetlands preservation as the creation of a benefit, rather than (as in many state courts) the prevention of a harm.[104] To reiterate, a benefit-creation characterization of wetlands preservation disposes a court to find a taking.

Cancelled land-purchase contract. The preceding addresses only claims that *land* was taken. What happens when a land owner suffers cancellation of a contract to buy his/her property, or the loss of a prospective contract, when the buyer learns that the parcel contains jurisdictional wetland? Is there a taking of the contract itself? In *Robbins v. United States*, such a claim was rejected.[105] "It is well settled," said the CFC, "that government action that merely frustrates expectations under a contract does not constitute a taking."[106] The court also noted that it was the contract parties, not the Corps, that caused the contract to be cancelled.

---

[101] For example, in both Marks v. United States, 34 Fed. Cl. 387 (1995), *aff'd without op.*, 116 F.3d 1496 (Fed. Cir. 1997), *cert. denied*, 118 S. Ct. 852 (1998), and Palm Beach Isles Assocs. v. United States, 42 Fed. Cl. 340 (1998), *appeal pending*, the CFC readily rejected on navigation servitude grounds the portion of a wetlands taking claim based on lands below the high water mark. *See also Good*, 39 Fed. Cl. at 96-97 (affirming *Marks* but holding that United States failed to show that all limitations on plaintiff's property overlapped servitude). At the Federal Circuit level, the status of the navigation servitude as a defense to takings is asserted in a non-wetlands decision: M & J Coal Co. v. United States, 47 F.3d 1148, 1153 (Fed. Cir. 1995).

[102] *Palm Beach Isles*, 42 Fed. Cl. at 351.

[103] 505 U.S. 1003, 1028-1029 (1992), citing Scranton v. Wheeler, 179 U.S. 14 (1900). *See also* United States v. 30.54 Acres of Land, 90 F.3d 790, 795 (3d Cir. 1996).

 Lucas, together with the navigation servitude decisions in note 101 *supra*, suggest that the Federal Circuit's 1986 rejection of the navigation servitude as a defense to regulatory takings claims is no longer good law. Florida Rock Industries, Inc. v. United States, 791 F.2d 893, 900 (Fed. Cir. 1986), *cert. denied*, 479 U.S. 1053 (1987). Running against the tide, however, is the CFC's 1999 ruling in *Florida Rock*, which spoke approvingly of this Federal Circuit assertion. 45 Fed. Cl. at 28 n.7.

[104] *Florida Rock*, 791 F.2d at 904 (Fed. Cir. 1986), 45 Fed. Cl. 21 (1999).

[105] 40 Fed. Cl. 381, *aff'd without op.*, 178 F.3d 1310 (Fed. Cir. 1998), *cert. denied*, 119 S. Ct. 2400 (1999).

[106] 40 Fed. Cl. at 385.

Cumulative impacts

It may happen that the loss of some wetland acreage in a particular area is seen by government regulators as ecologically acceptable, but that further losses are not. Thus, the first few persons seeking to fill in pieces of an extensive wetland may be granted permits, while the person who comes along next is denied.

Takings law does not accommodate this situation well. The takings cases repeatedly refer with disapproval to government actions that "single out" a property owner for different treatment than those similarly situated.[107] Thus, while the Corps of Engineers must, as part of its review of permit applications, consider cumulative impacts, its doing so may lead to denials that are hard to defend from a takings standpoint.

VI. Regulatory takings test: mitigation conditions

Though the large majority of wetlands/takings cases address outright permit denials (section V), such denials are actually quite infrequent in the federal and most state wetlands programs.[108] Far more often, the government wetlands agency offers to grant the permit — with conditions. Often, these conditions require the permit applicant to "mitigate" the environmental impacts of the proposed project, possibly at considerable expense. It behooves us, therefore, to examine the takings implications of these conditions.

In the section 404 program, mitigation generally means first, seeking to avoid to the extent practicable the adverse impact of the proposed development; second, minimizing to the extent practicable those impacts that cannot be avoided; and third, requiring compensatory mitigation for remaining impacts.[109] This is called "mitigation sequencing," and is an important component of state programs as well. Compensatory mitigation may take the form of restoration of existing degraded wetlands, creation of man-made wetlands, or use of an approved mitigation bank. Importantly, mitigation conditions may attach to activities under both individual and nationwide permits. Mitigation serves the national commitment to no net loss of wetlands while allowing reasonable development to occur.

But *how much* compensatory mitigation to require? While many section 404 permits require compensatory mitigation at a ratio of only 1:1 (one acre of restored or created wetland for each acre filled), or at most 2:1, occasional reports of much higher ratios exist. Perhaps unavoidably given the diversity of aquatic resource functions and values, the EPA-Corps Memorandum of Agreement provides little in

---

[107] *See, e.g.*, Nollan v. California Coastal Comm'n, 483 U.S. 825, 835 n.4 (1987); *Florida Rock*, 45 Fed. Cl. at 37.

[108] *See note 29 supra.*

[109] Memorandum of Agreement Between the Environmental Protection Agency and the Department of the Army Concerning the Determination of Mitigation Under the Clean Water Act Section 404(b)(1) Guidelines, 55 Fed. Reg. 9210 (Mar. 12, 1990).

the way of concrete guidance. The memorandum notes only that the amount of compensatory mitigation demanded of the landowner be "appropriate to the scope and degree of [the unavoidable impacts] and practicable in terms of cost, existing technology, and logistics ...." The compensatory ratio "may be greater [than 1:1] where the functional values of the area being impacted are demonstrable higher and the replacement wetlands are of lower functional value or the likelihood of success of the mitigation project is low." This guidance leaves Corps district engineers with much discretion.

Given their ubiquity, it is curious that mitigation conditions on wetlands permits have kept such a low profile in the takings cases. Perhaps the dearth of case law reflects the fact that mitigation conditions often are arrived at after protracted negotiations between applicant and agency, so that the applicant, having had a hand in the result, is likely to perceive it as reasonable. Then, too, developers generally would rather build than litigate.

Research reveals but one federal wetlands decision (reported) in which mitigation conditions figured significantly. In *Plantation Landing Resort, Inc. v. United States*, the court said it could not view a Corps permit denial as a taking when the denial was the result of plaintiff's having cut off negotiations with the Corps over mitigation requirements — especially where the Corps had provided several mitigation alternatives.[110] Thus, a certain amount of good faith negotiations over mitigation appears to be essential before filing a taking claim; a "my way or else" attitude is disfavored.[111] It would seem, however, that once an agency's minimum conditions become clear, a taking claim alleging that the project with those conditions is not economically viable should be possible. Indeed, a recent Endangered Species Act case holds that the landowner may ripen a taking claim without the one permit denial usually required (see section IV) if the mitigation conditions demanded up front by the government are prohibitive.[112]

Once the government's final, absolute-minimum conditions are reached, the takings test is presumably the same as for permit denials — that is, either *Lucas* or *Penn Central*. In some cases, however, the heightened scrutiny applied by the Supreme Court to exaction conditions on development permits might be appropriate. Heightened scrutiny demands that such a condition further the same objective as the permit to which it is attached ("nexus" requirement) and that the burden imposed on the applicant by the permit condition be "roughly proportional" to the impact of the proposed development on the community.[113] Though the Supreme Court recently

---

[110] 30 Fed. Cl. 63 (1993), *aff'd without pub. op.*, 39 F.3d 1197 (Fed. Cir. 1994), *cert. denied*, 514 U.S. 1095 (1995).

[111] Two cases from the wildlife protection area that make this point are Southview Assocs. v. Bongartz, 980 F.2d 84 (2d Cir. 1992) (taking claim unripe where state, in denying permit, indicated that reapplication with appropriate mitigation would be accepted, but landowner failed to reapply); Killington, Ltd. v. State, 668 A.2d 1278, 1282-1283 (Vt. 1995) (similar).

[112] Taylor v. United States, No. 99-131L (Aug. 18, 1999).

[113] *See* Nollan v. California Coastal Comm'n, 483 U.S. 825 (1987) (announcing "nexus"
(continued...)

gave the rough proportionality standard a narrow scope,[114] at least some conditions on section 404 permits arguably remain subject to it.[115]   CFC/Federal Circuit decisions have not yet explored this issue.   In any event, rough-proportionality challenges to Corps permit conditions should be rare if the Corps is complying with the EPA-Corps Memorandum of Agreement statement that compensatory mitigation should be "appropriate to the scope and degree" of the project's unavoidable impacts.[116]

Takings issues also have been raised in connection with mitigation banking. As with the transferrable development rights long used by local land-use agencies, the hope of mitigation banking proponents is that by imparting value to unusable wetlands, mitigation banking or credits trading may deflect takings claims.[117]

VII. Regulatory takings test: project delays

Two types of temporary takings actions have been brought based on delays in developing wetlands caused by the actions or inaction of wetlands agencies. Almost all the cases involve the federal section-404 program.

Processing delays

Courts have grappled with the sometimes lengthy processing time before a wetlands permit is issued, holding that the key factor in the temporary taking analysis is whether the wait was, under the circumstances, unreasonable or "extraordinary."[118]

---

[113] (...continued)
criterion); Dolan v. City of Tigard, 512 U.S. 374 (1994) (announcing "rough proportionality" criterion).

[114] City of Monterey v. Del Monte Dunes, Inc., 119 S. Ct. 1624, 1635 (1999).

[115] Under the 404 program, easements are usually recorded on mitigation property to permanently dedicate the property to mitigation. In *City of Monterey*, the Court left the rough proportionality test applicable to "exactions — land use decisions conditioning approval of development on the dedication of property for public use." *Id.*   Some have argued that *City of Monterey* leaves the rough proportionality test applicable as well to purely monetary exactions. Dollar exactions reportedly are not used by the Corps, except that the agency will accept payments to mitigation providers in lieu of mitigation performed by the wetland owner itself.

[116] *See* text following note 109 *supra*.

[117] *See generally* William J. Haynes II and Royal C. Gardner, *The Value of Wetlands as Wetlands: The Case for Mitigation Banking*, 23 Envtl. L. Rptr. 10261, 10262 (1993); Jeffrey Zinn, *Wetlands Mitigation Banking: Status and Prospects*, CRS Report 97-849 ENR. Mitigation banking thus raises the same issue posed by transferrable development rights: whether the taking determination depends on residual use or residual value. See note 91 *supra*.

[118] *See, e.g.*, Walcek v. United States, 44 Fed. Cl. 462, 467 (1999); 1902 Atlantic Ltd. v. United States, 26 Cl. Ct. 575, 581 (1992). *See also* Norman v. United States, 38 Fed. Cl.
(continued...)

Was it unduly protracted in light of the complexity of the regulatory scheme? Did the owner fail to take actions that might have shortened the processing time? To date, federal courts have held that waiting periods for section 404 permits up to two years did not, under the circumstances presented, work a taking.[119]

Teasing apart the delay attributable to the agency from that caused by the plaintiff can be pivotal to the case. In *Walcek v. United States*, all but one year of an eight-year span between first permit application and issuance of a limited permit was laid at the feet of the wetland owners.[120] Their applications, said the court, had lacked the requisite information and state permits, and they had opted for litigation over completing the application or submitting a scaled-down proposal. The one year of government-caused delay, it held, is not the sort of "extraordinary" delay that makes out a temporary taking, particularly where no bad faith or negligence is shown.

Agency error

Another delay scenario is when an agency's assertion of jurisdiction over a wetland, or its denial of a permit, is judicially set aside. In *Tabb Lakes, Inc. v. United States*,[121] the Corps of Engineers issued a cease-and-desist order requiring a developer to stop work until it obtained a section 404 permit, only to be judicially informed three years later that its claim of jurisdiction over the property was procedurally defective. The three-year delay caused no taking, said the Federal Circuit. The cease-and-desist order had specifically left the door open to development by obtaining a permit. Invoking a powerful principle for government planners, the court further cited the Supreme Court's assertion that "mere fluctuations in value during ... government decisionmaking, absent extraordinary delay, ... cannot be considered a taking."[122]

The result was the same where the takings challenge was to a judicially invalidated wetlands permit denial.[123]

---

[118] (...continued)
417, 427 (1997) (collecting cases).

[119] *1902 Atlantic*, 26 Cl. Ct. at 579 (15 months); Dufau v. United States, 22 Cl. Ct. 156 (1990) (16 months); Lachney v. United States, 22 Env't Rptr. (Cases) 2031 (Fed. Cir. 1985) (2 years).

[120] 44 Fed. Cl. at 468.

[121] 10 F.3d 796 (Fed. Cir. 1993).

[122] *Id.* at 801 (quoting Agin v. City of Tiburon, 447 U.S. 255, 263 n.9 (1980)). Similar to *Tabb Lakes* is Littoral Development Co. v. San Francisco Bay Conservation and Devpmt. Comm'n, 33 Cal. App. 4th 211, 39 Cal. Rptr. 2d 266 (1995). As in *Tabb Lakes*, the government agency's assertion of wetlands jurisdiction was invalidated. The resultant delay was held not a taking because the government's legal arguments, though erroneous, had been plausible, and because use of the property continued during the dispute.
Whether government errors should be considered a normal, to be expected, part of land use regulation processes, and hence not a taking, is in contention now in the state courts.

[123] *1902 Atlantic*, 26 Cl. Ct. 575.

The CFC and Federal Circuit consistently have held that "unauthorized" government actions cannot form the basis of takings actions against the United States.[124] The Federal Circuit recently clarified this rule, stating that not all erroneous federal actions are "unauthorized" — only those that are *ultra vires*, that is, either explicitly prohibited or outside the normal scope of the agency official's duties.[125] It is likely, then, that a permit action by the Corps of Engineers asserted to be unlawful merely because of a reasonable misinterpretation of section 404 could simultaneously be the subject of a taking action in the CFC.

Takings actions against state wetlands programs are much less likely to get embroiled in the question of whether the government action is *ultra vires*. Typically, the *ultra vires* or otherwise erroneous status of a government act is seen by state courts as irrelevant to whether a taking occurred.

Economic return

A source of confusion is whether a project's economic return *during* the restricted period should play a role in a taking analysis. The better view is that when a restriction is plainly temporary at the time imposed, the absence of any economic use during the period of restriction (reasonably limited) is not material. One reason is that Supreme Court takings cases rejecting the physical segmentation of property in takings analysis can be read to disfavor as well a narrow focus on the restricted segment of time.[126] Another reason is that the strong likelihood of future economic use when the restriction is lifted, supports present economic value.[127] Where, on the other hand, the development restriction is of presumptively indefinite duration, such as a permit denial on the merits, the property may be left with no development potential to sustain present market value, and a taking may indeed occur.

CFC and Federal Circuit decisions indicate no awareness of this distinction. The *Tabb Lakes* trial court, in addressing a temporary taking challenge to a Corps cease and desist order, homed in on the existence of lot sales during the development prohibition, and noted that plaintiff's tax returns during that period showed profitability.[128] Yet it was clear at the outset that the Corps order would terminate upon the occurrence of likely future events. And in another wetlands case, the CFC stated without qualification that in evaluating temporary takings claims, courts look at whether the delay was extraordinary *and* "whether the government's actions have

---

[124] The rationale is that such conduct by an official "will not ... represent the United States, and ... cannot create a claim against the Government." Hooe v. United States, 218 U.S. 322, 335 (1910).

[125] Del Rio Drilling Programs, Inc. v. United States, 146 F.3d 1358 (Fed. Cir. 1998).

[126] *See, e.g.*, Woodbury Place Partners v. City of Woodbury, 492 N.W.2d 258 (1992), *cert. denied*, 508 U.S. 960 (1993). See section VIII (Parcel as a whole).

[127] This raises yet again the question of whether the takings determination should key off a property's residual value or residual use, an issue noted earlier in connection with transferrable development rights and mitigation banking.

[128] 26 Cl. Ct. 1334 (1992). *aff'd*, 10 F.3d 796 (Fed. Cir. 1993).

temporarily deprived the property owner of all or substantially all economically viable use of their [sic] property."[129]

Should a taking be found based on permit denial, an eventual reversal of the denial decision does not undo the taking, but only defines the termination date for the period of the temporary regulatory taking.

VIII. Parcel as a whole

As noted, the frequently invoked *Penn Central* test for regulatory takings requires a court to consider, among other things, the extent to which the government action caused the property owner (a) loss of the property's economic value or use, and (b) frustration of his/her reasonable investment-backed expectations for the property. Both these factors are assessed in a relative, rather than absolute, sense. For example, a $1 million drop in land value due to a wetlands permit denial points much more strongly to a taking if that loss deprives the owner of substantially all the property's value, rather than only a modest fraction thereof. For this reason, it becomes critical for a court to define with care the precise physical extent of the property it will look at — in the lingo of takings law, the "parcel as a whole" or "relevant parcel."

The parcel as a whole conundrum is pervasive in the wetlands takings cases. Quite often, for example, a tract consists of both restricted wetlands and unrestricted, still developable uplands. Or the permit is denied for some, but not all, of the wetland on the parcel. The relevant parcel issue requires a court to ask whether the developable portion should be counted in the taking analysis.

The relevant parcel determination is often a make-or-break one — the litigant that prevails on this issue likely will win on the taking claim. The "total taking" rule of *Lucas* — elimination of all economic use of a parcel is a *per se* taking, if no "background principles" apply — buttresses this point. Deeming the wetland portion alone to be the relevant parcel increases the chances that the court will find elimination of all economic use, hence a taking, when the permit is denied.[130] Congressional proponents of property rights legislation are also aware of this issue,

---

[129] Walcek v. United States, 44 Fed. Cl. 462, 467 (1999).

[130] In *Tabb Lakes*, 10 F.3d at 802, the Federal Circuit refused to narrow the parcel as a whole to solely the wetlands portion of a tract, explaining that wetlands permit denials "would [then], ipso facto, constitute a taking in every case ...." *See generally* Stephen M. Johnson, *Defining the Property Interest: A Vital Issue in Wetlands Taking Analysis After Lucas*, 14 J. Energy, Nat. Res. & Envtl. L. 41 (1994).

The *Tabb Lakes* court was incorrect in asserting that a wetlands-only relevant parcel would *always* be a taking. Most obviously, development of some portion of the wetland might be permitted. More important, some wetlands activities of economic value do not require permits at all.

often writing into their bills a value-loss criterion for which agency actions are compensable that is measured against the *affected portion* of the property.[131]

The Supreme Court holds that takings law "does not divide a single parcel into discrete segments and attempt to determine whether rights in a particular segment have been entirely abrogated."[132] From this and other Court pronouncements, it seems that one may not exclude acreage from the parcel as a whole *solely to isolate the restricted portion* of a plaintiff's property. Thus, a court will spurn a taking claim when the wetland owner fails to show that economic use of the unrestricted upland portion of the same parcel is infeasible. The different regulatory status of the upland is not, of itself, a reason to exclude it.

The different-regulatory-status rule doubtless has inhibited many a wetland owner from filing a taking action. The intermingling of wetlands and uplands on most land parcels has meant there is generally an economic use remaining after the wetland has been ruled off limits.

Relevant factors

The preceding paragraphs leave open the door for plaintiffs to attempt whittling down the relevant parcel through many factors other than different regulatory status. Wetlands owners have argued that acreage should be excluded because it is (1) not contiguous with the regulated tract, (2) subdivided as different lots, (3) owned by a different, though related, entity, (4) owned by plaintiff in different form (e.g., legal title versus equitable title), (5) in a different zoning or tax assessment status, (6) acquired at a different time or through a different transaction, (7) beyond the scope of the permit being sought, (8) beyond the scope of the project for which the permit is sought, or at least capable of separate development, or was (9) sold off (or at least developed) before the permit was denied, or even before the regulatory scheme was enacted.

The CFC and Federal Circuit have been in the forefront on relevant parcel issues. An early federal wetlands decision took a broad view of the parcel as a whole. After asserting that contiguous uplands had to be included in the relevant parcel, *Deltona Corp. v. United States* suggested inclusion as well of sections of the original purchase that had been developed and sold off prior to the permit denial on the contested section.[133] In *Loveladies Harbor*, however, the CFC went with a narrow definition, refusing to factor in two pieces of the developer's original 250-acre purchase: the lots it had developed and sold off by the date of the alleged taking (193 acres), and

---

[131] *See, e.g.*, H.R. 925, 104th Congress (Contract with America bill passed by House), reintroduced in 106th Congress as H.R. 2550.

[132] Penn Central Transp. Co. v. New York City, 438 U.S. 104, 130-131 (1978). The Court most recently reiterated the sentiment in Concrete Pipe & Products, Inc. v. Construction Laborers Pension Trust, 508 U.S. 602, 644 (1993).

[133] 657 F.2d 1184, 1192 (Ct. Cl. 1981), *cert. denied*, 455 U.S. 1017 (1982).

developed but not yet sold upland lots that were not contiguous with the land for which the permit was denied (6 acres)[134]

On appeal, the Federal Circuit in *Loveladies Harbor* announced the position now followed in both federal and several state courts. In defining the parcel as a whole, courts should use "a flexible approach, designed to account for factual nuances."[135] So, it said, the divergent results in *Deltona* and *Loveladies Harbor* were consistent — simply the product of the different facts in each case. The Circuit affirmed the Claims Court's acreage exclusions, endorsing its newly minted rationale that land "developed or sold before the regulatory environment existed" should not be included.[136] The 193 acres had been sold, and the 6 upland acres at least developed, before the "regulatory environment" of Clean Water Act section 404 was enacted in 1972.[137]

Other recent uses of the *ad hoc* approach to relevant parcel determinations have proved less hospitable to landowners. In *Palm Beach Isles Assocs. v. United States,* the CFC held that the converse of the *Loveladies Harbor* rule was that the portion of plaintiff's property sold *after* the regulatory structure was imposed *should* be included in the relevant parcel.[138] Thus, where plaintiff sold a large upland portion of its tract in 1968, following expiration of its Rivers and Harbors Act of 1899 (RHA) permit and after the Corps started to enforce a broader RHA scheme, that portion was deemed part of the parcel as a whole — defeating the taking claim. Inclusion of the upland portion was also deemed appropriate because the permit denial giving rise to the taking action followed an application under not only section 404, but the RHA as well.

How the developer itself treated the acreage in question has proved key. For example, the fact that a tract owned by the plaintiff is not contiguous with the tract generating the taking claim normally is a reason not to include the first parcel in the parcel as a whole. In *Ciampitti v. United States,*[139] however, the Claims Court lumped a developer's wetland with a nearby, but noncontiguous, upland it owned that

---

[134] 15 Cl. Ct. 381, 391-93 (1988). The six acres of uplands were valued at $2.4 million near the time of the taking, compared with the $300,000 paid by the developer for the entire 250-acre tract. These dollar figures make plain that the court's exclusion of this small fragment of the original tract was essential to its finding of a taking.

[135] 28 F.3d 1171, 1181 (Fed. Cir. 1994). The decision in East Cape May Assoc. v. State of New Jersey, 300 N.J. Super. 325, 693 A.2d 114 (1997), contains a particularly extensive discussion of the parcel as a whole issue.

[136] 28 F.3d at 1181 (emphasis added).

[137] *But see* Broadwater Farms Joint Venture v. United States, 35 Fed. Cl. 232 (1996) (subdivision sector developed and sold off before *date of alleged taking* by Corps not included in relevant parcel, where no evidence of strategic behavior), *vacated and remanded*, 121 F.3d 727 (Fed. Cir. 1997) (unpublished decision, not citable as precedent, explicitly affirming lower court on relevant parcel issue).

[138] 42 Fed. Cl. 340, 361 (1998).

[139] 22 Cl. Ct. 310 (1991).

was "inextricably linked in terms of purchase and financing" with the wetland.[140] More conventionally, the Federal Circuit in *Forest Properties, Inc. v. United States*[141] found that the developer had treated its combined lakebottom/upland parcel as a single income-producing unit for purposes of financing, planning, and development. It could not now segregate the wetland portion, said the court, for purposes of its taking claim.

These cases were influential in a state case: *K&K Construction Co. v. DNR.*[142] There, the Michigan Supreme Court held that where a permit application contemplated a single comprehensive development encompassing three of four contiguous tracts in common ownership, the relevant parcel was "at least" those three tracts. The single development proposal negated the fact that the tracts were zoned differently.

K&K, *Ciampitti*, and *Forest Properties* say that the scope of a unified development plan sets the minimum size of the relevant parcel.[143] It does not, however, fix the maximum. In *Zealy v. City of Waukesha*,[144] the Wisconsin Supreme Court rejected the view that a land owner's anticipated use of contiguous parcels caps the size of the relevant parcel. This decision turned on the fact that the non-wetland acreage, whether or not part of the development proposal, formed a single contiguous parcel with the wetland portion.[145]

Wetlands decisions of the CFC and Federal Circuit have differed over whether individual subdivision lots in common ownership should be considered together for takings purposes. The more extended analyses, dealing with situations where the lots

---

[140] The planned integrated use of mainland and island tracts also gave rise to a single parcel as a whole, despite noncontiguity, in Town of Jupiter v. Alexander, 1998 Westlaw 634705 (Fla. App. Sept. 16, 1998), *rev. denied*, 729 So. 2d 389 (1999), a non-wetlands case.

[141] 177 Fed. Cir. 1360, 1365 (Fed. Cir.), *cert. denied*, 120 S. Ct. 373 (1999).

[142] 456 Mich. 570, 575 N.W.2d 531, *cert. denied*, 119 S. Ct. 60 (1998). As to *Forest Properties*, the text statement refers to the CFC decision in the case; the Federal Circuit decision on appeal, which affirmed the trial court in all key respects, came after the state high court's ruling.

[143] More recently, in Volkema v. DNR, 457 Mich. 884, 586 N.W.2d 231, *cert. denied*, 119 S. Ct. 590 (1998), the Michigan Supreme Court affirmed a judgment as "correct pursuant to K&K Construction ...." At the same time, the court disapproved the reliance of the court below on *Loveladies Harbor*. This cryptic language, offered with no explanation, probably should be read as underscoring the importance attached by the state high court to the scope of the developer's plans in setting the minimum bounds of the relevant parcel.

[144] 201 Wis. 2d 365, 548 N.W.2d 528 (1996).

[145] *Accord*, Brotherton v. DEC, 657 N.Y.S.2d 854 (Supr. Ct. 1997) (two parcels should be treated as a whole, even though bulkhead/fill plan involves only one, given contiguity and unity of use and ownership), *aff'd*, 252 A.D. 499, 675 N.Y.S.2d 121 (1998). *See also K&K Construction*, 575 N.W.2d 531 (rejecting *per se* rule excluding tract from relevant parcel because not part of development plan).

were purchased together and sought to be developed together, have strongly rejected individual consideration.[146] A state wetlands decision takes the same view.[147]

Strategic behavior

How a court formulates its relevant-parcel doctrine may well affect whether individuals arrange their land transactions so as to put themselves in the best position for bringing a taking action, should a permit someday be denied. This is the "strategic behavior" issue. For example, the developer might sell the nonwetland portion of its property before applying to fill in the wetland — then, if a permit is denied, claim a severe percentage loss in value as to the wetland. Or, the land owner might segment the development, as by separate acquisition, planning, and financing, submitting a separate permit application for each phase.

Thus far, the developer conduct described in the wetlands/takings cases reveals little in the way of sophisticated, planned well in advance, strategic behavior. Efforts to segment parcels for purposes of the takings analysis seem to be largely after the fact. Nonetheless, several courts have indicated awareness of the strategic behavior implications of their relevant parcel formulations.[148]

IX. Prior regulatory scheme ("notice rule")

Can the wetlands buyer have a reasonable expectation of being able to develop when it was "on notice" at time of purchase that a wetlands permit might have to be applied for, and could be denied? Or does such foreknowledge, without more, defeat the taking claim? If it does not, would pre-purchase knowledge of additional facts

---

[146] Tabb Lakes, Inc. v. United States, 10 F.3d 796 (Fed. Cir. 1993); Broadwater Farms Joint Venture v. United States, 121 F.3d 727 (Fed. Cir. 1996) (unpublished). Cf. Bowles v. United States, 31 Fed. Cl. 37, 41 n.4 (1994) (taking claim based on denial of section 404 permit for subdivision lot evaluated without considering plaintiff's ownership of ten adjacent lots obtained at same time).

[147] FIC Homes of Blackstone, Inc. v. Conservation Comm'n, 41 Mass. App. 681, 673 N.E.2d 61 (1996), rev. denied, 424 Mass. 1104, 676 N.E.2d 55 (1997).

[148] The United States pressed strategic behavior concerns in Loveladies Harbor v. United States, 28 F.3d 1171, 1181 (Fed. Cir. 1994). The court may have found merit in them, since the court's adopted rule — land developed or sold before the regulatory environment existed is excluded from the relevant parcel — could act to minimize strategic behavior. Later wetlands/takings decisions noting strategic behavior concerns are Palm Beach Isles Assocs. v. United States, 42 Fed. Cl. 340, 363 (1998), appeal pending; Forest Properties, Inc. v. United States, 39 Fed. Cl. 56, 73 (1997), aff'd, 177 F.3d 1360 (Fed. Cir.), cert. denied, 120 S. Ct. 373 (1999); Broadwater Farms Joint Venture v. United States, 35 Fed. Cl. 232, 240 (1996) (subdivision sector sold off before date of alleged taking by Corps not included in relevant parcel, where no evidence of strategic behavior), vacated and remanded, 121 F.3d 727 (Fed. Cir. 1997) (unpublished decision endorsing CFC's discussion of relevant parcel); and K&K Construction, Inc. v. DNR, 456 Mich. 570, 575 N.W.2d 531 (rejecting per se rule excluding tract from relevant parcel because not part of development plan; would encourage "piecemeal development"), cert. denied, 119 S. Ct. 60 (1998).

suggesting that a permit would be denied foreclose a viable taking suit? Need such knowledge be actual, or can it be imputed by law?

To the extent courts rebuff wetlands takings actions based on such a notice rule, those actions may become rare. As the years pass, fewer permit applicants will be able to argue that they bought before the enactment of the governing regulatory scheme, and thus escape the notice rule. Even now, the federal wetlands permitting program, and many state ones, are decades old.

Cases involving state and local wetlands programs

A number of state cases endorse a notice rule, holding that the existence of a wetlands (or other) regulatory regime at the time of land purchase forecloses any later taking claim that the purchaser (or its successors in interest) might have as a result of government actions under that program.[149] The issue is discussed in either of two places in the contemporary takings analysis: (1) as a threshold inquiry, per *Lucas*, into the extent to which the pre-existing regulation limits the property rights acquired, or (2) as a subsequent inquiry, per *Penn Central*, into whether the existence of such regime reduces the interference with reasonable investment-backed expectations when it is eventually applied to deny use of the property.

An example of a *Lucas* analysis is *City of Virginia Beach v. Bell.*[150] There, a municipal sand dune protection ordinance had been adopted two years before the property was acquired. No taking resulted from the ordinance's use to block the owner's development plans, said the court: "[Plaintiffs] cannot suffer a taking of rights never possessed." An example of a *Penn Central* analysis is *Claridge v. New Hampshire Wetlands Bd.*: "A person who purchases land with notice of statutory impediments to the right to develop that land can justify few, if any, legitimate investment-backed expectations of development rights ...."[151]

---

[149] But not a later challenge to the *validity* of the regulatory program. *See, e.g.*, Lopes v. City of Peabody, 417 Mass. 299, 629 N.E.2d 1312 (1994).

[150] 255 Va. 395, 498 S.E.2d 414, *cert. denied*, 119 S. Ct. 73 (1998). *Accord*, Wooten v. South Carolina Coastal Council, 333 S.C. 469, 510 S.E.2d 716 (1999); Brotherton v. DEC, 252 A.D.2d 499, 675 N.Y.S.2d 121 (1998).

[151] 125 N.H. 745, 485 A.2d 287, 291 (1984). *Accord*, Alegria v. Keeney, 687 A.2d 1249 (R.I. 1997); FIC Homes of Blackstone, Inc. v. Conservation Comm'n, 41 Mass. App. 681, 673 N.E.2d 61 (1996), *review denied*, 424 Mass. 1104, 676 N.E.2d 55 (1997); Namon v. State, 558 So. 2d 504 (Fla. App. 1990); Rowe v. Town of North Hampton, 131 N.H. 424, 553 A.2d 1331 (1989). The minority view, that regulatory foreknowledge does not disable the taking claim, is embodied in cases such as K & K Construction, Inc. v. DNR, 217 Mich. App. 56, 551 N.W.2d 413 (1996), *rev'd on other grounds*, 456 Mich. 570, 575 N.W.2d 531, *cert. denied*, 119 S. Ct. 60 (1998); and Vatalaro v. DER, 601 So. 2d 1223 (Fla. App. 1992). *Vatalaro* and *Namon*, both Florida cases, are difficult to reconcile.

The wetland owner faces a particularly uphill climb where the amount paid for the wetland clearly reflected diminished development expectations based on the existing regulatory program.[152]

Wetlands owners have also been disappointed in their attempts to avoid the prior-regulation defense by moving up the operative date of acquisition to a time before the regulatory program began. This has arisen in cases where the sequence of events was: (1) a corporation in which the plaintiff owns a large share acquires a wetland/beachfront property, (2) the regulatory regime at issue takes effect, (3) the corporation dissolves and transfers the land to the plaintiff-shareholder. Courts have rejected plaintiffs' arguments that the pre-regulation corporate acquisition should govern for takings purposes. Instead, they have noted the traditional separateness of the corporate entity, and held plaintiff to the later, corporation-to-shareholder transfer date.[153]

Cases involving the federal wetlands program

Like the state and local program cases, CFC and Federal Circuit decisions give importance to the legal landscape at date of property acquisition, barring takings whenever the application of a regulatory scheme to a property precedes purchase. More than the state and local cases, however, the CFC and Federal Circuit stress the effect of such regulation on the investment-backed expectations factor in the *Penn Central* test, rather than on the plaintiff's bundle of property rights.

In *Deltona Corp. v. United States*, the Court of Claims (now the Federal Circuit) first articulated the defense in a wetlands/taking case.[154] The developer, it said, *knew* when it bought the property that development could take place only with the necessary permit. More recently, the trial-level Claims Court spurned a taking action after noting that the developer had ample warning before purchase "that the property was encumbered by a likelihood it could not be developed."[155] In yet another

---

[152] *Compare* Gazza v. New York State, 89 N.Y.2d 603, 679 N.E.2d 1035 (purchaser who paid $100,000 for previously designated wetland worth $396,000 if unregulated cannot complain of taking when development permit is denied), *cert. denied*, 118 S. Ct. 58 (1997), *with* Gil v. Town of Greenwich, 219 Conn. 404, 593 A.2d 1368 (1991) (purchaser who paid $50,000 for previously designated wetland worth $80,000 if buildable *can* complain of taking, since discount might have reflected nothing more than anticipated difficulties of resolving tension between property's listing on residential subdivision map and wetlands constraints).

[153] City of Virginia Beach v. Bell, 255 Va. 395, 498 S.E.2d 414, *cert. denied*, 119 S. Ct. 73 (1998); Brotherton v. DEC, 252 A.D.2d 499, 675 N.Y.S.2d 121 (1998). Outside the wetlands area, the argument that a pre-regulation option to purchase a parcel bypasses the notice rule also has been rejected. Superior-FCR Landfill, Inc. v. County of Wright, 59 F. Supp. 2d 929 (D. Minn. 1999).

[154] 657 F.2d 1184 (Ct. Cl. 1981).

[155] Ciampitti v. United States, 22 Cl. Ct. 310, 321 (1991).

instance, the CFC confined the defense to instances when plaintiff lacks an "objectively reasonable" belief that it could build.[156]

The leading Federal Circuit endorsement of the notice rule arrived in 1994, in *Loveladies Harbor*. The investment-backed expectations factor of *Penn Central*, said the court, limits takings to "owners who ... bought their property in reliance on a state of affairs that did not include the challenged regulatory regime."[157] This now-canonical statement has thus far been construed as an absolute bar on takings claims based on land purchased after the critical date. Otherwise put, an absence of reasonable development expectations at time of acquisition dispenses with the need to consult the other *Penn Central* factors.[158] The *Loveladies Harbor* statement thus reflects the Federal Circuit's rejection of the predominant state-court approach, allowing preexisting laws to define away sticks in the plaintiff's bundle of property rights,[159] while achieving the same fatal result for the taking claim.

Other issues with the *Loveladies Harbor* doctrine are still being worked out. For example, precisely what is the date after which land acquisitions come with constrained expectations? This is particularly important for the federal wetlands permitting program, where the evolution from statutory enactment to regulations to wetlands delineation manual took many years.[160] Presumably, the determinative inquiry is when a regulatory scheme was known (or should have been known) by plaintiff to apply to his/her wetland. But what to make of the shifting terminology used in the decisions to specify the date — ranging from the onset of a "regulatory climate" to the (presumably much later) existence of an actual "restriction"?[161] And should events following acquisition – in particular, the increasing stringency of the

---

[156] Bowles v. United States, 31 Fed. Cl. 37, 51 (1994).

[157] 28 F.3d at 1177. The CFC and Federal Circuit have reaffirmed this principle several times since, in the context of section 404 cases. *See, e.g.*, Forest Properties, Inc. v. United States, 177 F.3d 1360, 1367 (Fed. Cir.), *cert. denied*, 120 S. Ct. 373 (1999).

[158] *See, e.g.*, Good v. United States, 189 F.3d 1355 (Fed. Cir. 1999) (absence of reasonable development expectations dispenses with need to apply other *Penn Central* factors), *pet. for cert. filed*; Broadwater Farms Joint Venture v. United States, 45 Fed. Cl. 154 (1999).

[159] *See, e.g.*, Forest Properties, 177 F.3d at 1366-1367; *Loveladies Harbor*, 28 F.3d at 1177.

[160] *Forest Properties*, for example, places importance on the date when the Corps' guidance governing section 404 permitting was issued: "[T]hose guidelines made it clear that filling wetlands to construct housing on the reclaimed land was disfavored ...." 177 F.3d at 1366. *Florida Rock*, on the other hand, focussed on earlier dates: the enactment of the Clean Water Act in 1972 and the administrative extension of Corps jurisdiction to wetlands such as the plaintiff's in 1977. 45 Fed. Cl. 21 (1999).

[161] Two recent opinions assert that the *Loveladies Harbor* formula looks not only at whether the "specific regulatory restrictions at issue" were in place when the land was bought, but also at the "regulatory climate" at that time. *Good*, 189 F.3d at 1361; Palm Beach Isles Assocs. v. United States, 42 Fed. Cl. 340, 357-358 (1998), *appeal pending*. Under this view, there can be a loss of reasonable development expectations even before the statute that is the basis of the taking claim has been enacted.

regulatory program – be considered with regard to long-delayed development efforts made by the property owner after such events?[162]

Another issue is whether the land owner's sophistication about regulatory restrictions on property should play a role in notice-rule cases. In many of the wetlands/takings cases, the CFC/Federal Circuit have buttressed the chronology (regulation preceded acquisition) by stressing that plaintiff, often a developer, was knowledgeable as to the possibility of future restrictions and/or expressly acknowledged when buying the property that permits would be difficult to obtain.[163] At the very least, the existence of a plaintiff sophisticated in matters of land use regulation makes it easier for the court to charge plaintiff with constructive knowledge of the relevant scheme.

Advisability of an absolute rule

Some observers argue that an absolute rule disabling takings claims in every instance where regulation predates purchase is unfair. For one thing, the regulatory landscape and the definition of a wetland may evolve after the wetland is bought in ways unforeseeable at time of purchase. This factor alone, they argue, makes it inequitable to reject takings claims as a hard-and-fast rule where the wetland was bought after some sort of wetlands preservation program was on the books. Even when the definition of a wetland has not changed over the relevant time span, the judgmental leeway in applying the definition can leave buyers unclear as to what they bought.[164] Finally, physical changes in the land may occur: what is a wetland when

---

[162] Yes, said *Good*, at least under the circumstances presented. The Federal Circuit noted that plaintiff "wait[ed] seven years [after land acquisition], watching as the applicable regulations got more stringent, before taking any steps to obtain the required approval." While such inaction does not preclude a taking, the court said, "it reduces [plaintiff's] ability to fairly claim surprise when his permit application was denied." 189 F.3d at 1362-1363.

[163] *See, e.g., Good*, 189 F.3d at 1357 (sales contract for wetlands property recognized "certain problems ... with the obtaining of State and Federal permission for dredging and filling operations"); Broadwater Farms Joint Venture v. United States, 45 Fed. Cl. 154 (1999) (plaintiff familiar with Clean Water Act wetlands program from previous development projects); Ciampitti v. United States, 22 Cl. Ct. 310, 321 (1991) (plaintiff knew before purchase that developing wetlands would be difficult; purchases reflect gerrymandering to avoid state-designated wetlands); Forest Properties, Inc. v. United States, 39 Fed. Cl. 56, 77 (1997) ("As a sophisticated real estate developer, [plaintiff] would be charged with knowledge of this [preexisting] regulatory scheme."), *aff'd*, 177 F.3d 1360 (Fed. Cir.), *cert. denied*, 120 S. Ct. 373 (1999).

[164] The text point applies to the federal section 404 program and the minority of state programs that do not adopt areawide wetlands delineations on officially filed maps, but rather leave it to the property owner to initiate the jurisdictional determination. (The Corps does rely on National Wetlands Inventory maps made available by the U.S. Fish and Wildlife Service, but only as a way to give a quick estimate of whether lands will be regulated.) By contrast, state programs that proactively offer wetlands delineation maps leave little room for doubt as to whether a parcel being considered for purchase contains jurisdictional wetland. It has been suggested that the section 404 program emulate this approach, to minimize post-purchase surprise, although there is obviously an added cost. *See generally* Association of State

(continued...)

the government denies the permit may not have been one when bought. The query in each case must be, is it reasonable to charge the land buyer with the expectation that the contingencies leading to restricted development of that land would in fact occur? (Some property rights partisans would go much further, arguing that the concept of expectations should be dropped from takings jurisprudence entirely. In this view, the buyer of property acquires all rights that the seller had, regardless of changes in the legal landscape since the seller acquired the property.)

The counter-arguments, supporting an absolute foreclosure of takings claims based on a pre-acquisition regime, are not without force. Surely, it might be contended, the development expectations on a given parcel have become more qualified since the first settler took ownership, perhaps centuries ago. Property rights evolve, and change in regulatory demands over time are a near certainty. And does not any discount in the price paid for a parcel due to the presence of wetlands reflect, in an efficient market, the purchaser's gamble that wetlands regulations will impose no roadblocks? If so, should the government have to rescue the purchaser, through compensation, when the wager turns out unfavorably?

Possible developer responses to notice rule

Two ways have been suggested for wetlands buyers to bypass the notice rule. One way is to have the *seller* submit the development application — if the seller's title predates the wetlands regulatory regime. After the permits are obtained, the property is conveyed to the buyer-developer. Another way is to use contingency contracts, under which the developer agrees to buy only if he/she can obtain the needed permits.

X. Intergovernmental issues: liability attribution and "before value"

Often, more than one level of government is involved at the same wetlands site. The existence of multiple government actors raises several issues for the takings analysis.

Liability attribution

Which government entity is responsible for a taking when two or more governments play a role in restricting the wetland's use? For example, who pays when permission to fill the wetland is denied by both state or local government, and the United States? Is the fact that the restriction is imposed under a delegated program a sufficient basis to impute takings liability to the delegating government? Does it matter whether a political subdivision of a state was coerced by the state, or merely enticed, into participation?

---

[164] (...continued)
Wetlands Managers, State Wetland Regulation: Status of Problems and Emerging Trends 14 (1994).

The chance of state or local takings liability may in part explain why few states have assumed responsibility for the federal section 404 program within their borders.[165] Possible support for this view is found in a recent court decision in which a delegated state (Michigan) initially offered the 404 applicant a very limited permit designed to satisfy federal EPA concerns. The applicant rejected most of the permit, and filed a taking action against the state. The state then issued a state-only permit with relatively few limitations, in effect notifying the wetland owner that any further quarrel it had was with the United States, not the state.[166]

The few cases to wrestle with liability attribution questions so far suggest that when the defendant-government's action is truly coerced, absolution will be granted. Thus, a state court granted a county's motion to be dismissed as a party to a taking case, since the county had acted to restrict the wetland owner under the direction and control of the state — that is, had acted as the state's agent.[167] By contrast, where a city prohibited development on beachfront lots under an ordinance that it had been authorized, but not required, by the state to adopt, the city, rather than the state, was the proper defendant.[168]

Arguably the denial of a federal wetlands permit based on prior state denials is an instance that falls in between the foregoing cases of direction and no direction. On the one hand, the Clean Water Act and Coastal Zone Management Act state that the Corps has no choice but to deny the permit.[169] (The administrative reality is somewhat different.[170]) On the other hand, the United States voluntarily imposed the denial requirement on the Corps in enacting those statutes. In the only case to address this matter, the court rejected the Corps' argument that the compulsory nature of the permit denial creates a *per se* defense to takings liability.[171] At the state

---

[165] So far, only Michigan and New Jersey have done so.

[166] Michigan Peat v. EPA, 175 F.3d 422 (6th Cir. 1999).

[167] Orion Corp. v. State, 109 Wash. 2d 621, 747 P.2d 1062 (1987) (en banc), *cert. denied*, 486 U.S. 1022 (1988). Reflecting the same principle, the state of Minnesota has mandated that whenever its counties impose wetlands restrictions pursuant to state requirements, any statutory compensation liability is to be borne by the state. 1996 Minn. Laws ch. 462, § 36.

[168] City of Virginia Beach v. Bell, 255 Va. 395, 498 S.E.2d 414, *cert. denied*, 119 S. Ct. 73 (1998). The importance of the non-mandatory nature of the state statute is not explicit in this decision, but seems reasonably implied.

[169] Clean Water Act section 401(a), 33 U.S.C. § 1341(a), and Coastal Zone Management Act section 307(c)(3), 16 U.S.C. § 1456(c)(3), both prohibit the Corps from granting a wetlands permit until the applicant has received specified state approvals, or state approval is waived or presumed through inaction.

[170] An issue of longstanding concern to the states is the fact that, if a state denies approvals under these statutes, the Corps does not necessarily consider the state's action sufficient cause to deny issuance of the federal permit. See Claudia Copeland, *Nationwide Permits for Wetlands Projects: Permit 26 and Other Issues and Controversies*, CRS Report 97-223 ENR, at 13 (1999). This fact obviously could undercut a we-had-no-choice defense to a taking action against the Corps.

[171] Ciampetti v. United States, 18 Cl. Ct. 548, 555-556 (1989). The court's ruling was despite

(continued...)

level, a taking claim has been brought against a state agency whose opposition allegedly compelled the Corps' permit denial.[172]

Whether the mere fact of delegation points the taking finger at the delegator has not been addressed.[173] To be sure, a state that takes over the federal wetlands program does so voluntarily, suggesting that takings liability would not transfer to the United States. If, however, delegated states are regarded as instrumentalities or extensions of the United States for program purposes, the picture becomes less clear.[174]

Finally, there is the issue of sequential regulation: say, for example, that a county bans development of a wetland under an agricultural zoning ordinance, after which the Corps of Engineers denies a section 404 permit for the parcel. Is the Corps liable even though development was previously prohibited? Is it sufficient that the necessary local permits would *likely* have been denied? It appears that this question has only been answered (in the wetlands cases) in its alter ego, as a valuation issue, per the following paragraph.

Restrictions reflected in property's "before value"

Suppose that a county adopts a comprehensive plan under which a wetlands development ban is applied to a given property. Later on, the Corps denies the owner a section 404 permit, who thereupon sues the United States for a taking. In this situation, the CFC held that where the local ban is only remotely linked to federal Clean Water Act requirements, the value loss induced by the local ban is appropriately reflected in the pre-permit denial value used in the takings analysis.[175] Using this lowered "before value," the court discerned no further value loss on account of the federal permit denial. Hence, there was no federal taking.

---

[171] (...continued)
the fact that Corps permit denials based on nonreceipt of state approvals are "without prejudice" — that is, subject to the wetland owner eventually obtaining such approvals.

[172] Ventures Northwest, Ltd. v. State, 914 P.2d 1180 (Wash. App. 1996).

[173] The CFC has indicated awareness of the issue, however. City National Bank of Miami v. United States, 33 Fed. Cl. 759, 763 and 763 n.4 (1995).

[174] Federal Circuit takings decisions outside the wetlands area have imputed state actions to the United States where the state, though acting voluntarily, was seen to be an agent or instrumentality of the federal program. Hendler v. United States, 952 F.2d 1364, 1378-1379 (Fed. Cir. 1991) (state acting pursuant to EPA access order under Superfund Act); Preseault v. United States, 100 F.3d 1525, 1551 (Fed. Cir. 1996) (en banc) (state accepting responsibility for trail management under federal Rails-to-Trails Act).

[175] City National Bank of Miami v. United States, 33 Fed. Cl. 759 (1995). *See also* Lakewood Assocs. v. United States, 45 Fed. Cl. 320, 339 n.12 (1999) (dictum to same effect, but without qualification that local prohibition lacks a linkage to federal section 404).

XI. Offers from speculators, conservation groups, and governments as evidence of property's "after value"

Speculators

Even if permit denial robs a wetland of all *immediate* economic use, it may retain value for persons willing to gamble that restrictions on the tract may change in the future. The Federal Circuit takes the view that "after value" necessarily includes the value of land to speculators.[176]

At the same time, post-permit-denial offers from speculators are adequate to establish residual value only if the speculator can reasonably be assumed knowledgeable of all regulatory restrictions. Offers from "suckers" — e.g., victims of fraud or persons unfamiliar with American law — must be discarded. This standard does not require a detailed inquiry into the sophistication of each buyer of a comparable parcel, said the Federal Circuit. Though clearly discrepant sales may be disregarded, "an assessor may not disregard an *entire* market as aberrational."[177]

The issue of whether a parcel's residual market value is sufficient to defeat a taking claim independent of the residual potential for immediate development has been playing out on several non-wetlands fronts. Property rights advocates have argued that it is *only* "turn dirt" potential that counts, and find support in *Lucas'* references to remaining "beneficial use." In *Suitum v. Tahoe Regional Planning Agency*, however, the Supreme Court suggested indirectly that residual value is relevant, even where no actual development of the subject lot is permitted.[178] Contrariwise, a Ninth Circuit ruling adopts the view that residual value, while relevant generally, is not a consideration when all immediate development has been prohibited.[179]

Conservation groups and governments

The CFC has given little weight to post-permit denial offers by conservation groups and governments to buy the wetland for preservation in its natural state. Stated the CFC in *Formanek v. United States*: "[A]n offer to purchase made by a conservation group which would maintain the property in its natural state is not a speculative, commercial, or recreational use which would refute plaintiffs' taking

---

[176] Florida Rock Industries, Inc. v. United States, 791 F.2d 893, 902-03 (Fed. Cir. 1986), *cert. denied*, 479 U.S. 1053 (1987).

[177] *Florida Rock*, 18 F.3d 1560, 1567 (Fed. Cir. 1994) (emphasis in original), *cert. denied*, 513 U.S. 1109 (1995).

[178] 520 U.S. 725 (1997). A three-justice concurrence by Justice Scalia took issue with the majority's suggestion. *Id.* at 747-750. Any residual value imparted by transferrable development rights, it said, is relevant only once a taking is found, as an offset to the constitutionally required compensation.

[179] Del Monte Dunes at Monterey, Ltd. v. City of Monterey, 95 F.3d 1422, 1432-1433 (9th Cir. 1996), *aff'd*, 119 S. Ct. 1624 (1999).

claim as a matter of law."[180] Other CFC-suggested grounds for ignoring such offers include that (1) the amount offered was far less than the land's fair market value prior to government restriction in question,[181] and (2) the offer was contingent on the availability of funds.

---

[180] 18 Cl. Ct. 785, 798 (1989). Though this decision only rejected the government's motion for summary judgment, the government's use of conservation group and government offers was rejected a second time after trial. 26 Cl. Ct. 332, 340 (1992) ("offers ... from nature conservationists do[] not establish that there exists a solid and adequate fair market value").

[181] *Formanek*, 26 Cl. Ct. at 340. *See also* Loveladies Harbor v. United States, 15 Cl. Ct. 381, 394 (1988) (finding that at $13,725, post-permit denial value of property based on possible conservation group or government purchase pointed to taking).

Natural Resources
Pages 211-220

INTERNATIONAL FOREST AGREEMENTS: CURRENT STATUS

Susan Fletcher

INTRODUCTION

Since the early 1980s, there has been extensive public concern about loss of forests around the world. Attention to the rapid rate of tropical deforestation accelerated around 1988 as concern about global climate change emerged; at the time, the extensive burning of forests in Brazil (and the consequent release of carbon dioxide into the atmosphere) was a major concern.

In the early 1990s, during preparations for the 1992 United Nations Conference on Environment and Development (UNCED) in Rio de Janeiro (known popularly as the Earth Summit), the United States was among the developed countries pushing hard for an international treaty on forests that would curb deforestation. However, it was politically infeasible to focus just on tropical areas, and the debate was enlarged to include all forests. Persistent concerns about sovereignty on the part of developing countries made agreement on such a treaty impossible. The Earth Summit produced instead a statement of forest principles, and a chapter on forests in Agenda 21, the 40-chapter action plan of the conference.

Over the past decade, there has been a proliferation of programs and declarations dealing with forests,[2] including the Earth Summit documents. However, the rates of deforestation and decline in forest health remain high, and forests are regarded as one of the most significant unresolved issues following the 1992 Earth Summit.

Generally, governments are at present split between those who continue to seek a global agreement on forests, and those who seek a regional approach. However, most nations recognize a need to formulate effective policies for "sustainable management" of forests. The reasons for this recognition are as follows:

- Rapid deforestation continues, especially in tropical countries, and forest health is declining, especially in industrialized countries.

---

[1] Carol Canada, Environment and Natural Resources Policy Division, assisted in the production of this report.

[2] See *Deforestation: An Overview of Global Programs and Agreements*, CRS Report 92-764 ENR, October 21, 1992.

- There is increased recognition of the importance of ecological services of forests, especially the complex ecosystems of old growth forests--as well as the economic (but often non-cash) value of non-timber forest products.

- However, there is a continuing clash between the major forestry and financial interests who seek income from tree harvesting, and those who wish to see other economic and social interests accommodated in forest management.

Among the major problems related to loss of forests are the following:

- Land conversion to agriculture and livestock grazing -- contributing to rapid deforestation -- in tropical areas;

- Declining forest health in temperate and boreal forests;

- Inadequate scientific knowledge of functioning of forest ecosystems and relationships of forests to climate change, hydrological cycles, etc.;

- Loss of subsistence systems for poor people with few sources of cash income; and

- Loss of biological diversity and options for future medicines.

Currently, a major focus of attention is the United Nations Commission on Sustainable Development (CSD), which in April 1995 established an Ad Hoc Intergovernmental Panel on Forests to conduct studies and report in 1997 with recommendations in several areas. This panel is likely to be the focal point for resolving major forest issues over the next two years. While the CSD panel is the major focus, however, a large number of other actions are underway. Some of the most active ongoing efforts are summarized below.

UNITED NATIONS CONFERENCE ON ENVIRONMENT AND DEVELOPMENT (UNCED)

During the Earth Summit, held in Rio de Janeiro in June 1992, two documents were developed that dealt directly with forest management issues and made recommendations to nations about how forest management could respond to international concerns about loss of forest resources around the world. These are the set of forest principles and the forests chapter of Agenda 21.

Forest Principles

Negotiations between nations seeking a binding global forest treaty and those who wished no constraints on their use of forests within their boundaries were difficult and contentious. The compromise emerging from the UNCED was a set of voluntary principles: "Non-Legally Binding Authoritative Statement of

Principles for a Global Consensus on the Management, Conservation, and Sustainable Development of All Types of Forests." The importance to many in the negotiations of assuring that this set of principles would not create any legal obligation is reflected in its title.

Critics of the principles note that they contain few calls for direct action that would halt deforestation, ensure that trade in forest products is based on environmentally sustainable practices, or commit to the adoption of a comprehensive world forest strategy. However, others, including some who were involved in the negotiating process, view the Forest Principles as an important statement of consensus, and a starting point for possible future negotiations.

The Principles begin with declarations that states have the sovereign right to exploit their own resources pursuant to their own environmental policies and the right to utilize, manage, and develop their forests in accordance with their development needs "on a sustainable basis." Among the 15 principles enunciated in the statement are the following:

- the full incremental cost of achieving benefits associated with forest conservation and sustainable development requires increased international cooperation, and should be equitably shared by the international community;

- new and additional financial resources should be provided to enable developing countries to manage, conserve, and develop their forest resources sustainably;

- the efforts of developing countries to strengthen the management, conservation, and sustainable development of their forest resources should be supported by the international community, taking into account the importance of redressing external indebtedness, particularly where aggravated by the net transfer of resources to developed countries;

- the access to and transfer of environmentally sound technologies on favorable terms, including concessional or preferential terms, should be promoted, facilitated, and financed in order to enhance developing country capacity to better manage, conserve and develop their forest resources;

- trade in forest products should be based on non-discriminatory and multilaterally agreed rules and procedures consistent with international trade law and practices. In this context, open and free international trade in forest products should be facilitated;

- unilateral measures to restrict and/or ban international trade in timber or other forest products should be removed or avoided; and

- reduction or removal of tariff barriers and impediments to better market access and to better prices for higher value-added forest products and their local processing should be encouraged to enable producer countries to better conserve and manage their renewable forest resources.

Agenda 21: Chapter on Forests

The most comprehensive document emerging from the lengthy UNCED process, Agenda 21 has 40 chapters intended to be an "action plan" for sustainable development into the 21st Century. Like the forest principles, Agenda 21 and all its chapters are not legally binding and represent an outline of desired voluntary actions. Chapter 11, *Combatting Deforestation*, outlines actions needed in four broad program areas:

- *Sustaining the Multiple Roles and Functions of Forests*: objectives include strengthening institutions, skills, expertise, and capabilities to formulate plans and implement policies;

- *Protecting, Conserving and Sustainably Managing Forests*: objectives include maintaining and expanding forests; devising national forestry action programs, conserving and sustainably managing forests; maintaining and increasing the biological, socio-cultural, ecological, climatic, and economic contributions of forests; and implementing the forest principles;

- *Promoting Efficient Utilization and Assessment*: objectives include recognizing the social, economic, and ecological values of forests; using forest resources efficiently, rationally, and sustainably; developing efficient and sustainable fuelwood and energy supplies; and encouraging ecotourism; and

- *Planning, Assessment, and Periodical Evaluations*: objectives include devising systems for assessment and periodic evaluations, and providing information to officials and communities.

Each program area includes sections on activities to be undertaken (such as expanding protected area systems, carrying out revegetation in appropriate areas, increasing protection of forests from pollutants, formulating scientifically sound criteria for management, conservation and sustainable development of all types of forests); data and information; international and regional cooperation and coordination needed; and means of implementation (such as financial and cost evaluation, scientific and technological means, human resource development, and capacity building).

UNITED NATIONS FOLLOW-UP TO UNCED ON FORESTS

The primary mechanism established to follow up on the implementation of Earth Summit decisions was the Commission on Sustainable Development (CSD). Recommended by Chapter 33 of Agenda 21 on Institutional Arrangements, the CSD was formally authorized by the United Nations General Assembly in December 1992, and established at the February 1993 meeting of the Economic and Social Council (ECOSOC). The CSD held its first meeting in June 1993 and will continue to meet on an annual basis.

The CSD is taking up clusters of issues at each of its annual meetings, and will have completed a review of all of Agenda 21 by 1997. At its third annual meeting in April 1995, the CSD took up issues related to Land, Desertification, Forests, and Biodiversity. As forests were regarded as one of the major unresolved issues on the CSD agenda, this meeting held significant interest for nations and interests that sought actions to further international cooperation on forest issues. After a flurry of meetings around the world hosted by a variety of nations, the CSD debated how to proceed on forests.

The final decision was to create an "Open-Ended Ad Hoc Intergovernmental Panel on Forests ... to pursue consensus and formulation of coordinated proposals for action." The panel is to meet at regular intervals, establish a program of work, report on an interim basis in 1996, and then produce a final report on conclusions, recommendations, and proposals for action to the CSD's 5th session in 1997.

The panel is scheduled to hold its first meeting in September 1995 in New York. The purpose of this meeting is to scope out program of work and to task relevant international organizations to carry out needed studies, etc. It is expected that various international organization, such as the United Nations Forestry and Agriculture Organization (FAO), the International Tropical Timber Organization (ITTO), the United Nations Development Programme (UNDP), and others will be assigned tasks and reporting responsibilities under the Panel's work plan.

The decision document outlined five issue areas for priority action:

- Implementation of UNCED decisions related to forests at the national and international level, including an examination of sectoral and cross-sectoral linkages;

- International cooperation in financial assistance and technology transfer;

- Scientific research, forest assessment, and development of criteria and indicators for sustainable forest management;

- Trade and environment relating to forest products and services, including labelling and certification, and how to make certification both fair and credible; and

- International organizations and multilateral institutions and instruments, including appropriate legal mechanisms. A possible recommendation for negotiation of global or regional agreements would be considered under this element of the work plan.

At present, most nations and forest-related non-governmental organizations (NGOs) consider this panel to be the primary focus of international and intergovernmental work on forests.

INTERNATIONAL TROPICAL TIMBER AGREEMENT (ITTA)

One of the major forest/timber-oriented international organizations is the International Tropical Timber Organization (ITTO), established in 1985 by the International Tropical Timber Agreement (ITTA), which was negotiated to be the primary commodity agreement governing trade in tropical timber. As such, the ITTA was not originally designed to address deforestation *per se*.[3] Moreover, it addresses only tropical timber trade, and trade is estimated to cause only a very small percentage -- about five percent -- of global deforestation.

Given its establishment just as international concern over tropical deforestation was building, however, the ITTO was the only binding international agreement focusing on this issue, and provided a unique forum for forest management policy discussion between countries both producing and consuming timber from tropical forests. As the mission of ITTO was shaped during the first five years of its existence, and in its two 2-year extensions (in 1990 and 1992), it became a vehicle for project activities, especially those geared toward reforestation and conservation in tropical forests. Environmental NGOs in several countries (mainly "Northern" countries that consume tropical wood) have exerted extensive pressure, with considerable success, on the ITTO to focus on environmentally sustainable forest management. It obtained a commitment from tropical timber producers (mainly "Southern" countries) to a voluntary goal of sustainable forest management by the year 2000 for all sources of tropical timber in international trade. In 1990, the ITTO established Guidelines for the Sustainable Management of Natural Forests.[4]

---

[3]For additional information on the background of the ITTA and ITTO, see *Deforestation: An Overview of Global Programs and Agreements*, CRS Report 92-764 ENR, October 21, 1992.

[4]International Tropical Timber Organization. *ITTO Guidelines for the Sustainable Management of Natural Tropical Forests*. ITTO Technical Series 5. ITTO, Sangyo-Boeki Centre Building, 2, Yamashita-cho, Naka-ku, Yokohama 231, Japan. December 1990.

After its initial five-year term, the ITTA was twice extended for 2 years. Then, in 1993, the parties entered into an intense and often contentious renegotiation to reinstate it before the March 1994 expiration date. This renegotiation replayed some of the North-South issues. There was an effort by some of the Southern producer countries to make it an all-forests agreement; some Northern consumer countries wanted to enshrine the goal of sustainable tropical forest management by the year 2000 in the ITTA agreement as a binding commitment.

The final March 1994 ITTA text settled on a compromise that kept the ITTA focused on tropical forests, and maintained sustainable management by 2000 as a voluntary goal. A separate statement was issued by Northern consumer nations stating their determination to achieve sustainable forest management of their own temperate and boreal forests by the year 2000. Many environmental groups seeking to broaden the agreement to all forests and to strengthen commitments to sustainable forest management expressed disappointment with the renegotiated agreement. However, others felt that the references to sustainable management in the text, while not creating formally binding action requirements, are a step in the right direction by acknowledging the importance of deriving traded timber from sustainably managed sources.

The renegotiated ITTA has not yet entered into force, and the United States has not yet ratified the agreement. Senate action is not required for commodity agreements, so approval by the Secretary of State is sufficient. The United States expects to ratify the agreement, but reportedly would prefer it to go into force in 1996, in order to assure that the 4 year review of its terms takes place in or after the year 2000.

The ITTA (currently operating under its original agreement until it has enough ratifications to enter into force) along with its implementing organization, the ITTO, remains the only binding international agreement on forests in effect at present, and it remains a focus of attention for those environmental and other interests seeking to gain global recognition of the importance of environmentally sustainable forest management.

WORLD COMMISSION ON FORESTS AND SUSTAINABLE DEVELOPMENT

During the Earth Summit meeting and through 1993 a proposal was circulated to establish a World Commission on Forests and Sustainable Development. It was hoped by its original sponsors, including Hon. Ola Ullsten, former Prime Minister and Foreign Minister of Sweden and George Woodwell of the Woods Hole Institute in Massachusetts, that it would serve as a "Brundtland Commission" for forests (a reference to the U.N. World Commission on Environment and Development headed by former Prime Minister Gro Harlem Brundtland of Norway which reported to the United Nations in 1987 and stimulated discussion that led to the Earth Summit).

It gained little support as a United Nations effort. However its sponsors continued their efforts as an NGO activity, and eventually the Commission was privately established in 1995. The Commission's inaugural meeting was June 5 - 6, 1995, at UNEP regional headquarters in Geneva, during which it defined its general mission as including support to national governments and providing a forum of the principal stakeholders in the global community in addressing constraints to implementation of forest decisions in Agenda 21 and the Forest Principles from the Earth Summit.

The co-chairs of the Commission are Ola Ullsten, former Prime Minister and Foreign Minister of Sweden, and Emil Salim, former Minister of State for Population and Environment of Indonesia. The Commission will hold five regional meetings and public hearings, through early 1997, concluding just before the 1997 CSD review.

The Commission has defined the following key issue areas:

- Identifying steps needed to shift from "timber" to "ecosystem" and multiple end-use based management;

- Government subsidies for transportation and pricing for timber;

- Actions needed to ensure more rapid implementation of newly emerging approaches to forest management;

- Strengthening scientific research needed to underpin criteria and indicators of sustainable management;

- Ensuring adequate resources for forest inventories, including non-traditional forest products and research into low impact harvesting technologies to improve forest regeneration;

- Reconciling conflicting perspectives on the role of forestry plantations and their potential to reduce pressure on old-growth forests;

- Protecting biodiversity; and

- Local participation and institutional reform.

With respect to tropical forests, issues identified by the Commission also include:

- government policies encouraging migration into forest areas;

- rights and welfare of indigenous forest dwellers;

- alternative livelihoods for shifting cultivators already in forest areas; and

- assuring that land conversion for agriculture occurs in areas conducive to sustainable agriculture.

FOREST STEWARDSHIP COUNCIL

In addition to actions by organized forest and environmental interests and by governments, there is evidence that consumer interest is growing in sustainable production of timber. Market demand for such timber is growing, and is commercially significant in many areas, including the United States and the United Kingdom. Reportedly, companies handling five percent of the U.K. market for wood products have committed to buying only timber products from well-managed forests by end of 1995; this is a share worth $2 billion.

A growing number of "certification" programs have been established to certify that timber products from specific forests have been produced in an environmentally sustainable manner. Some of these are self-certification by the owner of the resource, some are government efforts, some are programs of NGOs.

As the number of such certification programs has increased, the problem of assuring credibility has arisen. A private, NGO effort was mounted to establish consensus on how to certify the certifiers -- to provide guidelines and standards for certification organizations. Out of this effort came the Forest Stewardship Council (FSC), a voluntary effort involving NGO, industry, and government participants, which is negotiating a consensus on criteria that credible certification programs must meet.

So far, some 20 forests worldwide have been certified by seven independent certifiers as of March 1995. Some 20 other organizations are developing certification systems. FSC provides assistance to new certifiers in developing standards based upon public consultation, and auditing protocols that ensure transparency and independence. The FSC intends to undertake special efforts to build the certifier capacities in Southern countries.

Principles and criteria have been agreed upon within the FSC for natural forest management; new principles and criteria were drafted for plantations in December 1994. Other issues to which the FSC has indicated that it will turn include the relationship between land use conversions and certification, and certification of non-timber products.

CRITERIA AND INDICATORS: THE "MONTREAL PROCESS"

An underlying question, still largely unanswered, is what constitutes sustainable forest management. Criteria and indicators of sustainability have been under discussion in several fora, and as noted above in the discussion of the ITTO, some have been developed. In 1994, several countries came together in Montreal, forming the Working Group on Criteria and Indicators for the

Conservation and Sustainable Management of Temperate and Boreal Forests.[5]
Some international organizations and NGOs have also been a part of this
process.

In February 1995, these countries, meeting in Chile, endorsed a set of
criteria and indicators for sustainable forest management and conservation,
known as the Santiago Declaration. The process of defining operational
implications of these criteria is continuing among the parties to the Montreal
Process. A similar effort is underway among European nations under what is
termed the "Helsinki Process."

---

[5]Countries participating are Australia, Canada, Chile, China, Japan, the Republic of
Korea, Mexico, New Zealand, the Russian Federation, and the United States, which
represent some 90 percent of the world's temperate and boreal forests.

Natural Resources
Pages 221-232

MINING IN NATIONAL PARKS AND WILDERNESS AREAS: POLICY, RULES, ACTIVITY

Duane A. Thompson

INTRODUCTION

Since the establishment of the National Park and National Wilderness Preservation Systems, agencies of the Federal Government have faced the formidable task of reconciling two allowed, but fundamentally incompatible activities--hardrock mining and preserving lands as essentially untouched by development. Mining, usually involves major disturbance and sometimes permanent change of the environment, while management of national parks and wilderness areas seeks to minimize disruption of landscapes and wildlife habitats.

The competing demands for mineral extraction and land preservation/recreation have led to some of the more difficult and complex resource decisions faced by Federal policymakers. Today, vast highly-mineralized areas of the western United States, once coveted largely for their precious metals, are also highly regarded for their unique aesthetic values, habitats for endangered and other species, recreational use, or opportunity for solitude. Ironically, some of these areas are historic mining districts, that provided the raw materials for the industrial revolution in the mid-1800's. In many instances, servicing these mines stimulated the construction of railroads that later served the growing agricultural and commercial sectors of the Midwest and the Great Plains. More recently, however, the demand for raw materials and minerals to supply industrial needs has had to compete with or been supplanted by the demand for more recreational space, and the protection of woodlands and wildlife.

BACKGROUND ON MINING AND PUBLIC LANDS

Historically, a major incentive for the private sector to invest in mineral development originated with the Mining Law of 1866, which declared all mineral lands of the public domain open to exploration and occupation.[1] The 1866 Mining Law was superseded by the now greatly debated General Mining Law of 1872. The concepts of conveying rights and land title, contained in the earlier

---

[1] Act of July 26, 1866, 14 Stat. 251. Maley, Terry S., <u>Mining Law: From Location to Patent</u>, Mineral Land Publications, P.O. Box 1186, Boise, Idaho, 1985, p. 6.

Act, were generally included, but expanded by the 1872 Mining Law.[2] The Law states that:

> ...except as otherwise provided, all valuable mineral deposits in lands belonging to the United States, both surveyed and unsurveyed, shall be free and open to exploration and purchase, by citizens of the United States and those who have declared their intention to become such.

Individuals were assured exclusive rights to develop a mineral deposit upon location and establishment of value, and to profit solely from any development. In addition to mineral ownership passing to the claimant, the Mining Law contained provisions for title to the land (surface as well as subsurface) to pass to private hands as a "land patent." A claimant who has expended $500 worth of labor or improvement on a claim may apply for a patent and take title upon payment of either $5 or $2.50/acre depending on the type of claim--lode or placer, respectively. Other than requiring $100 annual expenditures (including value of work accomplished) by the claimant (to establish intent to develop) and assessing filing fees, the Federal Government did not participate in any profits from mineral development under the Mining Law. No royalties are paid to the Federal Government.[3]

The 1872 Mining Law did, however, differ from the earlier law by including the clause "except as otherwise provided," which expressly left the door open for subsequent limitations on mineral exploration and development. This language may have been a recognition by Congress that certain geological and geographical sites were so unique, fragile, and irreplaceable that they might be protected from any type of degradation, including mineral exploration and development. Only a few months earlier in 1872 Congress enacted legislation creating the first and one of our most magnificent national parks--Yellowstone.

The 1872 mineral disposal framework applied to virtually all minerals on Federal lands until 1920, when oil, natural gas, coal, and certain other bedded, defense related minerals were removed from location and patent laws and placed under a leasing system that required royalty payments to the Government.

The provisions of the early mining laws have led to litigation on many issues over the years. There is a substantial body of case law intended to interpret what originally may have been considered "simple" provisions and their application. Courts have been required to rule on such concepts as: the value and marketability of a mineral deposit; extra-lateral rights of a claimant or patentee; and whether a hypothetically "prudent man" would develop the ore

---

[2] Act of May 10, 1872; 17 Stat. 91; 30 USC 22. Inquiries involving legal issues relating to laws or regulations on mining in national parks or wildernesses may be referred to Ms. Pamela Baldwin, Legislative Attorney, American Law Division, Congressional Research Service.

[3] Some argue that the Federal government benefits from collection of corporate and income taxes associated with any mineral development. Others contest this concept.

body. For its part, when creating conservation areas, Congress has usually protected "valid existing rights." Determining what these are and reconciling mining with the laws establishing and protecting national parks and wilderness areas has been challenging, particularly with an almost infinite combination of geographic and legal circumstances associated with discovering, claiming, and patenting specific mineral deposits. Although legislative proposals have been introduced to clarify some of these issues, Congress, for the most part, has allowed the provisions of the laws to be interpreted through regulations and court decisions.

NATIONAL PARKS

From the very beginning, the national parks were established for current recreation and educational use while protecting them for the future. According to the Department of the Interior:

> Congress charged the national Park Service (NPS) with the responsibility of managing the various units that comprise the national Park System so as to preserve and protect the resources and values of those units for current and future generations.[4]

To achieve this goal of protection, the NPS has a number of management tools at its disposal. These include prohibiting certain activities, regulating activities to reduce their adverse effects, and purchasing private lands and/or mineral rights to prevent the onset of such activities. Consistent with the Park Service's mandate, when most park units[5] are created, the lands are withdrawn from mineral entry at that time.

However, the value of a park or wilderness, particularly in the West with its dry air and distant vistas, may be affected by the lands beyond the area's boundaries. Federal efforts to preserve the unspoiled nature of an area may be affected by activities including mineral development on adjacent or nearby lands over which the NPS or other Federal agencies have little direct control, absent acquisition or condemnation of the lands--an often lengthy and expensive process.

An example of land acquisition to protect park values has occurred at a nearby unit. While standing on a rock outcrop at Harpers Ferry, Thomas Jefferson remarked that the view was worth crossing an ocean to see.

---

[4] U. S. Dept. of the Interior, National Park Service. Mineral Laws and Regulations and the National Park System. Natural Resource Report NPS / MMB / NRR-89 / 01. Washington, D C: Dec. 1989. p. 1; see also 16 U.S.C. §1 and 1a-1.

[5] Park units include not only National Parks, but also National Monuments, National Recreation Areas, National Rivers, some Wild and Scenic Rivers, National Historic Parks, National Scenic Riverways, National Rivers and Recreation Areas, National Historic Parks and Preserves, National Seashores, and National Preserves.

Consequently, the Harpers Ferry National Historic Park has sought to acquire property rights, whether full title or scenic easement, to all lands within eyesight of "Jefferson Rock," some of which are several miles distant, to prevent commercial and residential development that arguably would destroy the scenic view.

Buffer zones have occasionally been proposed in which development activities that would detract from the aesthetic or natural values of an area could be either restricted or prevented altogether. This concept is very controversial and no legislation directly authorizing buffer zones has been enacted.

Typically, lands within the National Park System have been withdrawn from new mineral entry or location. However, many of the national parks and monuments were established with ongoing mining operations or other valid existing rights. Such rights may permit the holder to explore on or develop minerals in a claim or on patented lands, within park boundaries. A valid existing right may also exist in situations where privately-owned minerals underlie a federally-owned surface--the so-called "split estate." Holders of valid claims and patents may exercise their rights to develop the minerals, "subject to such regulations prescribed by the Secretary of the Interior as he deems necessary or desirable for the preservation and management of those areas."[6] According to the Bureau of Land Management (BLM), the location of a claim inside a park unit does not invalidate the right to go to patent. The BLM is only concerned whether the applicant has met the tests (marketability, etc.) to go to patent, first at the time the park is established and second, at the time application for patent is made.

In 1976, Congress enacted the "Mining in Parks Act" (P.L. No. 94-429, 16 U.S.C. 1901 et seq). This Act found and established as a matter of policy that, because of changes in mining technology, the continued application of the mining laws to areas of the National Park System conflicts with the purposes for which they were established and that all mining operations in areas of the National Park System should be conducted to prevent and minimize damage. The exercise of valid existing mineral rights on both patented or unpatented mining claims in System units was made subject to regulations the Secretary of the Interior deems "necessary or desirable for the preservation and management" of those areas. The ability to regulate mining varies, depending on the nature of the mining rights--generally there is less Federal control over lands fully owned by private parties than over unpatented mining claims.

The Act also required the recording of outstanding mining claims within System units and established a presumption of abandonment for claims that were not recorded. The payment of compensation was authorized for any owner found by a court to have suffered a taking of property compensable under the Constitution. However, according to the Geologic Resources Division of the National Park Service, recorded claims are presumed to be valid unless they are

---

[6] 16 U.S.C. §1902.

invalidated at either (1) the time the park unit is established, or (2) the time of the patent application. The Resources Division estimated total unpatented claims at 12,428 as of January 1995. In addition to this large number of unpatented claims, the Park System also contains 746 valid mineral patents.

Largely because of valid mineral rights existing when the NPS units were created, mining occurs in some national parks. The general mining regulations for national parks are contained in Title 36, Part 9, Subpart A (Mining and Mining Claims) and Subpart B (Nonfederal Oil and Gas Rights) of the Code of Federal Regulations (C.F.R.). Subpart A regulations cover a broad range of topics including, but not limited to: access permits (§9.3); surface disturbance moratorium (§9.4); recordation of mining claims (§9.5); transfer of interests (§9.6); assessment work (§9.7); use of water (§9.8); plan of [mining] operation (§9.9); plan approval (§9.10); reclamation requirements (§9.11); supplementation or revision of plan of operations (§9.12); performance bonds (§9.13); appeals (§9.14); use of roads by commercial vehicles (§9.15); penalties (§9.16); public inspection of documents (§9.17); and surface use and patent restrictions (§9.18). Subpart B, (Nonfederal Oil and Gas Rights) contains provisions similar to those above plus requirements unique to oil and gas well safety and proper disposal of well wastes.

The following table 1 lists national park units that have special mineral provisions, identifies relevant regulations for mining in the parks, and provides the most recent available information on the status of mining in the listed areas. It shows that 33 of 368 National Park System units have at least one mining activity occurring on them; at least 817 operations are ongoing, including 15 hardrock metals (primarily gold), 28 for sand, gravel, soil and similar substances, and 709 for nonfederal oil and gas.[7]

Table 1.National Park System Units with Special Mineral Provisions		
Name	**Special Provisions**	**On-going Operations**
Bering Land Bridge NP, Alaska	Part 9; Subparts A & B	5 (gold)
Kenai Fjords NP, Alaska	ditto(do)	1 (gold)
Cape Krusenstern NM, Alaska	do	1 (sand and gravel)
Lake Clark NP, Alaska	do	1 (gold)
Wrangell-St. Elias NP, Alaska	do	2 (gold)
Gauley River NRA, W. Va.	do	11 (nonfederal oil and gas)
New River Gorge NR, W. Va.	do	1 (coal); 2 (nonfederal oil and gas)
Upper Delaware, New York	do	5 (sand and gravel)
Cuyahoga Valley NRA, Ohio	do	1 (clay)
Hopewell Culture NHP, Ohio	do	1 (sand and gravel)

---

[7] Total number of national park units was retrieved from the National Park Service Website, "http://www.nps.gov/nps/".

Table 1.National Park System Units with Special Mineral Provisions		
Name	**Special Provisions**	**On-going Operations**
Saint Croix NSR, Wisc.	do	5 (sand and gravel)
Acadia NP, Maine	do	1 (sand and gravel)
Lake Chelan NRA, Washington	do	3 (sand and gravel)
Ross Lake NRA, Washington	do	3 (sand and gravel); 1 (topsoil)
Curecanti NRA, Colorado	do	1 (decomposed granite)
Big Cypress NPr, Florida	do	30 (nonfederal oil and gas)
Big South Fork NR&RA, Tennessee	do	210 (nonfederal oil and gas)
Chattahoochee River NRA, Georgia	do	2 (sand and gravel)
Obed Wild and Scenic River, Tennessee	do	2 (undisclosed); 244 (nonfederal oil and gas)
Alibates Flint Quarries NM, Texas	do	1 (nonfederal oil and gas)
Aztec Ruins NM, New Mexico	do	3 (nonfederal oil and gas)
Big Thicket NP, Texas	do	2 (sand); 15 (nonfederal oil and gas)
El Malpais NM, New Mexico	do	1 (cinder)
Hot Springs NP, Arkansas	do	1 (novaculite)
Jean Lafitte NGP & Pr, Louisiana	do	1 (nonfederal oil and gas)
Lake Meredith NRA, Texas	do	180 (nonfederal oil and gas)
Padre Island NS, Texas	36 CFR §7.75(h)--Mineral exploration and extraction. Regulations for the scope of mineral extraction, exercise of nonfederal oil and gas rights, and applicability of state laws.	14 (nonfederal oil and gas)
Poverty Point NM, Louisiana	Part 9; Subparts A & B	12 (nonfederal oil and gas)
Salinas Pueble Mission NM, New Mexico	do	1 (stone)
Death Valley NP, California/Nevada	36 CFR §7.26(a) through (e)--Limits claims to mining purposes only, provides restrictions for road construction, and water use.	1 (borax); 1 (gold); 20 (unspecified)
Joshua Tree NP, California	Part 9; Subparts A & B	1 (garnet and epkidote); 4 (precious metals)
Mojave NPr, California	do	28 (unspecified)
Saguaro NP, Arizona	do	1 (wulfenite and gold)

WILDERNESS AREAS

The Wilderness Act created the National Wilderness Preservation System in 1964, set out appropriate management direction, and was the first of many laws (total of 117 laws from 1964 through 1995) designating wilderness areas. The 1964 Act included a general policy statement for the use of designated wilderness areas: [8]

> In order to assure that an increasing population, accompanied by expanding settlement and growing mechanization, does not occupy and modify all areas within the United States and its possessions, leaving no lands designated for preservation and protection in their natural condition, it is hereby declared to be the policy of the Congress to secure for the American people of present and future generations the benefits of an enduring resource of wilderness.

Unlike national park lands, which are exclusively under the jurisdiction of the National Park Service in the Department of the Interior, wilderness areas, as stated in the Act, "shall continue to be managed by the Department and agency having jurisdiction thereover immediately before its inclusion in the National Wilderness Preservation System...." Consequently, lands in the wilderness system can be administered by Departments other than Interior (e.g., the Department of Agriculture, in the case of wilderness areas under the auspices of the Forest Service) and by other agencies within the Interior Department (e.g., the U.S. Fish and Wildlife Service and the Bureau of Land Management). A brief list of some of the major legislation expanding the wilderness system is contained in the table below. Many other statutes have designated wilderness areas.

Table 2. Major Wilderness Laws			
Title	**Public Law #**	**Date**	**Brief Description of Major Provisions**
The Wilderness Act	P.L. 88-577	1964	--defined wilderness for purpose of establishing and maintaining the Nat'l Wilderness Preservation Sys (NWPS). --specified that only Congress had authority to designate future wilderness areas. --required study of certain Forest Service, NPS, and national wildlife refuge lands. --special prov. allowed for mining on valid claims and mineral development on leases established before Dec. 31, 1983
"Eastern Wilderness Act"	P.L. 93-622	1975	--added 16 wildernesses in the East, implicitly easing the standards for areas in the East --designated roadless areas in the East should be included and managed as part of the NWPS
Federal Land Policy and Management Act	P.L. 94-579	1976	--the Bureau of Land Management joined the Forest Service, NPS, and Fish and Wildlife Service as a partner in wilderness review and management --existing uses such as mining, mineral leasing...permitted to continue in study areas subject to regulations set by the Secretary of the Interior

---

[8] P.L. 88-577 (16 U.S.C. §§ 1131-1136), Section 2(a).

Table 2. Major Wilderness Laws			
Title	**Public Law #**	**Date**	**Brief Description of Major Provisions**
Endangered American Wilderness Act	P.L. 95-237	1978	--added 16 areas to the NWPS --criteria for assignment changed to encourage the establishment of wilderness areas near large cities even though some of these areas had previously been influenced by man
Alaska National Interest Lands Conservation Act (ANILCA)	P.L. 96-487	1980	--added 56 million acres to the NWPS (most in units of the NPS and the National Wildlife Refuge System), nearly tripling total acreage --vast areas were authorized for further study --use of certain vehicles authorized and wilderness cabins to be maintained with some new cabins added
Colorado Wilderness Act	P.L. 96-560	1980	--set guidelines for livestock grazing in all national forest wildernesses --prohibited establishment of buffer zones around wildernesses --provided for release of remaining wilderness study areas to traditional management planning and uses

Generally, Congress permitted mineral-related activities in designated wilderness areas for 20 years following the enactment of the Wilderness Act in 1964. During that period, new mineral rights could be established. However, following December 31, 1983, new mineral rights could no longer be established, although Congress did permit prospecting in designated wilderness areas. [9] Valid existing mineral rights, some of which may have been established during the 20-year grace period, may still be exercised and developed in designated areas, subject to reasonable regulations to protect the wilderness character of the lands. [10]

Some literature asserts that mining in wilderness areas is an extremely complex legal issue, and that regulating exploration and mining activities is site-specific.[11] Maintaining the unspoiled character of wilderness can be especially confounded in the East, where the mineral estate has often been split from the

---

[9] The authority to establish new mineral rights in existing wilderness areas was actually terminated on September 30, 1981, through riders on the Dept. of the Interior Appropriations Acts for FY1982, FY1983, and FY1984.

[10] Mineral development has occurred in some national forest wilderness areas, but a comprehensive list of such developments is not available. Personal communication with Tom Klabunde, Legislative Affairs Staff, U.S.D.A. Forest Service, Washington, D.C., on December 5, 1995.

[11] Browning, James A., John C. Hendee, and Joe W. Roggenbuck, 103 Wilderness Laws: Milestones and Management Direction in Wilderness Legislation, 1964-1987, University of Idaho, College of Forestry, Wildlife and Range Sciences, Bulletin No. 51, October, 1988, pp. 6 and 7.

surface estate. [12]   Although the surface of a wilderness may be under the authority of a particular agency, the subsurface rights may have been severed and reside in private ownership. In these instances, a question of access for mineral development often arises. The Federal agencies generally cannot deny access to privately held mineral estate, but can regulate mineral activities to varying degrees.

Congress has generally pursued a situational approach and has adopted several approaches to mineral development. Congress has sought either to accommodate mineral development by drawing the boundaries of the wilderness to exclude highly-mineralized, potentially-developable areas or to avoid development by acquiring mining rights through purchase or exchange. The following Table 3. identifies wilderness areas and/or laws that contain special provisions on mining. As noted, no ongoing mining operations are currently occurring in wilderness areas.

Table 3. Wilderness Areas with Special Mining Provisions		
Name	**Special Provisions**	**On-going Operations**
River of No Return Wilderness. The Central Idaho Wilderness Act of 1980, P.L. 96-312.	Prospecting, exploration and development of mining of cobalt and associated minerals in the Clear Creek Special Mining Management Zone of the River of No Return Wilderness shall be permitted beyond the December 31, 1983 deadline, subject to regulations.	None noted.
San Rafael Wilderness P.L. 90-271.	Wilderness Act of 1964.	None noted.
San Gabriel Wilderness, P.L. 90-318.	Wilderness Act of 1964.	None noted.
Sawtooth National Recreation Area, P.L. 92-400.	The Secretary may acquire mineral interests in lands within the recreation area (which includes the wilderness) with or without the consent of the owner. Subject to valid existing rights, all federal lands located in the recreation area are withdrawn from location, entry, and patent under the U.S. mining law.	None noted.
Hells Canyon National Recreation Area, P.L. 94-199.	do.	None noted.
The Endangered American Wilderness Act of 1978, P.L. 95-237.	Extends the mineral exploration, patenting, and development period for the Gospel-Hump Wilderness from December 31, 1983, to December 31, 1988.	None noted.
Boundary Waters Canoe Area Wilderness, P.L. 95-495.	No mining of minerals owned by the U.S. is permitted; no exploration or mining of nonfederal minerals is permitted if such action would adversely affect navigable waters. The Secretary may acquire minerals and mineral rights owned by the private sector. Specific guidelines are provided for any mining activity or acquisition of minerals rights.	None noted.

---

[12] U.S. General Accounting Office. Private Mineral Rights Complicate the Management of Eastern Wilderness Areas. GAO/RCED-84-101. Washington, D.C.: U.S. Govt. Print. Off., July 26, 1984. 48 pp.

Table 3. Wilderness Areas with Special Mining Provisions		
Name	**Special Provisions**	**On-going Operations**
The Alaska National Interest Lands Conservation Act, P.L. 96-487.	(Misty Fjords National Monument Wilderness) The Secretary of Agriculture shall allow installation, maintenance, and use of navigation aids, docking facilities, and staging and transfer facilities associated with the development of the mineral deposit at Quartz Hill. Such activities shall not include mineral extraction, milling, or processing.	None noted.
Monongahela National Forest, P.L. 97-466.	(a) Exploration activities, including core drilling and use of mechanized ground equipment, is allowed in the Cranberry Wilderness to determine the value of the nonfederally owned mineral resources there, under regulations set by the Secretary of Agriculture. (b) The Secretary of the Interior is directed to acquire all nonfederally owned coal deposits and other minerals interests and rights within the Cranberry Wilderness, and such interests and rights outside the wilderness according to certain requirements. Guidelines are provided for the acquisition of these mineral interests and rights.	None noted.
The Vermont Wilderness Act, P.L. 98-322.	All federally-owned lands within the White Rocks National Recreation Area (which includes portions of the Big Branch and Peru Peak Wildernesses) are withdrawn from all forms of appropriation under the mineral and geothermal leasing laws.	None noted.
California Wilderness Act of 1984, P.L. 98-425.	Various sites within California. Mineral prospecting, exploration, development, and mining are permitted in the North Fork Smith Roadless Area under laws applicable to nonwilderness national forest lands.	None noted.
The Florida Wilderness Act of 1984, P.L. 98-430.	Specifies that phosphate leases shall not be permitted on Osceola National Forest (which includes the Big Gum Swamp Wilderness) unless: 1. the President defines need; 2. there is a procedure for public input; 3. the President specifies impacts; 4. the President specifies conditions and stipulations to govern any mining activity; 5. Congress approves the President's recommendation by joint resolution.	None noted.
The Wyoming Wilderness Act of 1984, P.L. 98-550.	Oil and gas exploration and development activities on the Palisades Wilderness Study Areas shall be administered under reasonable conditions to protect the environment under regulations and laws generally applicable to nonwilderness lands. Subject to valid existing rights, the Palisades Wilderness Study Area is withdrawn from all forms of appropriation under the mining laws.	None noted.
The Pennsylvania Wilderness Act of 1984, P.L. 98-585.	The Secretary of Agriculture is authorized to acquire land, including oil, gas, and mineral interests or scenic easements, within the wildernesses by various means.	None noted.
Arizona Desert Wilderness Act of 1990, P.L. 101-628	Private mineral rights within wilderness areas designated by this title be acquired as expeditiously as possible by the Secretary using existing authority to acquire such rights by exchange.	None noted.
Los Padres Condor Range and River Protection Act, P.L. 102-301	(a) Subject to valid existing rights, federally owned lands depicted on a map entitled "Mineral Withdrawal Area, California Coastal Zone, Big Sur--Proposed are generally withdrawn from mineral entry. (b) Subject to valid existing rights, all mining claims located within the withdrawal area shall be subject to such regulations as the Secretary of Agriculture may prescribe to ensure that mining will be consistent with the protection of scenic, scientific, cultural, and other resources of the area. In instances where a land patent is issued following the date of enactment, only title to the minerals will be conveyed.	None noted.

Table 3. Wilderness Areas with Special Mining Provisions		
Name	**Special Provisions**	**On-going Operations**
El Malpais National Monument, P.L. 100-225.	Section 504 provides for the Secretary of the Interior to exchange Federal mineral interests for private mineral interests--both described in detail within the section.	None noted.
Washington Park Wilderness Act of 1988, P.L. 100-688.	Subject to valid existing rights, the lands within recreation areas are withdrawn from...disposal...under the United States mining laws, and disposition under the United States mineral leasing laws: *Provided, however,* That within that portion of the Lake Chelan National Recreation Area which is not designated as wilderness, sand, rock and gravel may be made available for sale to the residents of Stehekin for local use....	None noted.

Natural Resources
Pages 233-238

FOREST HEALTH: OVERVIEW

Ross W. Gorte

Summary

The pine ecosystems in the intermountain West are considered by many to be unhealthy. While the data are inconclusive, studies show at least localized problems of timber mortality and dense stands of small trees, including a shift away from the fire- and drought-resistant pines in mixed conifer stands. The comprehensive land management planning processes of the Forest Service and the Bureau of Land Management were intended, in part, to address such issues, but to date, efforts by the agencies, the interest groups, and Congress have focused on separate authorities and funding for forest health activities -- salvage timber sales, prescribed burning, thinning, and other timber stand activities.

What Is the Problem?

Many of the forests in the intermountain West -- from the Black Hills of South Dakota to the Cascades and the Sierra Nevadas, and from the Canadian border to Arizona and New Mexico -- are dominated by pines, especially Ponderosa, Western white, and lodgepole pines. The pine ecosystems of the West are considered by many to be in unnatural and unhealthy conditions, with excessive numbers of trees and excessive tree mortality, leading to insect and disease epidemics and to increased risk of catastrophic fire.[1]

Timber mortality in the intermountain West has risen since 1976 -- in total, per acre, and as a percent of inventory.[2] Timber mortality (per acre and as a percent of inventory) is often higher on the national forests than on other timberlands. However, mortality on the national forests of the intermountain West appears to be no worse than on other timberlands – timber mortality in 1991 was higher than in 1976 in nearly all regions for all

---

[1] For a further discussion of this relationship, see CRS Report 95-511 ENR, *Forest Fires and Forest Health*.

[2] Data on timber mortality, timber inventory, and timberland area are from: Douglas S. Powell, Joanne L. Faulkner, David R. Darr, Zhiliang Zhu, and Douglas MacCleery. *Forest Resources of the United States, 1992*. Gen. Tech. Rept. RM-234. Ft. Collins, CO: U.S.D.A. Forest Service, Sept. 1993. 132 p. (Hereafter referred to as *Forest Resources, 1992*.)

landowner classes. Furthermore, timber mortality per acre is higher in the Pacific Coast States (Alaska, Washington, Oregon, and California), because the remaining dense old-growth stands have high mortality rates; timber mortality is a greater percentage of inventory in the Eastern regions (Northeast, North Central, Southeast, and South Central), because conifers have relatively short lifespans in the humid Eastern climates.

Although existing Forest Service data do not show abnormal timber mortality in the intermountain West, certain health problems might not be captured by those data. The Forest Service data are based on periodic inventories, typically on a 10-year cycle; thus, the 1991 data are, on average, at least 5 years old. If timber mortality in the intermountain West has risen because of the drought that began in the early 1980s, the data might not yet reflect that increase. Two other forest health problems also would probably not be reflected in the comprehensive timber data. One is excessive numbers of small trees, with little or no net growth, due to stand stagnation without mortality; this could be a particular problem for the Ponderosa and lodgepole pines, which are well adapted for dry and infertile conditions. The other problem, fuel buildup, is more likely in the intermountain West, because the arid conditions slow the decomposition of the wood.

The forest health problems of the intermountain region have been developing over a long period, although the deterioration of the forests may have been accelerated by the past decade of drought. The problem began with livestock overgrazing in the Western pine forests in the 1800s; this reduced vegetative competition for the trees, especially from grasses, some of which inhibit tree regeneration and growth. The problem has been exacerbated by logging, both before and since the national forests were established, that has emphasized cutting large-diameter old-growth pines, and leaving smaller trees and other species (particularly the true firs). However, the most significant cause may have been fire suppression over the past 75 years that virtually eliminated the natural cycle of frequent fires.

These anthropogenic factors have altered the Western pine forests. The pure pine forests (pure being defined by foresters as more than 80% of the trees in one species) have seen substantial increases in fuels and in seedlings and saplings. Historically, frequent, low-intensity fires in Ponderosa pine forests reduced the fuels and killed many of the seedlings and saplings. According to a recent study in northern Arizona, the Coconino National Forest averaged 23 trees per acre prior to settlement, but now has 851 trees per acre.[3] The frequency of stand replacement fires in lodgepole pine forests has also declined, leading to more trees and more fuels per acre than occurred prior to 1900.

The mixed conifer forests have been similarly altered, with substantial increases in the number of small diameter trees and in the quantity of woody fuel. However, the species composition of these forests has also changed, with much more Douglas-fir and true fir than existed 150 years ago. This is the result of logging the high-value species (the inland Douglas-fir subspecies is not nearly as valuable as the subspecies that grows along the coast and in the Cascades) and of suppressing the low-intensity fires (because pines are

---

[3]W.W. Covington and M.M. Moore. "Postsettlement Changes in Natural Fire Regimes and Forest Structure: Ecological Restoration of Old-Growth Ponderosa Pine Forests." In: *Assessing Forest Ecosystem Health in the Inland West*. [R. Neil Sampson and David L. Adams. eds.] New York, NY: Food Products Press, 1994. pp. 153-181.

less susceptible to damage from fire). Furthermore, the Douglas-fir and true firs require more water than the pines, and thus the stress of the decade-long drought has increased their susceptibility to insect and disease attack, and possibly set the stage for epidemics.

What Can Be Done About It?

Many people are interested in improving forest health -- for immediate and/or sustainable wood supplies, for reducing the risks of catastrophic wildfires, and/or for sustaining and protecting other outputs and values from the forests (*e.g.*, water quality, recreation, and "naturalness"). One principal goal of forest health improvement is to reduce biomass -- small-diameter trees, dead or dying trees, and existing woody fuels; in mixed conifer forests, shifting the species mix back to pine dominance may also be a goal.

Much of the attention on improving forest health has focused on the national forests in the intermountain West, where they account for 60% of the timberland. [4] At a forest or landscape level, this could be addressed through national forest planning. The Forest and Rangeland Renewable Resources Planning Act of 1974, as amended by the National Forest Management Act of 1976 (NFMA), requires the Forest Service to prepare integrated, coordinated land and resource management plans for units of the National Forest System.[5] These plans are prepared using an interdisciplinary approach, "to achieve integrated consideration of physical, biological, economic, and other sciences," and with the public's participation, to assure that relevant concerns and issues are addressed. Furthermore, the plans are to be revised "from time to time when . . . conditions in a unit have significantly changed, but at least every 15 years." Many forests are beginning the process of revising their plans, thus providing an opportunity to address forest health concerns in forest planning.

Some have criticized forest planning as being slow, expensive, and unresponsive to current problems.[6] To date, efforts to direct the Forest Service to improve forest health have generally been external to the planning process. Proposals and draft bills have either ignored national forest planning under NFMA, or directed forest health decisions to override existing plans.

Several tools exist for improving forest health. One of the most frequently mentioned is salvage timber sales.[7] Salvage timber sales can be used to remove dead, dying, and threatened trees from the forest, and therefore can be useful in reducing biomass and in controlling insect and disease infestations. However, since commercial interest reflects timber quality, salvage sales have limited potential for reducing small-diameter trees, and much woody material (limbs and needles) is left on the site. Environmentalists are also

---

[4]*Forest Resources, 1992*, p. 43.

[5]Respectively: Act of Aug. 17, 1974, Pub.L. 93-378, 88 Stat. 476; and Act of Oct. 22, 1976, Pub.L. 94-588, 90 Stat. 2949. 16 U.S.C. 1600-1614.

[6]See: U.S. Congress, Office of Technology Assessment. *Forest Service Planning: Accommodating Uses, Producing Outputs, and Sustaining Ecosystems*. OTA-F-505. Washington, DC: U.S. Govt. Print. Off., Feb. 1992. 206 pp.

[7]For more information on this tool, see CRS Report 95-364 ENR, *Salvage Timber Sales and Forest Health*.

concerned about salvage sales, because little is known about the ecological consequences of extensive salvage sale programs, because the current definition of salvage does not limit salvage sales to dead or dying trees, and because inappropriate logging has contributed to the current problem.

Another common tool is prescribed burning. This is using fire (set intentionally or occurring naturally) under prescribed weather and fuel conditions to reduce the quantity of woody fuel on a site. It can be an effective tool for converting organic matter to minerals, water, and carbon dioxide (and other gases), but protecting air quality (particularly from airborne particulates) often limits the timing, location, and amount of prescribed burning that can occur. Prescribed burning is also a poor tool for eliminating small-diameter trees, because it is indiscriminate about which (if any) trees remain, and can be a dangerous tool when weather conditions change.[8]

Other forest management techniques can also be used to improve forest health and reduce the risk of catastrophe fire. One activity is precommercial thinning, to cut down trees that are too small to have any commercial value. Release -- killing competing vegetation chemically or manually -- can reduce timber stand densities. Pruning can eliminate low-growing branches, thus removing a "ladder" for fires to reach the crowns of the trees while improving the value of wood growth. Fertilization can accelerate tree growth, possibly overcoming stand stagnation. Planting on mixed conifer sites can help reestablish the natural variation of native forests, both on cleared sites and in stands with relatively low densities.

Oftentimes, these various tools and techniques need to be used in combination to achieve the desired goal -- salvage with mixed-species planting or prescribed burning after precommercial thinning, for example. Indeed, none of these approaches is sufficient to improve forest health alone; rather, a coordinated program combining relevant tools and techniques is probably necessary to improve forest health in the pine ecosystems of the intermountain West. However, it should also be noted that most of these tools and techniques are expensive, and the total cost may limit the ability of the agencies to improve forest health.

Legislative Proposals

102nd-104th Congresses. Congress has addressed forest health legislation several times over the past few years. The first comprehensive bill, H.R. 4980 in the 102nd Congress, the National Forest Health Act of 1992, was introduced on April 9, 1992. After July 1 hearings before the House Agriculture Subcommittee on Forests, Family Farms and Energy, the bill was marked up and ordered reported, but a report was never filed, and Congress adjourned without further action on the bill. Several bills were introduced in the 103rd Congress: H.R. 229, the National Forest Health Act; S. 459, the Federal Forests Health Recovery Act of 1993; and S. 2456, the Forest Health Act of 1994. However, no hearings were held on any of these bills.

---

[8] A prescribed fire in Michigan in 1980 escaped when weather conditions changed, killing one person and destroying 44 homes and buildings. See: Albert J. Simard, Donald A. Haines, Richard W. Blank, and John S. Frost. *The Mack Lake Fire*. Gen. Tech. Rept. NC-83. St. Paul, MN; U.S.D.A. Forest Service, Sept. 1983. 36 p.

Following the severe wildfires in the intermountain West during the summer of 1994, the Administration proposed the Western Forest Health Initiative. [9] This program was, essentially, an acceleration of current planned, funded projects and of planned, unfunded projects, with improved coordination with the Environmental Protection Agency on monitoring, with the U.S. Fish and Wildlife Service and the National Marine Fisheries Service on endangered and threatened species, with the National Wildfire Coordinating Group, and with State Foresters. However, this program was also criticized as a weak response to the magnitude of the problem in the West.

Two bills in the 104th Congress addressed forest health. The first was the Emergency Salvage Timber Sale Program included in the 1995 Emergency Supple-mental Appropriations and Rescissions Act, P.L. 104-19, directing an increase in salvage timber sales, with expedited procedures. The program was controversial, because it prohibited most challenges to agency decisions and reinstated certain previously-halted timber sales in the Pacific Northwest.[10]

The other bill was the Federal Lands Forest Health Protection and Restoration Act, S. 391. The bill would have established a complicated program to:
(1)   review forest health conditions annually;
(2)   designate emergency and high risk areas;
(3)   select and publish a schedule of activities: (a) to arrest the decline of and to restore forest health; (b) to safeguard human life and property; (c) to protect natural resources; (d) to restore ecosystem integrity; and (e) to protect Federal investments and future revenues; and
(4)   notify the public and respond to comments and challenges under expedited procedures.

The Senate Energy and Natural Resources Subcommittee on Forests and Public Land Management held a hearing on the bill on March 1, 1995, but a markup scheduled for late April 1996 was postponed to allow negotiations on a bipartisan substitute. The negotiations concluded in June without an agreement, and the bill was reported by the Committee, but saw no floor action.

105th Congress. Several bills addressing forest health have been introduced in the 105th Congress. H.R. 2458, the Community Protection and Hazardous Fuels Reduction Act of 1997, would direct Forest Service and BLM programs of fuel reduction in high risk areas of the wildland/urban interface, undertaken through requirements on timber purchasers who would be compensated with credits that could be used to pay for the timber. (This would parallel the Forest Service's purchaser road credit system for building access roads; for a description of this program, see appendix E (pp. 40-41) of CRS Report 97-14 ENR, *The Forest Service Budget: Trust Funds and Special Accounts*.) The House Resources Subcommittee on Forests and Forest Health held hearings on the bill on September 23, 1997, and forwarded a marked-up version to the full committee on March 5, 1998.

---

[9]U.S. Dept. of Agriculture, Forest Service, State and Private Forestry. *Western Forest Health Initiative*. Washington, DC: Oct. 31, 1994. 66 pp.

[10]For more information on this program, see CRS Report 96-569 ENR, *The Salvage Timber Sale Rider: Overview and Policy Issues*.

H.R. 3530, the Forest Recovery and Protection Act of 1998, would enact a process for establishing standards and criteria, for identifying and ranking priority recovery areas, and for undertaking recovery projects on National Forest System lands. A scientific advisory panel would provide advice on the standards and criteria and on monitoring the results of the program. Projects would be funded with a new permanently-appropriated special account, the Forest Recovery and Protection Fund, which would receive moneys previously deposited in the Forest Roads and Trails Fund (*i.e.*, 10% of Forest Service revenues) plus any appropriations. The bill is a substitute for H.R. 2515, reported by the House Agriculture Committee on March 12, 1998 (H.Rept. 105-440, Part I); the House Resources Committee has waived its jurisdiction over federal forest lands to expedite floor consideration.

The Senate has not approached forest health directly in the 105th Congress. Rather, S. 1253, the Public Lands Management Improvement Act of 1997, would supplement both the National Forest Management Act of 1976 (NFMA; P.L. 94-588) governing Forest Service planning and practices and the Federal Land Policy and Management Act of 1976 (FLPMA; P.L. 94-579) governing BLM planning and practices. Forest health problems would then be addressed within the general planning and management guidance, as supplemented by S. 1253. The Senate Energy and Natural Resources Subcommittee on Forests and Public Land Management held several workshops on a draft bill in February and March of 1997, and hearings on the bill on October 30, 1997.

INDEX

Y

Yellowstone National Park, 4

Z

Date Due

BRODART, CO. Cat. No. 23-233-003 Printed in U.S.A.